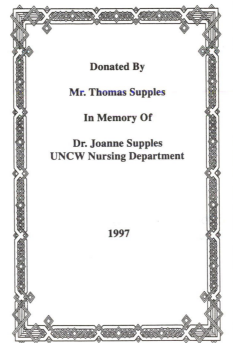

Managerial Ideology
and the
Social Control of Deviance
in
Organizations

Managerial Ideology and the Social Control of Deviance in Organizations

Richard M. Weiss

PRAEGER

New York
Westport, Connecticut
London

Library of Congress Cataloging-in-Publication Data
Weiss, Richard M.
  Managerial ideology and the social control of deviance in organizations.

  Bibliography: p.
  Includes index.
  1. Industrial management.   2. Social control.
3. Alcoholism and employment.   I. Title.
HD38.W4243   1986   658.3'144   85-19385
ISBN 0-275-92105-0 (alk. paper)

Library of Congress Catalog Card Number: 85-19385
ISBN: 0-275-92105-0

First published in 1986

Praeger Publishers, 521 Fifth Avenue, New York, NY 10175
A division of Greenwood Press, Inc.

Printed in the United States of America

The paper used in this book complies with the Permanent Paper Standard issued by the National Information Standards Organization (Z39.48-1984).

10 9 8 7 6 5 4 3 2 1

For Lynn

Contents

List of Tables

Preface

In the spring of 1985 the long-standing division within sociology went very public. In the Sunday *New York Times'* Week in Review section, a panel of five distinguished sociologists engaged in "Debating the Direction of a Discipline," prompted by the controversial denial of tenure to a qualitative (as opposed to quantitative) sociologist at Harvard whose book had won a number of prestigious awards.

Among the panelists was Daniel Bell of Harvard, who had been a supporter of this individual's candidacy. He contrasted "interpretive sociologists, who are interested in exploring general laws of society," with "positivists"—a term that serves in contemporary sociology as an epithet used by qualitative sociologists to describe those who are quantitatively-oriented. He commented "I believe that a return to interpretation is going on ... People get disappointed with what you can do with numbers. They are showing more interest in looking at the meaning of things." A panelist taking a similar view was Peter Berger, who contrasted "positivists" with "humanists." He characterized the humanists as "interested in the large questions of the workings of society" and the positivists as "quantifiers of minutiae."

The quantitative camp was represented by William Sewell, a leading figure in research on the "status attainment" process—perhaps the most prominent quantitative paradigm in the sociological literature of the mid-1970s. He argued that theoretical issues had not been forgotten by quantifiers, but that the complex, computer-based statistical analyses of large samples simply have taken energy away from purely theoretical work. The two remaining panelists viewed themselves as supporting both approaches. William Julius Wilson argued that the diversity of research styles should be a source of pride for the field, rather than conflict. Neil Smelser also argued for a balance of approaches, but expressed his concern that the quantifiers had fallen prey to a "fetishism of technique."

He further betrayed his sympathies by explaining that the lure of government research funding had pushed many sociologists over to the quantitative side, but that "there's still a large portion of the field that is basically sympathetic to human problems and human suffering."

I must admit that I do not understand this debate. Of course, I understand it in the sense that I have seen the arguments many times before, and I think that by now I comprehend the opposing viewpoints. Yet, I am still puzzled to read classification schemes in which the use of numbers disqualifies a social scientist from being "sympathetic to human problems and human suffering" or "interested in the large questions of the workings of society." Bell, defending the record of his junior colleague, argued that this young sociologist had been objected to "because he doesn't publish in the itty bitty academic journals." In fact, the scholar in question had never published in any of the major mainstream journals in sociology. Bell's contemptuous characterization of the *American Sociological Review* and the *American Journal of Sociology* as "itty bitty" and Berger's characterization of numbers-oriented sociologists as "quantifiers of minutiae" seem oddly dogmatic for those claiming to represent humanism.

Nor was the quantitative side of this debate very convincing. The view that quantitative sociologists have not disregarded theory and qualitative understanding of their subject matter might better have been exemplified by quantitative research other than Sewell's. The status attainment researchers were accused by Lewis Coser, in his presidential address to the American Sociological Association in 1975, of conducting work that not only was atheoretical, but whose substance was only barely sociological (rather, Coser implied, it might be an applied psychology of individual success).

Even Wilson and Smelser, who averred that both approaches are valuable, accept the idea that there are different styles, that some social scientists do quantitative research and that others conduct qualitative research. But if this split is recognized and accepted, why have the preponderance of graduate programs in which social scientists are trained required that all students take the courses in theory, methods, and statistics that provide the background for work in both of these styles? Are such requirements merely initiation rites or perhaps the result of a compromise among academics of differing methodological persuasions? My own preference would be to attribute their existence to an awareness that the production of good social science usefully might involve a combination of research styles. The history of the social sciences provides ample evidence of the value of organizing one's thoughts around a body of theory, working intensively at gaining an empathic insight into the human experience under study, and collecting and analyzing data that facilitate the determination of whether the phenomena observed are idiosyncratic and ephemeral or patterned and stable.

The social phenomenon addressed in this book is the process by which managers maintain control of their workforces. I have been guided by the theoretical work of Max Weber and the historical analyses of Reinhard Bendix, both of whom have pointed to the role of ideas in the process of social control. Although the role of ideology in contemporary organizations has been speculated upon before, it has been examined too broadly for consistent, nontrivial, relationships to be determined. To address that problem, this study looks at ideology concerning one topic, that of the concept of alcoholism. Managerial ideology is investigated here with a discussion of classical sociological theory, a description of alcoholism and "employee assistance" programs in business and industry, and a quantitative analysis of survey data from a large sample of U.S. corporations, to examine how and when these programs are used to achieve social control.

I admit to more than slight apprehension about the reaction to this attempt to employ both qualitative and quantitative styles of research in one book. Among the comments from a number of individuals who have kindly given their time and expertise in reading all or part of this manuscript has been the warning that my use of quantitative data provides opportunities for criticism of this manuscript by those who disagree with my conclusions or with the use of statistical procedures in general. My experience with some of those who read earlier versions of this book has confirmed the perspicacity of this warning: on two occasions, I was first told that what my subject really needed was one or two intensive case studies, and then told that my survey data on over 300 corporations' programs was of dubious representativeness and reliability. On two other occasions, I was told that the manuscript read too much like a dissertation. On probing for the specific meaning of that criticism, I was told that the book started out with a statement of the problem, presented the theory used to address the problem, provided data and analyzed them, and came to conclusions connecting the theory to the data. This characterization of my work as following the format of the leading publications in the field would hardly seem to be an unfavorable one, unless, of course, the leading journals are considered to be "itty bitty." Nor would data from over 300 corporations seem to suffer from problems of representativeness and reliability compared to one or two case studies, unless it is believed that the quantification necessary to distill all of the data collected from hundreds of firms necessarily prevents sociologists from "looking at the meaning of things," and transforms them into "quantifiers of minutiae."

In the social scientific study of organizations, the schism between qualitative and quantitative research seems to be across time as well as across individuals. Perhaps because of frustration with the failure of quantitative research paradigms to provide clear-cut answers, and perhaps because of the uninterest of consulting clients in recommendations for practice that are based on complicated statistical procedures, there has been a shift away from quantitative and toward qualitative work. This shift happens to have coincided with a shift over the past decade in which many of those engaged in the social science of organizations have moved from traditional academic disciplines, primarily psychology and sociology, into schools of business.

Thus, un-disciplined, organizational researchers have been rediscovering (and publishing in their specialty journals) approaches that psychologists and sociologists confronted many decades ago; some of these were found not to be useful and have largely disappeared from the literature, and some have by now been developed to a high level of theoretical and methodological sophistication. For example, although debates conducted in the sociological literature some decades ago substantially resolved issues concerning the value of functionalist and evolutionist theories, the mainstream of what lately is called "organization science" seems to be reconstructing these debates de novo. Similarly, social psychologists have spent decades cumulating a body of knowledge on the correspondences among attitudes, norms, and behaviors, yet those in the organization sciences have seemingly disregarded the consistent development of this literature, examining these same concepts, often unwittingly, in a series of temporarily popular topics such as "organizational climate," "organizational commitment," and "organizational culture."

During this decade I have had the good fortune to have teachers and graduate school and faculty colleagues who have illustrated, in their words and their deeds, the changing nature of the field. There are far too many individuals to name all of them here, but I do hope that they know how I feel about them.

One person whom I especially would like to thank is Lynn Miller, who took time from her own research and writing to read and comment on this manuscript. Her human sensitivity and rigor as a social scientist have set high standards for me. I thank her, and the others who have given generously of their counsel.

A genuine sociology of organisations as presented in the relevant works of Weber and Marx would not stop with investigations of organisational structures, technology and the role of managements and experts. It would also cover various other topics, such as the nature and function of personnel practices and procedures, mechanisms of management control, the impact of organisational experience on members' attitudes and aspirations, and the nature and role of organisational ideologies (Salaman 1978, p. 546).

1

Introduction and Overview

This study examines the interplay of organizational structures and processes with certain ideas espoused by corporate executives. In particular, it examines the ideological justifications of bureaucratic authority, a topic that was addressed by Max Weber in *Wirtschaft und Gesellschaft* and by Reinhard Bendix in *Work and Authority in Industry*. For these twentieth century theorists, and for Marx and Hegel as well, the study of bureaucracy played a central role in the sociological analysis of systems of domination. This book is directed toward aiding in the reclamation of that role for the contemporary social science of organizations.

The particular vehicle to be employed in the examination of these issues from classical social theory is an analysis of programs in business and industry that, according to their proponents, have been designed to identify and rehabilitate alcoholic and other "troubled" employees. This book questions organizations' claims about the purposes of these programs and investigates whether, under certain conditions, managements have motives that are at the least mixed, and that include social control of their workforces.

In this analysis of the nature of social domination, a variety of materials are brought together. These include an examination of the historical development of theories of organization and of social control, an analysis of written documents issued by companies to explain their alcoholism programs, and reviews of the literature on the nature of alcohol abuse problems in general, and the means by which they are dealt with in the workplace in particular. Specific hypotheses are then derived from these materials and are examined through quantitative analyses of detailed survey data regarding the operations and outcomes of alcoholism and "employee assistance" programs among a large sample of U.S. corporations. This chapter is intended to provide a brief overview of the theoretical and empirical issues that are addressed in later chapters.

This book begins with an analysis of Weber's writing on bureaucracy that argues for a very different understanding of those essays than that which has had such a strong influence on the development of the sociology of organizations in the United States. An attempt will be made to demonstrate that Weber's concerns were far closer to those of other social theorists than to those of management consultants (as is often taken to be the case). That is, his focus on control and the role of ideas in the control process are argued here to be core concerns of Weber and others writing in what C. Wright Mills called the classic tradition in sociological theory. Guided by these concerns, this study examines job-based alcoholism programs to address hypotheses concerning the use of managerial ideologies that facilitate the control of deviant behavior by redefining it as a medical problem.

The chapter following this introduction offers an analysis of the social structure to which some of Max Weber's best-known writing was directed, the bureaucracy. It contends that most discussions of bureaucracy in the one and a half centuries between the first coining of the term and Weber's writing on that topic concentrated on its relationship to the political structure. Only occasionally was commentary about bureaucracy concerned with its efficiency relative to other forms of administration. Moreover, most such remarks were criticisms of bureaucracy's intrusiveness and nonresponsiveness, and had been commonplace in Europe as far back as the eighteenth century. In fact, the word bureaucracy was invented as a mocking pejoration of this form of administrative apparatus.

The historical development of state power and the role of the state's administrative apparatus was a central controversy in the mainstream of European intellectual thought. This controversy, it is argued here, is most likely to have been Weber's primary concern in his writings on bureaucracy. It will also be contended that Weber's contribution to the debate on political power was later read as a prescription for effective organizational functioning, an erroneous understanding that resulted, at least partially, from the inaccurate English translation of Weber's work by Talcott Parsons. The chapter will detail how Parsons' functionalist orientation helped to transform Weber's analysis into a set of prescriptions that formed the basis for a research paradigm that has been highly productive empirically. Yet, because of those errors, the research that has been inspired by his version of Weber appears to be irrelevant to the theoretical concerns that animated Weber's attention to the study of organizations.

Additional reasons for the misconception that Weber's essays on bureaucracy were primarily directed toward problems of efficiency will also be addressed—in particular, the misunderstandings of his use of the terms *rationality* and *ideal type*. A great many contemporary social scientists appear to believe that Weber used the term *ideal* to mean something like perfect and that he used the term *rationality* to mean something like "optimally oriented toward goal attainment." It will be argued here, however, that *ideal* was an analytic rather than an evaluative term in Weber's methodology and that Weber employed the term *rationality* in a variety of ways, only one of which fits common usage.

These dilemmas in the translation of Weber suggest that the sociologists in the United States, primarily students of Parsons and Merton, who criticized what they perceived as Weber's lack of attention to "bureaucratic dysfunctions" were neither accurately assessing Weber's intended contributions nor making a novel contribution of their own. Similarly, the frequent characterization of Weber as the first to catalogue bureaucracy's structural features is inconsistent with the historical record, as he was preceded by Hegel, Schmoller, and even administrative policy manuals in Prussia.

Contrary to the various misconceptions and misinterpretations, Weber's work appears actually to have been focused on the means by which individuals or groups exercise power over others. His writings addressed the concerns of his historical predecessors, who debated the relative importance of ideas versus objective interests. According to the materialist viewpoint, societal development is governed by action based on the material interests of dominant groups; sets of beliefs are merely consequences of the interests of the powerful. Conversely, the idealist perspective views ideas as having a prime causal influence on the development and nature of social structures; a shift in religious beliefs, for example, might be seen as a cause of changes in the structure of intergroup relations in a society.

Weber's analysis of bureaucracy attempted to contribute to this debate on the true nature of the government administrative apparatus, considered a pivotal element in the analysis of social domination, by demonstrating the value of both idealist and materialist perspectives. The idealist pole of that debate was Hegel's view that the administration served to guarantee that the general will of the population would be served. A materialist inversion of Hegel's argument was propounded by Marx, who argued that the government apparatus served, in fact, to guarantee domination by those in possession of the material resources of society. Although Marx strenuously disputed Hegel's idealist analysis of bureaucracy, he was not a simple materialist. Very clearly, he viewed beliefs as important factors in historical change, as indicated, for example, by his concern with the problem of "false consciousness" among the proletariat. However, because he viewed ideas as emanating primarily from demands of the economic substructure, Marx assumed them to be oriented toward the self-interests of the ruling class and, therefore, most likely to be distortions of reality.

Specifically addressing this long-standing debate, Weber agreed with Marx's contention that a bureaucracy was a mechanism that served social control purposes for a dominant individual or clique. However, Weber added that this domination would be accomplished more easily if a set of ideas could convince those being subordinated that the advantageous situation of the dominant group was legitimate. Weber's explication of an ideal type model of a rational-legal bureaucracy, in which he described a set of structural features—hierarchical authority, written rules, and so on—that complemented one of the three categories of legitimating ideologies that he had proposed, was intended to illustrate how social ideas and social structures combine to effect domination. Also consistent with Marx's position, Weber viewed ideas and interests as mutually causal. However, he disputed the Marxian notion that ideas expressed by groups or their representatives should be assumed to be untruthful. He advocated, instead, their empirical study, as exemplified in his well-known analysis (1930) of the social structural correlates of the Protestant Reformation.

Reinhard Bendix, in *Work and Authority in Industry,* applied the Weberian perspective on the process of social domination to a study of the ideas used by management during the development of industrial society. Noting that one aspect of bureaucratic structure, complexity, was a source of control problems, rather than a response to them, he hypothesized that increasingly complex organizational differentiation along with increasing size create control problems requiring the use of managerial ideologies to maintain effective domination.

The research reported here endeavors to test the viewpoints of Weber and of Bendix on the relationships among administrative structures, ideologies, and domination. Organizational administration and processes of domination and control are familiar topics of research, but ideology has been more resistant to empirical investigation. This study, rather than attempting to assess a global ideology of management, restricts its focus to managerial viewpoints on one topic. It is argued here that the problem referred to as alcoholism provides especially appropriate subject matter for an examination of the role of ideology. Given the lack of societal consensus concerning the accuracy of the various explanations of the set of problems associated with the ingestion of alcohol, a variety of "ideologies of alcoholism" actively compete.

Four differing alcoholism ideologies are analyzed: the moral, sociological, psychological, and medical explanations of alcohol problems. They are evaluated in terms of both the empirical evidence and the political interests arrayed for and against each of them. Next, programs in work organizations that have been instituted with the stated intention of identifying and rehabilitating employees with alcohol problems are described. Originally called alcoholism programs, they have almost always accepted clients with other "behavioral-medical" problems, such as drug abuse and marital difficulties. In recognition of this (and, perhaps, for additional reasons, pertinent to their social control function) their charter typically has been expanded in recent years, and they are now more frequently called "employee assistance programs"("EAPs"). This description will suggest that one of the most frequently espoused alcoholism ideologies in these programs' training sessions and educational literature is the medical model, which holds that alcohol problems constitute a medical disease very much like cancer, diabetes, or tuberculosis.

However, the medical model of alcohol problems happens to be the one for which the systematic scientific evidence has found the least support and the greatest amount of clear disconfirmation. This book suggests that in many firms the adoption of the medical disease model of alcoholism has resulted neither from chance nor from an especially sympathetic approach to alcohol problems; rather, the promotion of this scientifically discredited view constitutes the use of an ideology that is helpful for the social control of the workforce. The data that will be presented constitute an attempt to demonstrate that under the guise of treating "the disease of alcoholism" many corporate managers have been able to use a serious health problem, the abusive overconsumption of alcohol, to construct a generalized mechanism of deviance sanctioning.

This has been accomplished, it is argued here, through the application of some extraordinary theories concerning the symptoms of, and appropriate therapy for, alcoholism. Those firms whose alcoholism and employee assistance programs promote the disease model of alcoholism also generally allege that the major symptoms of what this viewpoint represents as an invariably progressive, irreversible, and fatal disease, are absenteeism from and lateness to work, and low work productivity. The use of these diagnostic symptoms provides a justification for labeling as alcoholic any employees who perform poorly, and for forcing them (a "therapeutic" strategy necessitated by what is said to be another of the disease's supposed major symptoms—denial) to enter the company program.

Once in the program, employees may be referred to treatment, which most typically consists of mandatory attendance at meetings of Alcoholics Anonymous. The major emphasis of "the program," however, is likely to consist of monitoring cooperation with this putative treatment assistance by measuring improvement in the "symptoms of the disease"—that is, clients' absenteeism, lateness, and productivity are observed very closely. A lack of improvement in these "symptoms" is taken as an indication of a lack of cooperation with the program, and companies often cite what they construe as employees' uncooperativeness as justification for firing them. Thus employees who perform poorly are diagnosed as alcoholic, and if their job performance improves they are pronounced recovered—with no reference at any point in the process to any use (much less abuse) of alcohol. Conversely, those who perform poorly and are diagnosed as alcoholic, but who do not improve their job performance sufficiently, are likely to be fired—not because they are alcoholics, companies may claim, but because they are said not to have participated wholeheartedly in the "help" that their employer has offered.

A review of research pertinent to the efficacy of this approach provides little reason to believe that absenteeism, lateness, and poor productivity are reasonably reliable indications of alcohol problems. However, even though these job performance symptoms may be unrelated to alcoholism in the great majority of cases, research does show that forcing people into "treatment" for alcoholism leads to improvement in their work behavior. This procedure of forcing treatment, under the threat of job loss, is referred to as "constructive confrontation" (originally, "constructive coercion") and is a cornerstone of a great many corporate programs. Unfortunately, although constructive confrontation leads to improvements in job behavior, there is no evidence that such coercion causes salutary changes in alcohol consumption.

To examine further the operation of employee assistance and employee alcoholism programs, and to help address the hypotheses concerning the relationships among ideology, structure, and control that were derived from Weber's and Bendix's formulations, analyses of survey data will be reported. More than 300 large U.S. corporations responded to questionnaires requesting details of the structure and outcomes of their alcoholism or employee assistance programs, along with data on the organizations' structure, and on beliefs held by the program administrators and the corporations' senior personnel executives. Analyses of the relationships between elements of bureaucratic structure and executives' perceptions of problems in controlling employee job performance will be presented, both to examine Bendix's view that certain aspects of organizational structure and context contribute to control problems and Weber's assessment of the role of other structural elements as responses to such problems. Supplementing the qualitative data presented in earlier chapters, the quantitative analyses attempt to demonstrate empirically that the medical disease model of alcoholism does serve management as an ideology useful for social control. More specifically, Chapter 8 examines the hypothesis that in organizations whose contexts and internal structures create control problems, management will state that the impetus for the alcoholism program was a concern about controlling work performance. Further, it examines the hypothesis that organizations experiencing problems with control over employees' work performance will respond both structurally, by altering bureaucratic mechanisms, and ideologically, by adopting an alcoholism program based on the medical disease perspective.

The concluding chapter reviews this study's use of classical sociological theory for organizational analysis, comparing it to current fashions in organization theory. It contends that recent "innovative" theoretical perspectives are actually rediscoveries of a number of the ideas advanced in the earliest stages of the development of organizational sociology in the United States, discussed earlier in the book as based on misreadings of Weber and other major European social theorists. It suggests that the weaknesses that led to the disappearance of these early paradigms are equally evident in their modern reincarnations. This study hopes to demonstrate that theories that have continued to be of central concern to social scientists in general can be fruitful bases for the social scientific analysis of formal organization.

2

Theoretical Foundations of the Sociology of Organizations

The contemporary sociology of organizations derives primarily from the analysis of developing governmental administrative institutions in France and Prussia during the seventeenth and eighteenth centuries. The growth of these mechanisms appears to have been related, in a general sense, to the monarchs' increased needs for control arising from the larger and more diverse geographic areas and populations under their domination.

In the particular case of France, the assignment of permanent, salaried officials to virtually all regions of the country was instituted originally as a more efficacious alternative to tax farming. In Prussia the major administrative innovations occurred more than half a century later, following that state's defeat by Napolean in 1806. The earlier, collegial *Kabinettsystem* of officials who advised the ruler and made decisions in a relatively collective manner was replaced by the *Einheitssystem* of clear, hierarchical responsibility and authority.

The appellation commonly given such devices was *bureaucracy,* a term that appears to have been coined in 1745 by Vincent De Gournay (Krygier 1979). His usage of the word was entirely pejorative, denoting a form of government run by meddlesome, self-serving officials (the term *bureau* referred to a type of desk blotter favored by French government officials). Indeed, the typical use of the term in Europe during the eighteenth and nineteenth centuries centered on the arrogation of state power by officials. A corollary of the perception that bureaucratic functionaries lacked concern for serving the interests of the public was the view that they failed to function efficiently in their official capacities. Consequently, another referent of the term bureaucracy became that of an inefficient device for carrying out the state's business.

Although such unfavorable characterizations were the rule, there is one particularly notable historical exception. In *The Philosophy of Right*

(1952) Hegel attempted a response to the problem posed by Rousseau in *The Social Contract* (1951) concerning the division between private and public interests (i.e., between civil and political life, or rights and responsibilities), which Rousseau spoke of as the distinction between *homme* and *citoyen.* Hegel argued that the government administrative apparatus was the mechanism of societal integration through which this duality could be unified. The thesis and antithesis in his dialectical analysis were, respectively, the state and civil society. In Hegel's terminology, the state referred to the universal will of the general populace, as embodied in and expressed by the monarch, the government's executives, and the legislature. Opposing the general will was civil society, by which he meant those elements of the social structure in which self-interests determine the nature of individuals' social relations, such as in a private business.

Stated in this manner, Hegel's notion of civil society appears isomorphic to the Hobbesian *bellum omnium contra omnes.* However, Hegel viewed these ego interests as achieving some measure of social-political unity through the "corporations," the pivotal structure of civil society. Using this term in its contemporary sense, it is not clear how the existence of corporations deters economic competition. However, in Hegel's era the term "corporation" signified guildlike associations of individuals within an occupation or trade, structures through which economic competition was regulated and coordinated. Further defining the concept of civil society, Hegel categorized societal self-interests into three *stande* (literally, statuses, translated as social estates or classes): the substantial (or agricultural) estate, the formal (or business) estate, and the civil servants.

As suggested by his categorization of the civil servants as representative of civil society, and of the executive power, the other arm of government administration, as representative of the state, Hegel considered the bureaucracy to be uniquely representative of both elements of society. He contended that, as the one group whose concerns were those of both the particular and the general interest, the collectivity of individuals engaged in the administration of the state constituted the synthesis integrating these dialectically-opposed aims, and were thus *der allgemeine stand* (typically translated as "the universal class").

Having posited that the government administrative apparatus was the key integrating mechanism in society, Hegel proceeded to discuss the specific characteristics that made it particularly capable of serving this role. In doing so, he provided a set of structural and processual features of bureaucracy that predates, by roughly a century, Weber's highly parallel yet better known essays on this topic. The word bureaucracy did not appear in Hegel's writing, very probably because of its negative connotations. However, the following sections from Hegel's discussion make a number of points that typically are presented in textbooks as Weber's contribution to management theory, such as the advisability of task specialization and hierarchy and the need for salaried officials appointed on the basis of technical qualifications, who perform their duties in an impersonal manner.

> Division of labor occurs in the business of the executive . . . the business of government shall be divided into its abstract branches manned by special officials as different centers of administration (1952, par. 290).

> The nature of the executive functions is that they are objective and that in their substance they have been explicitly fixed by previous decision . . . individuals are not appointed to office on account of their birth or native personal gifts. The objective factor in their appointment is knowledge and proof of ability. Such proof guarantees that the state will get what it requires; and since it is the sole condition of appointment, it also guarantees to every citizen the chance of joining the class of civil servants (1952, par. 291).

> The state does not count on optional, discretionary services . . . it is just because such services are optional and discretionary that the state cannot rely on them, for casual servants may fail for private reasons to fulfill their duties completely, or they may arbitrarily decide not to fulfill them at all but pursue their private ends instead. . . . What the service of the state really requires is that men shall forgo the selfish and capricious satisfaction of their subjective ends; by this very sacrifice, they acquire the right to find their satisfaction in, but only in, the dutiful discharge of their public functions. In this fact, so far as public business is concerned, there lies the link between universal and particular interests which constitutes both the concept of the state and its inner stability (1952, par. 294).

> The security of the state and its subjects against the misuse of power by ministers and their officials lies directly in their hierarchical organization and their answerability; but it lies too in the authority given to societies and Corporations, because in itself this is a barrier against the intrusion of subjective caprice into the power entrusted to a civil servant, and it completes from below the state control which does not reach down as far as the conduct of individuals (1952, par. 295).

> But the fact that a dispassionate, upright and polite demeanor becomes customary is (i) partly a result of direct education in thought and ethical conduct. . . . (ii) The size of the state, however, is an important factor in producing this result, since it diminishes the stress of family and other personal ties, and also makes less potent and so less keen such passions as hatred, revenge, etc. In those who are busy with the important questions arising in a great state, these subjective interests automatically disappear, and the habit is generated of adopting universal interests, points of view, and activities (1952, par. 296).

The best-known response to Hegel's contention that bureaucracy constitutes a universal class, resolving the dilemma posed by Rousseau, is that of Marx. His *Critique of Hegel's 'Philosophy of Right'* (1970) argues that the bifurcation of civil and political life was of recent origin (completed in the bourgeois revolution in France) and that Hegel's analysis did not constitute a resolution, but merely an acceptance, of the social alienation implied in such a split. In attacking Hegel's highly favorable analysis of the functioning of the government administration, Marx strongly criticized the view that bureaucracy serves as a force for societal integration and accommodation of the general will. Rather, Marx viewed the government bureaucracy as an instrument of social division and particular interests and denigrated Hegel's essay as failing to go beyond merely flattery of the Prussian state. According to Marx, "What Hegel says about 'the Executive' does not merit the name of a philosophical development. Most of the paragraphs could be found verbatim in the Prussian Landrecht" (1970, p. 44). In addition, he contended that "Hegel gives us an empirical description of the bureaucracy, partly as it actually is, and partly according to the opinion it has of itself" (1970, p. 45).

Marx had been raised in a region of Germany and in a social milieu in which Prussian hegemony (which Hegel's writing represented) characteristically was viewed with some antipathy. Consequently, it is not surprising that, rather than conforming to Hegel's significant choice of the terms "executives" and "civil servants," he inserted the clearly pejorative "bureaucracy." Marx argued that the notion that the Prussian bureaucracy served the general interests of society was merely a cloak for an institution whose true function was to enforce the domination of particular class interests over those of the general will. He thus disagreed with Hegel's assertion that bureaucratic functionaries constituted a "universal class," serving to reunify social divisions. Rather, he viewed those engaged in the operation of the bureaucracy as a transitory and parasitic class, which would cease to exist when the alienative, class-based, capitalist society was transcended.

Consistent with this analysis, Marx paid relatively little attention to bureaucracy in his later writings. However, he did not reject Hegel's concept of a universal class; rather, he transformed it into the crucial dynamic of social change in his materialist inversion of Hegel's dialectic. He posited that historical change occurs when one class can, for a period, identify its own interests with the universal interests of society; in turn, the feudal class and the bourgeoisie were universal classes, according to Marx. He theorized that the next stage in this historical progression, the proletarian revolution, would be qualitatively different from previous changes in the class structure. Calling the proletariat the ultimate universal class, he argued that this revolution would signal the end of class society (including such elements as a parasitic class of bureaucrats), rather than a substitution of new class dominancy relations for old ones.

Although Marx's view that the bureaucracy was a temporary, parasitic class might have been expected to direct attention away from the study of bureaucracy, one of its effects was to inspire the most well-known writing on this topic, that of Weber. With more of an historicist orientation than Marx, Weber saw society as stratified on a greater number of dimensions than only that of differing relationships to the means of economic production (in particular, he added political and status group dimensions). Accordingly, domination, the process by which the system of stratification is created and maintained, need not be class domination, nor rooted in the production process. Weber stated that "Not every case of domination makes use of economic means; still less does it always have economic objectives" (1968, p. 212).

Weber did set two general conditions for the exercise of domination. One was the existence of an administrative staff: "normally the rule over a considerable number of persons requires a staff . . . that is, a special group which can normally be trusted to execute the general policy as well as the specific commands" (1968, p. 212). The second condition he proposed as necessary for domination was the belief of those subordinated in the legitimacy of the relationship:

> Experience shows that in no instance does domination voluntarily limit itself to the appeal to material or affectual or ideal motives as a basis for its continuance. In addition every such system attempts to establish and to cultivate the belief in its legitimacy. But according to the type of legitimacy which is claimed, the type of obedience, the kind of administrative staff developed to guarantee it, and the mode of exercising authority will all differ fundamentally (Weber 1968, p. 213).

Having identified the "type of legitimacy which is claimed" as the key to the means of subordination, Weber offered three pure types of legitimate domination, that based on rational, traditional, and charismatic grounds. He argued that each of these corresponds to a particular mode of administration:

> *Rationally regulated* association within a structure of domination finds its typical expression in bureaucracy. *Traditionally* prescribed social action is typically represented by patriarchalism. The *charismatic* structure of domination rests upon individual authority which is based neither upon rational rules nor upon tradition (Weber 1968, p. 954).

Thus, in Weber's view, when social interaction is based on rational grounds, domination is legitimated (and thus transformed from power into authority) through a bureaucratic means of administration. Of the three modes of legitimate domination this one was of the greatest interest to Weber; writing at the beginning of the twentieth century, he considered rational authority to be the historically ascendant ideational basis of legitimation. In particular, he saw authority based on "formal rationality" (one of Weber's categories of rationality, discussed below) as having an elective affinity with capitalism, primarily because of the capitalists' requirement of calculability of financial affairs.

Weber employed this analysis of the correspondence between the rise of capitalism and the tendency toward rationalized modes of domination to reinterpret Marx's theory of alienation. In contrast to Marx, Weber argued that the separation of laborers from the product of their labor in the capitalist industrial process did not indicate that capitalist social relations of production were uniquely alienating. Rather, he viewed this separation as an instance of the general process of rationalization, and suggested that analogous processes of bifurcation occur in noncapitalist contexts, such as the military and even the university:

> Through the concentration of [the ownership of laboratories and other such research facilities] in the hands of the privileged head of the institute the mass of researchers and instructors are separated from their "means of production," in the same way as the workers are separated from theirs by the capitalist enterprises (Weber 1968, p. 983).

For Marx bureaucracy was merely a superstructural embodiment of the class-based, and therefore alienating, production system. For Weber bureaucracy was the most crucial instrument of the advancing predominance of formally rational action, the type of action that he saw as a cause of the combination of separation and surrender that Marx appears to have intended in his use of the term *alienation* (Schacht 1970). Weber therefore contended that the crucial leverage point in social domination would not be control over the means of production, but over the means of administration of various forms of collective social action.

THEORY AND RESEARCH ON ORGANIZATIONS SINCE THE TRANSLATION OF WEBER

The discussion to this point has suggested that the preponderance of writing on bureaucracy has been concerned with its relationship to processes of power and domination. Nevertheless, this focus seems to have been lost in the contemporary social sciences, as seems evident in the interpretations made of the most significant of these analyses, that of Weber, and in the uses to which his work has been put.

Max Weber's writings on bureaucracy seem to have been largely misunderstood by social scientists in the United States, and this misunderstanding has been of substantial consequence for the direction of the sociology of organizations through the 1950s, 1960s, and the early part of the 1970s. At least three factors seem to share responsibility for the development and persistent popularity of this view of Weber: Talcott Parsons' mistranslation of Weber's introduction to *Wirtschaft und Gesell-*

schaft; the general misunderstanding of Weber's concepts of ideal type and rationality (also partly attributable to Parsons); and the desire of social scientists in the United States to identify empirically researchable subject matter.

The Influence of Talcott Parsons on the Sociology of Organizations

Parsons' only specific writing (1956a, 1956b) on the sociology of organizations and bureaucracy was a two-part essay written at the invitation of the editor of the newly-founded *Administrative Science Quarterly.* As Pfeffer (1976) has noted, the specific elements of Parsons' approach to the analysis of organizations has had only a minimal impact on organizational sociology. However, his general intellectual influence has been crucial, despite a background that provided him with questionable credentials for such a role.

Many details of his academic training have been provided by Parsons himself in an autobiographical article (1970). He wrote that, after studying economics and biology as an undergraduate at Amherst College, he was uncertain of his career direction and accepted a relative's offer to pay for a year of postgraduate study in Europe. From 1924 to 1925 Parsons attended the London School of Economics, where he received his first exposure to the social sciences, studying under the functionalist anthropologist Bronislaw Malinowski and the evolutionist sociologists Hobhouse and Ginsburg. Still uncertain of his career goals at the end of that year, he took advantage of a fellowship that provided support for study at a German university. He enrolled at the University of Heidelberg, in whose intellectual community Max Weber had participated from 1896 to 1919 (although Weber's official faculty tenure was irregular and brief due, especially, to mental illness). By no means, however, had Parsons chosen Heidelberg because of an interest in pursuing Weberian scholarship; indeed, prior to arriving in Heidelberg he had not heard of Weber. The specific link between Parsons and Weber was Edgar Salin, who had studied with Weber and taught Parsons.

Learning that three semesters of course work and a thesis were all that were required for the doctorate at Heidelberg, Parsons decided to continue past the fellowship year to complete the degree. He wrote a dissertation, "The Concept of Capitalism in the Theories of Max Weber and Werner Sombart," on a topic that appears to have been highly consistent with the interests in that intellectual climate. As Shils (1970) has noted, the relatively little attention paid to Weber's work by German academics in the years following his death in 1920 was restricted to two areas: his writing on the *Methodenstreit* (a "crisis" over the appropriate nature of social scientific research methodology; current disputes over the relative merit of qualitative and subjective versus quantitative and objective techniques are strikingly similar); and his contribution to the debate over the historical synchronicity between the Protestant Reformation and the rise of capitalism. Shortly after writing the thesis, Parsons published his English translation of Weber's *The Protestant Ethic and the Spirit of Capitalism* (1930), the work that had been central to Parsons' thesis. This was not the first English translation of Weber; in 1927 a collection of the lectures Weber presented at the University of Munich in 1919, translated by Frank Knight, was published under the title *General Economic History.* However, Parsons' appointment in 1927 to the Harvard faculty provided the institutional basis for the dissemination of Weber's ideas.

But was Parsons, an individual whose exposure to social science theory was somewhat brief and narrow, the most appropriate interpreter of Weber's work? By his own admission the young Parsons was far from fluent in German, a particular predicament in light of the difficulty of Weber's prose. Weber's wife and biographer, Marianne, has cautioned that:

> He was entirely unconcerned with the form in which he presented his wealth of ideas. So many things came to him out of that storehouse of his mind, once the mass [of ideas] was in motion, that many times they could not be readily forced into a lucid sentence structure. . . . After all, let the reader take as much trouble with these matters as he had done himself (Marianne Weber 1950, p. 350).

Reinhard Bendix, perhaps the most astute of Weber scholars, has concluded:

> The plain fact is that Weber's work is difficult to understand. Whatever may be said in justification of long sentences and scholarly qualifications is not enough to explain the characteristic "style" of Weber's sociological writings, which tends to bury the main points of the argument in a jungle of statements that require detailed analysis, or in long analyses of special topics that are not closely related to either the preceding or the ensuing materials (Bendix 1960, p. 18).

Faced with both the limits of his own training and the complexities of Weber's writing, Parsons may well have tended to make translations consistent with theoretical perspectives with which he was familiar. This is not to suggest that any distortion was necessarily volitional on Parsons' part; rather, such an approach may have helped to provide what Parsons felt was a conceptual consistency not very apparent in the original. To assess the appropriateness of Parsons' highly influential view of Weber, his translations will be compared here with those of others.

Weber's major writings on bureaucracy were contained in a manuscript that was unfinished at his death, and was subsequently published as *Wirtschaft und Gesellschaft* (1922). Sections of this work, including the detailed essay on bureaucracy, were published in English in 1946 in a collection of Weber's essays translated by Hans Gerth and C. Wright Mills. The following year, Henderson and Parsons' translation of the first four chapters of *Wirtschaft und Gesellschaft* was published under the title *The Theory of Social and Economic Organization*. These chapters constituted the "conceptual exposition" for the 16 chapters and appendix that followed. As Parsons noted in the introduction to that translation, its publication had been delayed a great many years; indeed, he had discussed this work a decade previously, in his classic *The Structure of Social Action* (1937). His interpretation of Weber appears to have been influential in the training of his early graduate students, and Wren (1979) noted that Parsons introduced even Chester Barnard to Weber's work.

A complete English translation of *Wirtschaft und Gesellschaft* did not become available until 1968, in an edition edited by Guenther Roth and Claus Wittich, entitled *Economy and Society*. Its version of Chapter 3, which contains the introductory essay on bureaucracy, was based on Parsons' original translation. However, the differences between Parsons' and Roth and Wittich's published versions suggest a systematically expressed disagreement as to Weber's theoretical focus. Parsons' translation appears to be highly consistent with the theoretical orientations to which he had been exposed at that early point in his career: Malinowski's functionalism, and the neo-Kantian idealism he began to read after arriving at Heidelberg (see Munch 1981). Consistent with those perspectives, Parsons interpreted Weber's essays on bureaucracy as concerned with how rule codification, task specialization, and hierarchical authority systems facilitate the effective functioning of organizations and societies, and with the role of value consensus in that process. In contrast, Roth and Wittich presented Weber as an analyst of the roles of material and ideal interests in the process of social domination.

Certainly the best-known difference between Parsons' and others' translations of Weber is the interpretation of the term *Herrschaft*. Bendix (1960), Gerth and Mills (1946), Cohen, Hazelrigg, and Pope (1975), and Antonio (1979) translated the term as domination. Parsons, in lone dissent, translated it first (1947) as imperative coordination and later (1960) as leadership. The crux of the debate, which last reoccurred in Parsons' response (1975) to Cohen, Hazelrigg, and Pope, derives from Parsons' view that normative consensus, whether expressed through law, religion, or administration of states and enterprises, was the focus of Weber's concerns. Reviewing Bendix's biography of Weber, Parsons wrote:

> The term [*Herrschaft*], which in its most general meaning I should now translate as "leadership," implies that a leader has power *over* his followers. But "domination" suggests that this fact, rather than the integration of the collectivity in the interest of effective functioning ... is the critical factor from Weber's point of view. The former interpretation

[does not represent] the main trend of Weber's thought . . . the preferable interpretation . . . is represented especially by his tremendous emphasis on the importance of legitimation (Parsons 1960, p. 752).

Other interpreters of Weber, however, have considered legitimated *Herrschaft* only one possible means of producing compliance to one's will, and have argued that he did not see social control as necessarily predicated on the consent of those who are subordinated. Cohen, Hazelrigg, and Pope (1975), as an example, found strong support for this view, citing Weber's statement:

It is by no means true that every case of submissiveness to persons and positions of power is primarily (or even at all) oriented to this belief [in legitimacy]. Loyalty may be hypocritically simulated . . . on purely opportunistic grounds, or . . . for reasons of material self-interest. Or people may submit from individual weakness and helplessness (Weber 1968, p. 214).

Comparing Roth and Wittich's with Parsons' translations of Weber on domination and on bureaucracy reveals a number of subtle influences of their own theoretical orientations in addition to the much discussed dissensus over the translation of *Herrschaft*. In the discussion of the relationship between domination (imperative control for Parsons) and legitimacy, Roth and Wittich translated Weber as stating: "Every form of domination implies a minimum of voluntary compliance" (1968, p. 212). Parsons' version of that same passage reads: "A criterion of every true relation of imperative control, however, is a certain minimum of voluntary submission" (1947, p. 324). Parsons, who used Weber as the basis for the development of a "Voluntaristic Theory of Action" (1937, pp. 473–694), here emphasizes Weber as propounding a "certain minimum," that is, a baseline of voluntary acceptance of control. For Roth and Wittich, it was merely "a minimum," that is, not very much voluntary acceptance is required. For Parsons, what is volunteered is "submission," that is, "a yielding or surrendering of power" (Gove 1976). For Roth and Wittich, however, there is only voluntary "compliance," that is, "conformity in fulfilling formal requirements" (Gove 1976). Thus, two rather different understandings of Weber's perspective on control have been presented: in Parsons' version control is predicated on a certain baseline of voluntary surrender; Roth and Wittich viewed it as founded merely on a minimum of voluntary conformity.

Responding not to Marx, but to the "vulgar Marxists" of his own era, Weber continued his analysis of the requisites of a system of social control by pointing out that material factors alone do not generally provide a stable basis for a system of domination. According to the Roth and Wittich translation, Weber did concede to the Marxists that "in certain exceptional cases" material factors "alone may be decisive" (Weber 1968,

p. 213). Parsons' version gives even less significance to the role of material (as opposed to affectual or ideal) concerns, translating the first part of the above statement (Weber 1947, p. 325) as "in certain exceptional *temporary* cases" (emphasis added).

Weber's writing linked the rise of capitalism not only to a shift in religious ideas, but to the rise of bureaucratic administration of enterprises. In the Roth and Wittich translation, this connection is unequivocal: "capitalism in its modern stages of development requires the bureaucracy" (Weber 1968, p. 224). However, this view, that the development of bureaucracy was related to the growth of an economic structure, suggests a material rather than normative basis for bureaucratic authority, and in Parsons' translation the connection between a capitalist economy and bureaucratic administration is presented as more tenuous. He translated Weber as having stated that "capitalism in its modern stages of development strongly tends to foster the development of bureaucracy" (Weber 1947, p. 338).

Weber continued his analysis of the administrative aspects of domination by arguing that "bureaucratic administration means fundamentally domination through knowledge" (1968, p. 225). The exception to that rule provided by Weber has, once again, distinctly different meanings in the two translations. In the Roth and Wittich version, Weber is translated as having stated:

> Superior to bureaucracy in the knowledge of techniques and facts is only the capitalist entrepreneur, within his own sphere of influence. He is the only type who has been able to maintain at least relative immunity from subjection to the control of rational bureaucratic knowledge. In large scale organizations, all others are inevitably subject to bureaucratic control, just as they have fallen under the dominance of precision machinery in the mass production of goods (Weber 1968, p. 225).

In this translation the issue is domination over persons through technique. Weber points out that only the entrepreneur, at the top of the organization, is not controlled by the bureaucracy, which constrains the behavior of all others in the administrative hierarchy as surely as modern machinery constrains the behavior of production workers. In the following version by Parsons, this passage becomes merely a melancholic recognition of the ascendance of technical administration, as heralded by the capitalist entrepreneur:

> Bureaucracy is superior in knowledge, including both technical knowledge and knowledge of the concrete fact within its own sphere of interest, which is usually confined to the interests of a private business— a capitalist enterprise. The capitalistic entrepreneur is, in our society, the only type who has been able to maintain at least relative immunity from subjection to the control of rational bureaucratic knowledge. All the rest

of the population have tended to be organized in large scale corporate groups which are inevitably subject to bureaucratic control. This is as inevitable as the dominance of precision machinery in the mass production of goods (Weber 1947, 339–40).

Certainly these two versions of the same passage are different, but is there reason to conclude that one more accurately conveys Weber's meaning? Parsons' version compares poorly, first of all, on the basis of coherence. Whereas Roth and Wittich noted the superiority of the entrepreneur over the bureaucracy, Parsons noted that bureaucracy is superior but never indicated to what it is superior (indeed, the syntax of his first sentence is very unclear). What was deemed inevitable in Roth and Wittich's version was that everyone except the entrepreneur will be subjected to bureaucratic control in the large-scale organization. Weber, pursuing his analysis of systems of domination, then noted that bureaucratic control was analogous to machine control of production. In Parsons' version, however, the same passage does nothing to advance or clarify the theorist's argument. Parsons translated Weber as referring to the growth of machine-paced industrial work as inevitable, but rather than providing an illustration of an historical process having theoretical significance, the passage serves merely as an observation of one more unfortunate historical occurrence.

Still, even though the material on bureaucracy was contained in a major section of his book, concerning what he called *The Sociology of Domination,* Weber *may* have been simply expressing a pessimistic vision of the future (which he did indeed hold), rather than analyzing domination. However, the beginning of that section made his primary purpose in discussing bureaucracy quite clear. It started with a discussion of the role of legitimacy and the three pure types of legitimate domination. This was followed by a discussion of what Weber considered to be the most crucial of those types for modern society, rational-legal domination. He then supplied eight fundamental precepts of this form of legitimate domination, the last of which reads, in Roth and Wittich's text:

> Legal authority can be exercised in a wide variety of different forms which will be distinguished and discussed later. The following ideal-typical analysis will be deliberately confined for the time being to the administrative staff that is most unambiguously a structure of domination: "officialdom" or "bureaucracy" (Weber 1968, p. 219).

Thus bureaucracy was analyzed because it was the clearest example of the structural form taken by rational-legal domination. In Parsons' version, however, this idea is buried; his interpretation of Weber's justification for the lengthy and highly detailed discussion of bureaucracy was simply that it provided an example of how the coordination that is necessary for effective functioning of social collectivities may be accomplished:

> The following analysis will be deliberately confined for the most part to the aspect of imperative coordination in the structure of the administrative staff. It will consist in an analysis in terms of ideal types of officialdom or "bureaucracy" (Weber 1947, p. 332).

The differences detailed here between the views of Weber contained in Parsons' writing and those contained in all other interpretations of Weber indicate consistent differences. Only Parsons did not view Weber's analyses of bureaucracy as a discussion of domination, and only Parsons has held the functionalist view of Weber as concerned with the best means by which to achieve "the integration of the collectivity in the interest of effective functioning." Nevertheless, despite his lone dissent and the inhospitability of Weber's text to his interpretations, it is Parsons' interpretation of Weber that has been of overwhelming influence in the development of the sociology of organizations in the United States. A major reason for this influence is likely to have been Parsons' tenure on the Harvard faculty for almost half a century, a status that not only lent credibility to his translations, but, as Mullins (1973) has noted, also afforded Parsons the opportunity to influence students who themselves became prominent.

Conservative Social Theory at Harvard and the Development of Two Schools of Organization Theory

The direction of the research paradigm that was based upon Parsons' translation of Weber was influenced by additional intellectual currents at Harvard in the 1930s. These perspectives can be detected in the work of Parsons' early students, the first and most noted of whom was Robert Merton. His essay on "The Unanticipated Consequences of Purposive Social Action" (1936) was a major program statement for not only his own subsequent research, but for that of his own graduate students as well. Indeed, much of the history of the sociology of organizations can be traced to the work of Merton (1940) and his students Peter Blau (1955), Alvin Gouldner (1954), and Philip Selznick (1949). As March and Simon (1958) observed in their classic analysis of major research reports in the young field of organizational theory, these studies were "remarkably similar." In each case Merton's idea that social actions have latent as well as manifest functions was applied to the Parsonian understanding of Weber's analysis of bureaucracy. These studies reported that adherence to the characteristics of what their authors believed was Weber's prescriptive model of bureaucracy did not necessarily contribute to effective organizational functioning; rather, strict adherence to those tenets led to unanticipated, dysfunctional consequences. For example, Gouldner (1954) found that the imposition of a formal rule stipulating the specific number of permitted absences per year resulted in poorer attendance, as many employees absented themselves for the maximum number of days allowed. Similarly, Blau (1955) described how regulations that specified a particular quantifiable performance measure as the basis for employee appraisals caused employees to work to meet that one standard, but to ignore other stated goals of the organization. The common general theme of these studies seems to have been that formal, rational structures could not be presumed to ensure efficiency, because of their failure to account for the less formal and less rational conduct of the individuals who make up organizations.

These analyses were misdirected as criticisms of Weber, who (as discussed later in this chapter) most probably would have concurred with their views of the dubious efficiency of formal organizations. However, the explanations advanced by Merton, Gouldner, and Blau for these failures of bureaucratic administrative mechanisms provide considerable insight into the intellectual influences, in addition to functionalism, on the writing of Parsons and his students.

During the 1930s Parsons was associated with what came to be known as the Harvard "Pareto Circle." Lawrence Henderson, a bio-chemist who had joined the faculty of the Harvard Business School to work with the Industrial Fatigue Laboratory, had been contemptuous of social science prior to reading Pareto at the suggestion of an entomologist friend. Fascinated by Pareto, Henderson employed a variety of formal and informal settings to proselytize for his newly found faith. According to Hacker (1955), in Henderson's hands Pareto's social thought took on an even more conservative form than it had in the formulations of its author (who had been a supporter of Mussolini, a member of his government, and an acknowledged source of Mussolini's political philosophy). Henderson represented Pareto as arguing that those who were not among society's elites were nonlogical, acting on the basis of emotions rather than in their own best economic interests. They were thus seen as in need of an elite to guide them, or, to use the candid language Henderson employed in lectures to students at the Harvard Business School, to manipulate them (see Hacker 1955). The group that formed around him has been character-ized as consisting mostly of politically conservative Harvard faculty, very few of whom had training in the social sciences, who apparently were seeking intellectual refuge and legitimacy in the face of the left-wing climate on that campus during the 1930s (Keller 1984). The poor regard in which Pareto's sociological theories were held by social scientists seems not to have been attributable simply to Pareto's anti-Marxism. In addi-tion, sociologists have viewed it not as sociological theory but as post hoc application of a crude instinct psychology, in which stories of unsuccess-ful social actions are presented as proof that certain people are nonlogical (Zeitlin 1968).

The other major figure in this group, along with Henderson, was Elton Mayo, Henderson's colleague at the Business School and good friend. The Industrial Fatigue Laboratory was funded by the Laura Spelman Rockefeller Memorial Foundation (later the Rockefeller Foundation), and Mayo, who had worked for the Rockefellers previously, had been brought to Harvard as its founding director. Mayo held only a liberal arts baccalaureate, having dropped out of medical schools on three occasions (Trahair 1984), but Dean Donham's formal request to President Lowell for Mayo's appointment to the Harvard faculty seems to have embellished on his educational attainment. It apparently stated that he held a master's degree, and implied that he had completed medical school. Mayo, who furnished his office at Harvard with medical paraphernalia, had his secretary dress in a nurse's uniform, and allowed others to address him as "Dr. Mayo," did little to disavow these exaggerations (Trahair 1984).

Perhaps the major theme in Mayo's social theorizing was one that, in his view, was based on the work of Emile Durkheim. Mayo argued (1933) that the dissolution of traditional preindustrial society, with its tight structure and clear and unquestioned leaders, had created a state of anomie among the masses. He proposed that the modern industrial corporation could replace the traditional village as the source of individuals' satisfaction of their most basic needs, those of human contact and social relatedness (as opposed to more economically "rational" concerns). However, this is a substantial misrepresentation of Durkheim, who did not view modern society as eliminating social solidarity, but as causing a qualitative change in its bases, from solidarity based on "mechanical" adherence to common norms, to solidarity based on "organic" functional interdependencies. Even more problematic for Mayo's view, Durkheim (1933) insisted that capitalist industrial enterprises were a pathological form of modern society and could never serve as an instrument of social solidarity.

According to Parsons (1970), it was Elton Mayo who had originally prompted him to take up the study of Freud's work. Freudian theory, with its emphasis on the role of unconscious motives, is highly congenial with the Harvard group's understanding of Pareto. This is particularly the case in Freud's later, more sociological work (such as *Civilization and Its Discontents* 1930), in which Freud contends that the masses, recognizing their inability to control their id impulses, accept the superego function exercised by leaders and by a structured society. Although, given the zeitgeist of the 1930s, it seems likely that Parsons would have come across Freud without Mayo's advice, Parsons' link to Mayo's perspective on organizations has been significant for the direction of the sociological analysis of organizations.

Despite the dubious accuracy of the Harvard group's understandings of Pareto and Durkheim, an ideologically conservative amalgam of these ideas, along with the highly complementary views of Freud, were used by Mayo to dignify his interpretations of the putative experiments conducted at the Western Electric Company's Hawthorne Works from 1924 to 1933. Indeed, despite an overabundance of evidence that his interpretation is not accurate (see Bramel and Friend 1981; Franke and Kaul 1978; Rice 1982), it is still widely accepted. Mayo interpreted the Hawthorne study data as showing that workers increased their output in response to attention and approval from supervisors and coworkers, rather than in response to financial incentives. He offered these supposed facts as confirmation of his views that worker motivation was not economically rational, but was more accurately described as irrational, nonlogical, or unconsciously motivated, and that group behavior was best understood as oriented toward mechanical solidarity. In short, the functioning of organizations was said not to be explainable merely by reference to formal, planned, rational structures and processes, but must also take into account the informal "human relations" on the job.

Mayo's discovery, in the 1930s, that human social interactions influenced workers' behavior did not in fact constitute a novel theoretical insight. In the United States this observation goes back, at the least, to Frederick Taylor. Although Taylor generally is characterized as having treated task design, selection, training and financial incentives as the major determinants of productivity, he devoted considerable attention to instances of output restriction resulting from norms informally agreed upon and enforced by the workers (Braverman 1974). In Europe, as discussed earlier, the notion that people's idiosyncrasies and interests can impair their effectiveness as functionaries in organizations formed the basis for most of the pre-Hegelian critiques of bureaucracy. Indeed, by the 1920s European research on these phenomena had gone far beyond the Hawthorne researchers' simple rediscovery that behavior such as output restriction occurred. For example, Max Weber (1924) had conducted survey research that investigated the relationship between output restriction and a variety of personal background variables.

Thus, the findings of the Harvard group may not have been especially novel, may have been addressing a political rather than a social scientific agenda, and may have been based on inaccurate interpretations of the theories they were said to be investigating and on careless interpretations of the experimental evidence. Nonetheless, in establishing the modern sociology of organizations Parsons' student Merton and Merton's own students appear to have employed the "new" facts about the limits of organizational rationality revealed in these studies to explain how unintended consequences always intervened to invalidate what they had been told were Weber's prescriptions.

Merton's group originally had attempted to disconfirm the view that application of the entire model of bureaucracy would lead to improved organizational functioning. One of his students, Peter Blau, extended this critique by dissecting the Weberian model into its elements. He argued that not only could Weber's general model be subjected to empirical disconfirmation, but so might its separate components (Blau 1956). He stated that the bureaucratic model

> includes not only definitions of concepts but also generalizations about the relationships between them, specifically the hypothesis that the diverse bureaucratic characteristics increase administrative efficiency. Whereas conceptual definitions are presupposed in research and not subject to verification by research findings, hypotheses concerning relationships between factors are subject to such verification. Whether strict hierarchical authority, for example, in fact furthers efficiency is a question of empirical fact, and not one of definition (Blau 1956, p. 34).

The following year, Blau set a specific research agenda:

> It is possible to test the hypothesis implied by Weber that administrative efficiency is the result of a combination of various characteristics in a bureaucracy, provided that empirical data on these characteristics and on efficiency can be obtained for a large sample of bureaucratic organizations (1957, p. 67).

Two years later Udy (1959) reported his findings that the model that had been extrapolated from Weber could appropriately be treated as multidimensional. He found, for example, that organizations having numerous hierarchical levels did not necessarily have similarly large divisions of labor or bodies of formal rules. The insights that "Weber's model" could be tested by comparing data from many organizations, and that the elements of that model were variables that might or might not co-vary and might or might not be associated with administrative efficiency, served as the foundation for the paradigmatic sociology of organizations for virtually the next two decades. Representative of these "tests" of "Weber's model" are studies by Blau and Schoenherr (1971), Child (1972a), Hage and Aiken (1967), Hall (1963), Meyer (1972), and Pugh and his associates (1968, 1969).

Not only did the various influences at Harvard in the 1920s and 1930s spawn the "Weberian" analysis of organizations, but they seem to have been substantially responsible for the development of the major competing perspective on the sociology of organizations as well, a viewpoint epitomized by the richly detailed qualitative descriptions of life in organizations conducted originally by a group of scholars at the University of Chicago. The beginnings of this perspective are associated with one of Mayo's disciples, W. Lloyd Warner, who had been very strongly influenced by the anthropologists Malinowski and Radcliffe-Brown. Whereas Parsons' contact with Malinowski had been brief, leaving an influence on Parsons' theoretical viewpoint but not on his choices of problems and methods, Warner was an anthropologist, coming to Harvard fresh from ethnographic field research on Australian aborigines. Eventually realizing that he would not be granted tenure at Harvard (Trahair 1984), Warner accepted a position at the University of Chicago. As the first director of that university's Committee on Human Relations in Industry, his anthropological perspective combined with the qualitative, micro-social research orientation of Chicago sociology (discussed in more detail in the next chapter) to inspire many of the most engaging early qualitative analyses of the social structure of work organizations. Warner was succeeded as director of that committee by his former doctoral student, William Foote Whyte, who, as a Junior Fellow at Harvard during the period when the Society of Fellows was directed by Lawrence Henderson, had also been a member of the Pareto Circle.

Whyte, a major contributor to these studies, has observed (1965) that members of the Chicago group eventually wanted to move beyond the findings that could be derived from intensive analyses of one case; by roughly the end of the 1950s, these studies had largely been eclipsed by the research of Blau and others working in Blau's quantitative framework. Perhaps, after discovering that there were some gross similarities between social interactions in modern organizations and those in primitive tribes, such as the existence of rituals and myths, there was not much more to say. However, as this book's final chapter will discuss, boredom with the apparently atheoretical "Weberian" analysis of organizations seems to have been at least partly responsible for a return in recent years to the Chicago approach of Warner's era.

Despite their dryness, the "Weberian" studies have created a substantial base of knowledge about the structure of organizations; for example, it has been repeatedly established that as organizations increase their number of employees, they tend to develop more hierarchical levels, specialized activities, and written procedures. If for no other reason than that they constitute an increased understanding of a social structural, supra-individual phenomenon, the findings of these studies are of sociological interest. However, they do not address the issue central to Weber's analysis of bureaucracy, that of domination. Parsons' general biasing of Weber's texts away from a concern with control, and toward that of collectivity integration in the pursuit of effective functioning, appears to be a major cause of this misdirection. However, in addition to the problems of translating words such as *Herrschaft,* incorrect understandings of two other key terms in Weber's writing—ideal type and rationality —have greatly compounded organizational sociology's difficulties in getting at the heart of Weber's analysis of domination.

"Rationality" and the "Ideal Type"

The acceptance of Parsons' functionalist perspective appears to have been facilitated by the seeming straightforwardness of the interpretation of "rationality" and "ideal" (as in "ideal type"). It appears that most English-language readers of Weber assume that he discussed bureaucracy as "ideally rational," which they have taken to mean "perfectly efficient." This view is consistent with Parsons' interpretations of these terms, but, once again, his translation is open to question. In his brief essay on Weber's methodology in his introduction to *The Theory of Social and Economic Organization,* Parsons (1947) argued emphatically for a view of Weber as a voluntarist (that is, as one who emphasizes the social integrative function of directed human choice):

> It is inherent in the frame of reference of "action" which is basic to Weber's whole methodology, that it is "normatively oriented." The actor is treated as not merely responding to stimuli, but as making an "effort" to conform with certain "ideal," rather than actual, patterns of conduct. . . . The ideal type . . . states the case where a normative or ideal pattern is perfectly complied with (p. 12).

In *The Structure of Social Action* (1937, p. 75) Parsons had defined *normative* as referring to action involving sentiments of a desirable end-state (that is to say, the way things *should* be). In the passage quoted above he treated *normative* and *ideal* as synonymous, thus representing Weber's ideal types as prescriptive models. This conception of the ideal type fits congenially with his interpretation of Weber's ideal type model of bureaucracy as a prescription for effective functioning. It fits very poorly, however, with Weber's own statement (in apparent anticipation of such misunderstandings) of what the purely analytical model that he referred to as the ideal type actually was:

> We should emphasize that the idea of an ethical *imperative,* of a "model" of what "ought" to exist is to be carefully distinguished from the analytical construct, which is "ideal" in the strictly logical sense of the term. It is a matter here of constructing relationships which our imagination accepts as plausibly motivated and hence as "objectively possible" and which appear as adequate from the nomological standpoint (Weber 1949, pp. 91–92).

Parsons had discussed Weber's methodological essays in detail in *The Structure of Social Action* and it is difficult to understand how this caveat, offered therein, was missed. Parsons' other bases for interpreting Weber as engaged in advocacy of bureaucratic organization, however, are more readily comprehended. In discussing the ideal type model Weber repeatedly used the term *utopia,* which Parsons (and others) may well have taken to mean "any visionary system of political or social perfection" (Gove 1976). But that usage would have contradicted the passage quoted above. The more correct understanding is probably that of Mannheim, writing in 1929, who noted that the then "contemporary connotation of the term 'utopian' is predominantly that of an idea which is in principle unrealizable" (1936, p. 177).

Rationality is another term that seems to have helped persuade Parsons to conclude that Weber's model of bureaucracy was a prescription for effective functioning. As was the case with the term *utopia,* Weber did not clarify his use of the term sufficiently for Parsons, who accused Weber of leaving his meaning unclear:

> Now the term rationality is used as pointing to certain specific criteria distinguishing some kinds of action from others. Weber unfortunately does not give us an explicit statement of these criteria, but they can be inferred from his discussion. An act is rational in so far as (a) it is oriented to a clearly formulated unambiguous goal, or to a set of values which are clearly formulated and logically consistent; (b) the means chosen are, according to the best available knowledge, adapted to the realization of the goal. The question of efficiency, a very important one in defining rationality, is not introduced by Weber at all until Chapter II and then only in a very limited context (Parsons 1947, p. 16).

Other commentators, however, have been able to discern a more clear, although more differentiated, use of the term by Weber. Although there is some dissensus over the precise number of categories of rationality and their boundaries, it is generally agreed that Weber employed a variety of types of rationality (Giddens 1971; Kalberg 1980; Swidler 1973). In not all of those types did Weber fit the voluntarist mold into which Parsons wished to place him.

For example, one category of rationality was formal rationality, the application by experts of intellectually analyzable, knowledge-based rules. It is this form of rationality to which Weber referred when stating that "bureaucratic administration means fundamentally the exercise of control on the basis of knowledge. This is its specifically rational character" (1947, p. 339), and "Bureaucratic authority is specifically rational in the sense of being bound to discursively analyzable rules" (1947, p. 361). It is crucial, however, not to assume that the sense of the word *rationality* conveyed in these brief passages was necessarily linked to efficiency or organizational goal attainment. Albrow, who has written the most detailed analysis of Weber's essays on bureaucracy, has stated that "Weber frequently referred to the fact that formal rationality did not guarantee what he called material rationality. Indeed, the most perfect formal system might operate to defeat the purposes and values which animated it" (1970, p. 64). Further, Albrow has contended

> that efficiency was for [Weber] a foreign term. It appears in many translations of Weber's work but this reflects more the preconceptions of the translator who cannot conceive of rationality in the organization except as efficiency, than any consistent usage by Weber of a term equivalent to efficiency (1970, p. 64).

WEBER AND BUREAUCRACY IN CONTEMPORARY
ORGANIZATION THEORY

Despite the various problems that have been identified with the Parsonian perspective on Weber, it seems to constitute the dominant framework for the contemporary analysis of organizations. Least surprisingly, it appears in the writing of Parsons' own students. For example, his student Leon Mayhew provided this concise restatement of the view of Weber taken by Parsons: "Bureaucratic organization is essential to modern political organization because it is the means by which collective energies can be mobilized in the efficient pursuit of deliberately chosen collective goals" (1971, p. 147).

The influence of Parsons on Merton and his students such as Gouldner, Blau, and Selznick has already been discussed. In turn, these writers have themselves become important sources on Weber for others. For example, Chris Argyris, a highly influential management theorist, quoted from Gouldner to point out that "it is important to keep in mind that Weber conceived of bureaucracy (formal organization) as 'the most efficient form of social organization ever developed' " (1957, p. 71). Blau's student, Richard Scott, explained "Weber's central message" in terms that both emphasized Blau's own research program and characterized Weber as prescriptively inclined, stating that:

> He viewed each bureaucratic element as constituting the *solution* to a problem or defect contained within the earlier administrative systems. Further, each element operates, not in isolation, but as part of a system of elements that, in combination, were expected to provide more effective and efficient operation (1981, p. 69).

Of course, misunderstandings of Weber's essays on bureaucracy are not limited to Parsonians. Typically, writers have attempted to convey the general theme that Weber called his model of bureaucracy "ideal" and "rational" and so must have been recommending the model's application as an efficient way to conduct organizational affairs. Some authors go into substantial detail concerning what they believe to have been the precise meanings of the terms in Weber's work. In explaining the ideal type, Osborn, Hunt, and Jauch wrote:

> To understand Weber's view it is important to realize that he attempted to describe ideal types much like a human anatomy text outlines the perfect human form. Some of Weber's critics claim that he is too idealistic. And by design he is (1980, p. 80).

In the view of Bobbitt, Breinholt, Doctor, and McNaul:

When we set up something as an *ideal type,* we are taking a normative position; i.e., we are making an assumption about *what should be,* what is right or proper. Weber viewed the bureaucracy as an ideal type because he felt it had certain advantages over other organizational forms (1978, p. 65).

Defining Weber's usage of the term *rationality* in his analysis of bureaucracy, Klein and Ritti stated that "*rational* here means 'for reasons of competence' or 'for greater effectiveness' rather than simply reasonable" (1984, p. 76).

In some cases Weber's theory of bureaucracy is explained in terms of its relationship to other "classical management theories." Kochan, for example, noted that "like the scientific management researchers, Weber presented an 'ideal type' or 'one best way' model of organization" (1980, p. 12). According to Szilagyi, "Like Taylor, Weber believed that the key to an organization's survival was through mechanisms that increased the *efficiency* of its activities. . . . In other words, Weber promotes the 'one best way' to structure all types of organizations" (1984, p. 289). Similarly, Gibson, Ivancevich, and Donnelly asserted that "Both Fayol and Weber described the same kind of organization, one that functioned in a machinelike manner to accomplish the organization's goals in a highly efficient manner" (1985, p. 489).

Probably the most typical representation of Weber's analysis of bureaucracy is simply to outline the elements of the model and to state that Weber believed that their usage would lead to efficiency. Bedeian, writing under the heading "Max Weber: Bureaucracy as the Ideal," stated that Weber regarded bureaucracy "as the most modern and efficient organization yet developed" (1984, p. 60). According to Duncan, "Max Weber . . . cites many cases of how the hierarchical, or pyramid structure leads to organizational efficiency" (1978, p. 14). Champion wrote that "the bureaucratic model prescribes a list of essential components which must be present in organizations in order for maximum efficiency to be obtained" (1975, p. 33). Miner's view is that Weber "believed that in its pure form, undiluted by other types of authority and forms of organization, bureaucracy represents the most efficient form of organization possible" (1985, p. 64). Robbins stated that Weber "sought to describe an ideal organization—one that would be perfectly rational and would provide maximum efficiency of operation" (1983, p. 189).

Views such as these portray Max Weber as a sort of turn-of-the-century management consultant. A number of these themes are brought together by Zey-Ferrell, who wrote:

The most influential proponent of the bureaucratic model was Max Weber. He argued for the maximization of organizational efficiency as a consequence of legitimate, rationally-based authority. Weber had little regard for practices of favoritism based on status (especially family connections) and hiring of personal friends and saw bureaucratic organizations as correcting such practices (1979, p. 48).

Champion covered much of the same territory, making a particular effort to impress the reader with Weber's practical perspicacity.

Weber believed that members of organizations should not relate to one another on a personal basis.... Again, nepotism becomes the target of Weber's analysis as he specified that employees be selected on the basis of their abilities.... Each employee should have jurisdiction over his own work activity.... Weber also believed strongly that rules of law would enable people to make decisions more objectively ... each person should develop a high level of competence (1975, pp. 34–35).

Descriptions of Weber as a writer of platitudinous how-to-manage advice seem to derive in part from the influence of the Parsonian perspective, in which Weber is interpreted as having prescribed a mechanism designed for functional efficiency. Although many of the writings that have been cited here could be characterized as the necessarily superficial work of textbook writers, by no means have all of these authors depended on secondary sources for their analyses of Weber. In a number of cases, their discussion is accompanied by all or part of a passage from Weber that states:

Bureaucracy—is, from a purely technical point of view, capable of attaining the highest degree of efficiency, and is in this sense formally the most rational known means of carrying out imperative control over human beings. It is superior to any other form in precision, in stability, in the stringency of its discipline, and in its reliability (Weber 1947, p. 337).

The passage above is from Parsons' translation, much of which permits, indeed promotes, an interpretation of Weber as prescribing a mechanism that would facilitate efficient functioning. However, in the passage above, the term *efficiency* (which Albrow has argued is inappropriate in any case) is connected to bureaucracy only "from a purely technical point of view." Weber immediately clarified just what type of rationality he meant, by explaining that bureaucracy "is in this sense formally the most rational." By characterizing bureaucracy as an example of formal rationality, Weber was indicating his confidence that such an administrative arrangement would no doubt lead to more precise, stable, disciplined, and reliable operation. Nevertheless, he did not mean to indicate that such procedures would invariably lead to desirable end-states. In his view, action taken without regard to goals and values (that is, action that was not substantively rational) did not provide sufficient conditions for organizational effectiveness. Thus, it is not correct to view Weber either as having believed that bureaucratic structure yields a maximal output for a given level of inputs (in other words, that it is efficient) or as having "sought to pin down the characteristics that lead to a successful institution" (Schwartz 1984, p. 15).

In some cases this misunderstanding of Weber has taken the form of an imaginative folklore of the social sciences, such as Bennis' assertion that "bureaucracy is a term invented by Max Weber" (1970, p. 1). More recently, Medeiros and Schmitt wrote that "The basic dimensions of this 'bureaucracy as machine' model were first stated by the architect of 'ideal-type' bureaucracy, Max Weber" (1977, p. 21). Berkly informed readers that "The burgeoning of bureaucracy ... was a gradual process. However, like most social movements, it gained impetus when it acquired a major theoretician. The theorist in this case was Max Weber" (1978, p. 31).

Some authors have created an historical context to help explain why Weber would advise such a form of organization:

> Weber saw it [bureaucracy] as the fairest, most rational and logical form of organization possible. Weber's Germany was run very much on a "traditional" basis. Jobs were handed out on the basis of who you were related to and knew, and how much influence you had. In light of this type of system, it is easy to understand why he preferred a more "rational" and impersonal system of organization (Stuart-Kotze 1980, p. 267).

> Weber attempted to replace a system of patronage for staffing management positions with a system based on competence and rationality of administration. At the time, organizations largely reflected the hierarchy of social classes that existed *outside* of them. This meant, of course, that only certain individuals, by luck of birth or acquaintance, could gain management positions (Anderson 1984, p. 51).

Max Weber, however, does not seem to have shared this view of what his concerns were. In an essay published in the *Frankfurter Zeitung* in 1917 he wrote:

> Surpassing all [previous organizational systems], the Germans perfected the rational, functional, and specialized bureaucratic organization of all forms of domination from factory to army and public administration. For the time being the Germans have been outdone only in the techniques of party organization, especially by the Americans (Weber 1968, p. 1400).

In the majority of the books cited here, the presentation of Weber is followed by a critique of his work, the substance of which is generally to accuse Weber of disregarding the ways in which internal and external uncertainties vitiate the efficiency that Weber purportedly claimed for bureaucracies. For example, Altman, Valenzi, and Hodgetts listed the elements of Weber's "description of the ideal bureaucracy" and then wrote:

> If one were to structure an organization along bureaucratic lines, the design would look very good—at least on paper. However, failure to consider the human element would cause all kinds of problems. As a result, Weber's bureaucratic characteristics merely provide us with a point of departure. The needs of the organizational personnel and the demands of the external environment have to be accommodated (1985, p. 343).

Szilagyi stated that "A careful examination of Weber's work reveals an absence of the word 'environment' " (1984, p. 291). In order to make this same general critique, Dessler (1980) provided a very different view of the facts concerning Weber's perspective on organizational environments. Explaining that Weber was "writing during the 1920's" (ghostwriting perhaps—he had died in 1920), Dessler noted Weber's comment that bureaucracy improves administrative reaction time and wrote that "one of the ironies in the development of organization theory is that bureaucracy, which has come to mean a ponderous and unadaptive organization, was originally advocated as the best form for dealing with a changing environment" (1980, p. 26).

It would thus appear that Weber was ignorant of either the effects of environmental uncertainty on bureaucracies or their appropriateness for responding to such variability are highly inconsistent with what Weber actually wrote; indeed, they impugn his common sense. The impact of situational variability on bureaucratic structures was obvious to Weber. However, his writing on bureaucracy was not intended to be read as a management development treatise, and he was eminently clear in stating that a discussion of the real-world pitfalls of bureaucratic structures was not appropriate in *Wirtschaft und Gesellschaft*. Weber stated that "The fact that the bureaucratic apparatus also can, and indeed does, create certain definite impediments for the discharge of business in a manner best adapted to the individuality of each case does not belong into the present context" (Weber 1968, pp. 974–75).

It would thus appear that Weber serves, at least for pedagogic purposes, as a "straw man"; he is the historical foil against which are posed the present-day "enlightened" acknowledgments of "the human factor" and of the necessity of flexibility in the face of "change."

For research scholars, the effect of treating Weber's writings on bureaucracy as a set of empirical hypotheses has been to add some intellectual luster to the sociology of organizations (or "organization theory," as it is called in schools of business), a subfield that has suffered from considerable theoretical impoverishment. Indeed, sociology in general has been plagued by the difficulty of finding subject matter that is, on the one hand, a supraindividual level phenomenon and, on the other, amenable to empirical investigation.

Other than the work of Weber, however, the contemporary sociology of organizations exhibits a noticeable dearth of theoretical foundations. Frequently, textbooks' discussions of Weber are included in the same section as discussions of the pronouncements of the "classical administrative theory school," a grouping of the assorted writings of a number of aging executives who deigned to share their experience-based guidelines as to what they confidently believed was the best way to manage. For example, Henri Fayol, the most prominent member of this "school," listed basic principles of effective organization, such as specialization and centralization. However, his formulation of the application of these principles has been of very limited use to either management practitioners or to scholars interested in hypothesis testing. Centralization, for example, was said to be most effective when there was neither too much nor too little of it. Similarly, his list of the "functions of management," such as planning, controlling, and commanding, is of questionable practical value. For example, Fayol stated that, in order to command, managers should eliminate the incompetent, set a good example, and aim at making unity, energy, initiative, and loyalty prevail among the organization's personnel. Although long on strictures such as these, the writings of Fayol and of the other classical theorists are short on the specifics of how these patently appropriate aims might be accomplished.

Ironically, given its redirection from theoretical issues of social control to managerial concerns with efficiency, the origins of the "Weberian" sociology of organizations in the United States had a great deal to do with the development of theory. Parsons' student Merton, in conducting and directing the early, seminal studies of bureaucracy, was addressing his own agenda on what the direction of social theory should be. Parting company with attempts at grand theory, Merton believed that sociological theory should start with "theories of the middle-range," from which micro-level and macro-level theory could then be developed. He saw the study of bureaucracy as providing an excellent setting for middle-range theorizing; as a social setting in which individuals and society interact, he viewed its study as holding the promise of bridging that interstice. In fact, Merton (1957) cited his students' research on bureaucracy as the best extant examples of the utility of the "theories of the middle-range" perspective.

Thus, in light of this subfield's original focus on systematic theory development, it is particularly regrettable that the study of organizations should degenerate into banal prescription. This chapter has attempted to demonstrate that the nature and role of formal organizations were of central interest in the origins of modern social theory, and has maintained that the focus, in a number of theoretical paradigms, on systems of domination and control has been lost in the contemporary sociology of organizations. The following chapter attempts to articulate further the connection between theories of bureaucracy and sociological theory in general, by endeavoring to reintegrate the theoretical concerns that motivated Weber's analysis of bureaucracy with the historical concerns of sociologists in the United States.

3

Ideology as a Social Control Mechanism

Weber's contribution to the debate over the nature of domination and control in society, a theoretical edifice in which his analysis of bureaucracy is a cornerstone, is paralleled by another stream of sociological theory, the literature on "social control." Among the most important mechanisms of social control, as seen in the tradition that runs from the writing of Marx, to that of Weber, and then to Bendix, is ideology. This chapter begins with a discussion of the concept of social control, primarily as it developed among sociologists in the United States, and addresses its relevance for the present study. It then examines Marxian and Weberian analyses of the role of ideology in social control. Next, the recent history and current status of managerial ideologies, used to facilitate control of the workplace, are traced. Finally, some limitations of contemporary organizational control strategies are outlined, along with the characteristics of an ideology that might further strengthen managerial hegemony.

THE SOCIAL CONTROL TRADITION IN THE UNITED STATES

The term *social control* has been widely diffused to sociologists in the United States, primarily through the writings of scholars associated with the sociology department at the University of Chicago. Among these sociologists was E. A. Ross, who, between 1896 and 1901, published 20 articles in the *American Journal of Sociology* that analyzed the various mechanisms that sustain the social order. In his book *Social Control,* Ross defined this concept as "concerned with that domination which is intended and which fulfills a function in the life of the society" (1901, p. viii). For Ross, and for other early twentieth-century American sociologists working in the social control tradition, the peaceful social order of preindustrial life was a paradise that had been lost to criminals, avaricious capitalists, and other social actors whose behavior deviated from the presumed societal consensus for harmonious social relations. The desirability of that earlier social order was an assumption and a starting point for these theorists, who then took up the sociological task of analyzing those social structures that seemed to function as mechanisms to reproduce the social order attributed to preindustrial societies. From this perspective, disharmonies (i.e., conflicts) were seen as the result merely of deviant norms and behaviors.

Despite this early intellectual leadership, Lemert (1967) contended that "the concept of social control has never been defined to the full satisfaction of sociologists." A major source of this dissatisfaction may have been the difficulty in distinguishing this term from the central concerns of other founders of modern sociology. Both the Chicago School's conception of social control and the perspectives of theorists such as Durkheim appear to have been rooted in Rousseau's romanticism and in the work of Saint-Simon and Comte, who followed directly in Rousseau's tradition. The theoretical perspective of both the early French sociologists and the Chicago sociologists was centered around their view that modern society, with its ever-increasing differentiation of tasks (and therefore of interests), had destroyed the natural social order of human cooperation. This is not to say that either the Chicago School theorists or Durkheim viewed all premodern societies as superior bases for human social interaction; Durkheim (1933), in fact, considered the modern form of society as potentially more humane. However, in both perspectives the maintenance of harmony in modern society was seen as requiring specific formal mechanisms: for Durkheim, those that promote "organic solidarity," and for the Chicago School, those that maintain "social control."

The essential problem in the work of the Chicago School is not only the same as that of Durkheim, Janowitz (1975), and Melossi (1983), but of Marx and Weber as well. Once again, the similarity seems to be attributable to the common derivation of their foci from Comte's concern about the impact of industrialization on social solidarity. That is, the Chicago sociologists' interest in deviance from societal norms was paralleled by the theoretically crucial discussions of anomie, alienation, and formal rationalization in the writing of Durkheim, Marx, and Weber, respectively. Indeed, Janowitz, although not advocating such a stance, observed that "one can translate much of the corpus of sociological writings on macrosociology into the language of the social control framework" (1975, p. 87). Thus, the focus of the social control perspective may be seen as indistinguishable from the most basic interests of Marx, Weber, and Durkheim, the three most important figures of modern sociology.

In order to differentiate the social control perspective from other approaches, the most frequent contemporary use of the term has been more narrow than its earlier extension to virtually all aspects of the structure and organization of modern society. For example, Coser and Rosenberg stated that "social control refers to those mechanisms by which society exercises its dominion over component individuals and enforces conformity to its norms and values" (1969, p. 97). Clinard also defined social control in terms of the actions taken to ensure norm conformance. He argued that "by observing the operation of sanctions, or in other words, social control . . . we can infer the nature and the limits of acceptable and nonacceptable behavior implicit in given norms" (1963 p. 18).

Societal response to failures to conform with norms is the focus, as well, of what is perhaps the most influential modern theoretical statement on social control, that of Parsons in *The Social System* (1951). Parsons' emphases in that book, on consensus in society and on mechanisms to maintain the prevailing social order, are consistent with the structural functionalist perspective that has been suggested in the previous chapter as having been a legacy of his European training (under Malinowski, in particular).This is not to say, however, that sociologists trained in the United States were unsympathetic to that approach. Indeed, Ross, in defining social control as "domination which is intended and which fulfills a function in the life of society" clearly aligned himself with that perspective. Although structural functionalism has been characterized as supportive of political conservatism (Gouldner 1970), Ross' personal history would seem to suggest that this was not his intent in employing that theoretical framework. Rather, those in the Chicago School tradition simply saw social controls, such as educational systems, as helping to maintain conformity with the will of the general populace, as expressed through operative norms that had been consensually, or at least democratically, derived.

As noted in the introductory chapter, however, the present study examines the maintenance of social order in business and industrial organizations, settings in which the formal norms have not been established through the consensus of all participants, but by those who manage the firm. Social control in these settings is thus most likely to refer to mechanisms to ensure conformity with the will of corporate management. Needless to say, the large body of laws and regulations by which society has endeavored to apply social controls to corporations suggests that the will of management may not necessarily be identical to that of the wider public. In this setting the Chicago School approach, which assumes a consensually-based set of norms, seems inappropriate, at the least. Centered on the societal reaction to deviance, this theoretical perspective would appear likely to underplay the dynamic of conflicting interests inherent to authoritarian social settings.

Despite the similarities between the Chicago School and Parsonian approaches to social control, the latter perspective has contributed insights that are central to the analysis to be presented here. Pitts (1968), elaborating on Parsons' discussion of the institutional patterns that attempt to prevent and/or manage deviance, argued that ideology serves an important function in social control by clarifying the substantive content of norms. Additionally, he maintained that the redefinition of many forms of deviance as medical problems facilitates social control by providing a basis for reliable negative sanctioning.

These two contentions of Pitts are the foci of this book's analysis of ideology, which argues that under certain conditions many corporate managers have effectively combined the two elements of social control strategy that he has proposed. Specifically, this study hopes to demonstrate how organizations have promoted an ideology advocating that a wide variety of deviant behaviors in organizations be thought of as symptomatic of a medical problem that is widespread among the employee population but that can be treated if its victims are identified.

Although this book will use the term social control, its analyses will, for the reasons presented above, be guided primarily by the European rather than the Chicago School developments of the traditions of Rousseau, Saint-Simon and Comte. Writers in the historical mainstream of European social-political thought, although sharing the attention of those in the United States to the problem of social order, pursued a different analytic focus. Rather than conceiving of deviance as generally dysfunctional, and investigating the means by which it could be eliminated, they examined the mechanisms by which a variety of conflicting interests are accomodated and those by which some interests win out over others. Following in this tradition, described in the next section, this study will examine the social structures and processes through which competing collectivities attempt to exercise social control; in particular, it will examine managerial control strategies in the context of the interaction between organizational structures and ideologies.

IDEOLOGY AND SOCIAL CONTROL IN EUROPEAN SOCIAL THOUGHT

The term *domination,* central to Ross' definition of social control, was central as well to Max Weber's discussion of bureaucracy. As has been shown, a particular interest in Weber's sociology of domination, as in most of his writing, was the long-standing debate over the relative primacy of ideas versus material interests in the process of historical change.

From Kant's response to the British empiricists, up to Hegel, the German philosophical tradition had been primarily idealist. Ludwig Feuerbach, a "Left Hegelian," reversed the causal ordering in Hegel's analysis of the relationship between ideas and real, material structures. As applied in his masterwork, *The Essence of Christianity* (1957), Feuerbach's transformative criticism posited material factors as the cause of ideas or "spirit."

Feuerbach is perhaps most important as the source of Marx's materialism.* He was nonetheless criticized by Marx, in the "Theses on Feuerbach" (1977), and by Marx and Engels in *The German Ideology* (1947), for viewing individuals as perceiving and acting in social isolation, a stance that directed attention away from the political ramifications of materialism. Marx also criticized Feuerbach for holding to an overly rigid materialism, which denied the reciprocal effects of ideas and actions. This is illustrated in the third of the 11 theses, in which Marx stated that "The materialist doctrine that men are products of circumstances and upbringings, and that, therefore, changed men are products of other circumstances and changed upbringing, forgets that it is men that change circumstances, and that the educator himself needs educating" (Marx, p. 156 in McLellan 1977). For Marx, although ideas primarily are the result of material interests, they may be employed to further those interests:

> The ideas of the ruling class are in every epoch the ruling ideas: i.e. the class, which is the ruling force of society, is at the same time its ruling intellectual force. The class which has the means of material production at its disposal, has control at the same time over the means of mental production, so that thereby, generally speaking, the ideas of those who lack the means of mental production are subject to it. The ruling ideas are nothing more than the ideal expression of the dominant material relationships, the dominant material relationships grasped as ideas (Marx and Engels 1947, p. 61).**

The related notions in Marx's work, exemplified above, that beliefs have an existential basis and are distorted to further particular interests, are the two most frequent conceptions of the term *ideology* in Marx's writing. Weber was aware of the polemical implications of Marx's usage of the term and although much of Weber's work addressed the idealist-materialist dispute over the sources of social order and change, a debate in which Marx's contributions were considered by Weber to be central, Weber used the word ideology very infrequently. In his essay on objectivity in the social sciences (Weber 1949), he implied that a reason for

---

*Another source is Helvetius, who wrote (1758): "our ideas are the necessary consequences of the societies in which we live."

**Some commentators (for example, Plamenantz 1970) seem to have interpreted Marx's statements about the significance of ruling class control over the "means of mental production" to mean that because they own the newspapers (and other communications media), the ideas available to the public are only those that the ruling class chooses to print. This is unlikely, however, to have been the meaning Marx intended. According to Marx, the application of ideas to the ends of the ruling class only occurs after the division of labor has proceeded to a separation of mental and physical work, with the ruling class performing the former, and those subordinated, the latter. Mental production, then, refers not simply to the specific manufacture of ideas, but to all the ideas on which the relations of production are predicated.

this nonusage was his view that social scientists should not engage in evaluations of their subject matter, but should examine the world-views of individuals and groups on their own terms. He viewed Marx's understandings of various political-economic phenomena as narrow and thus inaccurate and misleading guides to reality (and, therefore, to real-world applications), but maintained that they were nevertheless extremely useful when considered as ideal types (that is, as conceptual exaggerations with which reality is usefully compared).

The best-known applications of Weber's approach to the role of ideational factors are contained in his writings on the sociology of religion. For example, in *The Protestant Ethic and the Spirit of Capitalism* (1930), Weber attempted to fill in the historical details around the previously observed synchronicity of the rises of capitalism and Protestantism. His major theoretical thrust was to reject the adequacy of one-way and monocausal explanations for capturing the mutually causal nature of this phenomenon. Because Marx had emphasized the effects of real structures on ideas, Weber, as a moderate corrective (probably aimed more at "vulgar Marxists" than at Marx), took the opposite approach and emphasized the impact of religious ideology on economic structures. Weber's view, shared with Marx, that ideas simultaneously reflected and affected the social actions of individuals and collectivities is perhaps best illustrated in his essay "The Social Psychology of World Religions." He stated: "Not ideas, but material and ideal interests, directly govern men's conduct. Yet very frequently, the 'world images' that have been created by 'ideas' have, like switchmen, determined the tracks along which action has been pushed by the dynamic of interest" (Weber 1946, p. 280).

Although Marx's acknowledgment of the role of ideas is more difficult to find in his "mature" writing, this does not indicate that there was a shift in his views. Engels, in a letter to Joseph Bloch, denied the notion that Marx ever became purely an economic determinist, stating that "Marx and I are ourselves partly to blame for the fact that the younger people sometimes lay more stress on the economic side than is due to it. We had to emphasize the main principle vis-a-vis our adversaries, who denied it" (in Feuer 1959, pp. 399–400). In that letter, Engels attempted to clarify Marx's position:

> According to the materialist conception of history, the ultimately determining element in history is the production and reproduction of real life. More than this neither Marx nor I has ever asserted. Hence if somebody twists this into saying that the economic element is the *only* determining one he transforms that proposition into a meaningless, abstract senseless phrase. The economic situation is the basis, but the various elements of the superstructure . . . [e.g.] philosophical theories, religious views [etc.] . . . also exercise their influence upon the cause of the historical struggles and in many cases preponderate in determining their form. There is an interaction in all these elements (in Feuer 1959, pp. 397–98).

Thus it would appear that Marx and Weber differed not so much over the causal direction of the relationships, but over the question of how data concerning ideas were to be treated. According to Marx, ideas, because they were primarily products of the economic substructure, were necessarily so biased by self-interest as to be—presumptively—not worth taking at face value. In contrast, rather than assuming the ideas of those in positions of dominance to be self-serving lies, Weber felt that research could clarify which sets of ideas were falsifications and which were not. He therefore argued for a nonevaluative social science that treated the relations between interests and ideas as empirically problematic, to be investigated with a posture oriented toward as accurate as possible an understanding (*verstehen*) of the perspective of the social actors under study.

MANAGERIAL IDEOLOGY AND SOCIAL CONTROL

In *Work and Authority in Industry* (1956), Reinhard Bendix continued the analysis of the role of ideas in social control, examining the particular conditions under which a set of ideas serving to advance the interests of a dominant group would be promulgated. Consistent with Marx and Weber, Bendix started from the premise that domination is easier if those subordinated can be rendered willing to accept the relationship as, in some sense, right and proper (in Weber's terminology, *legitimate*). More specifically, he argued that coercive sanctioning of noncompliant behavior is unlikely to result in managerial directives being perceived as legitimate, and that management's control could be facilitated by promoting a set of logically consistent ideas that offer a justification for the existing social relations.

Bendix's subject matter was the means by which entrepreneurs and managers during the era of industrialization were able to justify to their workers the need for discipline and subordination. In examining this issue he analyzed the "ideologies of management," which he defined as "all ideas which are espoused by or for those who exercise authority in economic enterprises, and which seek to explain and justify that authority" (Bendix 1956, p. 2). Moreover, Bendix took a Weberian perspective on the nature of ideology, stating, "I depart from the identification of 'ideologies' with false or misleading ideas" (1956 p. 443). For Bendix, managerial ideologies were neither necessarily based on the exigencies of the relations of production, nor were they necessarily false. However, he did view such ideologies as oriented toward the legitimation of a system of domination.

In *Work and Authority in Industry* Bendix extended Weber's general formulation that the requisites of domination are an administrative structure and a legitimating ideology. Addressing "the managerial problems which typically result from the growing size and complexity of organizations" (1956.p. 244), he hypothesized that, as these factors make domination more difficult, managers respond with both the alteration of existing bureaucratic administrative mechanisms and the greater use of managerial ideologies to achieve this domination. According to Bendix:

> The internal bureaucratization of economic enterprises has had significant consequences. The few who command must control but cannot superintend the execution of their directives. They are bound to delegate more authority as the size of enterprises and the number of persons in positions of some responsibility increase.... Managerial ideologies are a response to the problems of coordination and direction in large-scale enterprises... [which] are thought to aid employers or their agents in controlling and directing the activities of workers (1956, p. 9).

The purpose of the present study is to continue Bendix's line of inquiry, narrowing the focus to the ideological ramifications of one particular issue, and subjecting it to both qualitative and quantitative analyses. This study will follow Bendix's usage of "ideologies of management," and the term ideology will be employed, in general, in a manner that emphasizes its role in the social control process. A discussion of ideology that provides a further elaboration of how the term will be used in the present study is that of Johnson (1968)—although it is offered here with an important caveat. Whereas the present study treats ideology as serving the interests of whatever group promotes it, Johnson, taking a Parsonian functionalist viewpoint, maintained that ideology may be functional for the entire social system. In defining ideology, Johnson stated that "Ideology consists of selected or distorted ideas about a social system or a class of social systems when these ideas purport to be factual, and also carry a more or less explicit evaluation of the 'facts'" (1968, p. 77). In addition, he noted that "The basic function of ideology... is to define a particular program of social action as legitimate and worthy of support" (1968, p. 81). Johnson also maintained that:

> Ideology may help a social system to achieve greater integration or greater adaptation or adaptive capacity. In this sense, it may be functional. For one thing, an ideology is likely to be a relatively simple definition of a complex situation—too simple, perhaps, by scientific standards, but for that very reason able to "explain" difficulties for a large number of people and able to activate them according to a common definition of the situation and a common plan (1968 p. 83).

Johnson's observation that ideologies aspire to be accepted as factual, when considered along with the frequent definition of ideologies as falsehoods, presents something of a conundrum for would-be ideologists. Although they may do their best to present sets of beliefs as factual, those beliefs are likely to be received with skepticism to the extent that they are perceived as being supportive of the communicator's own material interests.

Logically, it would seem that successful attempts to facilitate social control through the appeal to legitimating ideologies might share two characteristics. First, the truth or falsity of the central factual components of the ideology should be difficult for the targets of this influence attempt to assess. For example, an argument that corporate executives, despite their high salaries, have the same material standard of living as the average citizen would be unlikely to convince many people of the fairness of the current economic system; a look at the cars in the reserved spaces in the company parking lot or a drive through an "executive neighborhood" would quickly disconfirm such an idea. However, the notion that executives pay for their prestige and power with a much higher level of stress than those making less money and having fewer responsibilities is both plausible and, in light of their relatively narrow personal experiences, difficult for most individuals to assess. Although this idea apparently is untrue (see Boroson 1978), the scientific evidence addressing it is not readily accessible to those who have not been trained to read research.

Bendix's discussion of the use of social Darwinism as an ideology of management provides another example. The belief that social roles are biologically predetermined is both plausible and highly resistant to disproof, as is suggested by the periodic ebbing and flowing of social Darwinist scientific perspectives such as sociobiology (Wilson 1975). This particular example illustrates, as well, the second likely characteristic of a successful ideology: that it present principles applicable to a broader context than just the one involving material interests of the ideologist. The use of the social Darwinist "survival of the fittest" doctrine as a justification for the internal stratification of the industrial social order involved an appeal stating that this principle governed patterns of dominance and subordination not only in the workplace, nor even in the larger society, but among all nonhuman species as well.

Bendix recognized that managerial ideologies were not static but were subject to dialectical progressions. For example, he described how the emergence of the internal contradictions of the social Darwinist ideology led to its supersession by, and synthesis into, the New Thought Movement. Bendix identified half a dozen managerial ideologies used from the beginning of rapid industrialization in the United States during the 1880s to the time of his writing in the mid-1950s. He concluded his analysis with a discussion of the "human relations" ideology, which posited that labor-management cooperation formed the basis for the satisfaction of workers' basic, though often irrational, human needs for social esteem and connectedness. As stated by Davis, in a somewhat more contemporary manner:

> Human relations is the integration of people into a work situation that motivates them to work together productively, cooperatively, and with economic, psychological and social satisfactions. . . . Human relations is motivating people in organizations to develop teamwork which effectively fulfills their needs and achieves organizational effectiveness (1967, p. 5).

Davis' human relations view of the industrial order as a nonzero sum game where what's good for General Motors is not only good for the USA, but for each of GM's workers, is certainly an appealing ideology. Although widely accepted as an appropriate striving of management, it has been difficult to translate into successful managerial practice. For example, decades of research on the hypothesis that higher levels of satisfaction cause higher levels of work performance have suggested that an important tenet of the human relations ideology—the notion that happy workers are productive workers—is largely incorrect.

Nevertheless, if efforts to increase workers' desires to be more productive have not been dramatically successful, it may not mean that the human relations ideology is not practicable; rather, attention to the development of cooperative social relations may simply not be sufficient to elicit high performance levels. Current prescriptions for managers generally suggest that there are a variety of needs that work can fulfill, and recommend finding ways to make the satisfaction of these needs contingent upon successful performance. In addition, current theories emphasize that the ability, as well as the motivation, to carry out the task is a precursor of effective performance. Such a view has been elaborated by Morley:

> More than motivation is needed if a person is to produce the behavior necessary to the accomplishment of a particular task. He must also be capable of doing so; that is, he must possess the technical and social skills and knowledge needed for the task, and be in a state of sufficient health to carry it out (1971, p. 58).

Writing fifteen years ago, Morley argued that corporate attention to these ideas was essentially in its infancy. However, it would appear that developing employees' technical and social skills had already become fairly salient for many firms, at least as indicated by the type of organizational consulting activities that were popular at that time. For example, T-group training, which claimed to aid in the development of interpersonal skills, was a common activity in many corporations (Back 1972), particularly during the mid- to late-1960s. As T-groups went out of style in the 1970s, many "organizational development" specialists shifted their interests to "job redesign" or "work restructuring," the focus of which has been, in many cases, to increase the technical knowledge of the shop floor worker (Gibson, Ivancevich, and Donnelly 1985).

Although the original tenets of the human relations ideology may not have been supplanted, they appear to have been supplemented. Mayo's (1933) and Barnard's (1938) original formulations of the human relations perspective justified managerial authority on the grounds that managers had the skills to provide a setting in which the crucial human needs of their employees could be fulfilled through cooperation in the joint worker-manager endeavor. Their contention that the overarching need of workers was for meaningful affiliation with a primary social group, rather than for mere money, led to greatly increased attention to the worker as a "whole man," rather than a focus on simply the economic relationship between workers and managers. Since the 1930s, theories in psychology have emphasized motives such as the human drive for competence (White 1952) and for attaining self-actualization (Maslow 1954). Consequently, considerations of the "whole man" now include concern for workers having an opportunity to achieve feelings of technical and social competence. Despite this shift, however, the ideological thrust is the same as that of the Harvard group of the 1930s; in return for producing profits for the corporation, workers are offered a setting in which they may achieve the social and psychological gratifications that are claimed to be the most highly valued goals of these nonelite members of society.

Concern with Employee Health

Morley (1971) noted that one additional factor affecting employees' motivation to produce is their health, a concern that fits readily into the modern variant of the human relations ideology. In the past, managements have not always received wide public approval for their attempts to influence their employees' central life values. For example, efforts by early industrialists to dictate their workers' habits in such areas as dressing, eating, and attending church were abandoned amidst complaints of inappropriate "paternalism" (Brandes 1976). However, to the extent that management attempts to influence behavior for which there is a widely held public value, and which is demonstrably related to the completion of "a fair day's work," such efforts may succeed. Intuitively, the maintenance of sound health seems to be both a widely held value and a generally-accepted prerequisite for adequate job performance. Thus managerial interventions in matters related to employees' health might have a good chance of being accepted as legitimate. Indeed, in recent years various forms of such managerial interventions have proliferated and have been well received (Allen 1980). These have included not only insurance coverages, but programs and facilities, such as on-site gyms, oriented to primary prevention of health problems. A healthier workforce is of clear benefit to both individual employees and to employers, making these programs among the best examples of the actualization of the human relations ideology's promise of mutual advantages for labor and capital.

Although such welfarist measures may help to promote a generally greater tolerance of the political-economic status quo, they are usually not able to ameliorate adequately the day-to-day social control problems faced by management. For example, management has reported that its leading discipline problem is absenteeism (Bureau of National Affairs 1973). Although improved employee health may lead to reduced sickness absenteeism, it is generally recognized that absenteeism constitutes a form of work withdrawal behavior that will not be eliminated by good health (Miner and Miner 1977; Muchinsky 1977; Nicholson 1977).

If absenteeism, as well as other behaviors inimical to the interests of management, such as lateness, poor relations with peers and supervisors, and low productivity, could be construed as employee health problems, managerial interventions to control employee behavior would appear more justified. As noted earlier, the Parsonian sociologist Pitts has characterized the medicalization of deviance as one of the most promising social control techniques, stating that: "No doubt medicalization has resulted in extending immunity from punishment to certain culprits. However, it would seem that medicalization is one of the most effective means of social control and that it is destined increasingly to become the main mode of *formal* social control" (1968, p. 391).

Unfortunately for management, it is by no means clear which specific illness causes this variety of deficient job behaviors. Nonetheless, attempts at such an explanation have been made, but, emphasizing psychological or developmental deficiencies, they have tended to have a rather heavy-handed, normative tone. This is well illustrated by the views of the medical director of the Kerr-McGee Corporation, writing in the *Handbook of Modern Personnel Administration*; "Chronic absentees are largely immature malcontents who may not have had the opportunity to mature properly or simply have not yet learned the lesson that true happiness and satisfaction in life come mostly from conscientious work performed to the best of one's ability" (Sternhagen 1972, p. 61).

It has been argued here that two factors are conducive to the success of an ideology as an "aid to employers or their agents in controlling and directing the activities of workers" (Bendix 1956, p. 9), that is, as an instrument of social control: the difficulty of assessing the accuracy of the set of ideas, and their broad applicability. Because there is in fact no illness whose particular symptoms so neatly legitimate close monitoring of job performance in the name of "treatment," it might serve management's needs to claim that one exists. This alleged illness preferably would be one whose etiology, symptoms, course, and appropriate treatment were open to debate, and at the same time one that was widely recognized and accepted as a serious health problem. And preferably, managements' conception of this illness would be consistent with (or at least not contradict) a conception of the problem that is popular among the broader public. The chapters that follow argue that alcoholism, particularly the idea that it is a medical disease, fits this description and that this medical disease ideology of alcoholism is being used in many organizations to facilitate social control in the workplace.

4

Ideologies of Alcoholism

The problems associated with the ingestion of alcohol have long been subject to a wide variety of interpretations. No single explanation of why it eventuates in adverse long-term consequences for some persons and not for others has won wide public or scientific acceptance. In the absence of such a consensus, the proponents of the various approaches to the problem have competed for support for treatment, prevention, and research activities in a manner that has often been more akin to processes of political mobilization than to scientific discourse (see Weiner 1981).

This chapter will describe the major competing models that attempt to explain the condition that is usually referred to as alcoholism. These models will be considered in terms of the interest groups that would be likely to favor each of them, and in light of the systematic evidence for and against each perspective. In particular, the models will be evaluated on the basis of whether they "define a particular program of social action as legitimate and worthy of support" and are "able to 'explain' difficulties for a large number of people and able to activate them according to a common definition of the situation and a common plan"—that is, in terms of their usefulness as ideologies.

Following Tarter and Schneider (1976), the four types of explanations for problems associated with alcohol ingestion to be discussed here are the moral, psychological, sociological, and medical models. Following the usage of Orcutt, Cairl, and Miller (1980), these explanations will be referred to as alcoholism ideologies.

THE MORAL MODEL

"The moral concept of alcoholism," historically the earliest of the four perspectives, "saw the drunkard as a sinner, a weak individual, a degenerate who did not possess the inner strength to abstain from intoxicating beverages" (Howland and Howland 1978). The validity of the moral model is difficult to assess, as it generally does not focus on measurable etiological agents. Rather, its description of alcoholics as sinners or degenerates suggests that it is essentially an accusation of deviance from societal norms and values. However, if it is not useful in the treatment or scientific study of alcohol problems, it may serve a role for the larger society. As Dentler and Erikson (1959) have pointed out, the establishment of deviant roles, with a suitable number of occupants, may serve important social integrative functions by identifying the limits of what is held to be acceptable behavior. This is illustrated by Cherrington's analysis (1920) of the history of the moral model of alcoholism in the United States. He argued that during the colonial period relatively little attention was paid to conspicuous overconsumption of alcohol, and that it was only after the Revolutionary War that the public expressed much disturbance over drunkards. He interpreted this as indicative of a desire to reimpose a clear social hierarchy and set of social norms in the aftermath of the war's disestablishment of the former class structure. Similarly, Gusfield (1963), in his analysis of the development of the American temperance movement, contended that the desire for greater clarification of social boundaries contributed to the increased inclination to label certain individuals as degenerates and sinners.

In contemporary, secularized societies the view that individuals with alcohol overconsumption problems are immoral sinners would seem to be low in social desirability. However, research indicates that this view is by no means extinct. Linsky's content analysis (1970) of the responses of 305 adults in Vancouver, Washington, to an open-ended question about the most probable cause of alcoholism found that 9 percent of the respondents considered alcoholism to be a result of weak moral character. When he asked respondents to select, from ten alternatives, the most effective means of "getting alcoholics to stop drinking," he found that 15 percent selected "the use of more willpower." A survey reported by Mulford and Miller (1964) found that, of the 1,213 adult Iowans who responded, 31 percent indicated that they would apply the term "morally weak" to alcoholics, and 60 percent said that they would characterize them as "weak-willed" (multiple responses were permitted). Tolor and Tamerin (1975) found that 135 part-time graduate students (most of whom were teachers) gave the "moral weakness" explanation of alcoholism an average score of 1.67 on a scale for which 1 indicated strong disagreement and 4 indicated strong agreement. Thus, although their subjects were largely in disagreement with this perspective, they did not reject it completely. Weiss (1980) found that, of 1,306 corporate senior personnel executives, 51 percent expressed at least slight agreement with the statement that alcoholism can result from "weak character." Most recently, and perhaps most surprisingly, Tournier reported that in his sample of 157 alcohol and drug abuse workers "most . . . still believe that alcoholics . . . can somehow will themselves to recovery" (1985, p. 47).

The research evidence suggests that the view that alcoholics are of deficient character still appeals to a fairly wide segment of the population. Indeed, it is possible that the low social desirability of admitting to this opinion results in an underestimate, in the survey data reviewed above, of the model's actual level of support. Nevertheless, it is not at all clear who would wish to actively promote the view of alcoholics as sinners and weak-willed degenerates, other than perhaps certain segments of the religious sector. Although Tournier found that, in response to a survey instrument, alcoholism counselors indicated agreement that drinking problems were a matter simply of personal willpower, it seems highly unlikely that they would advance such a perspective in their professional roles.

For the most part the moral model of alcoholism seems to have met the fate of similarly stigmatizing interpretations of other human frailties. Much as the training for those born with deficient mental abilities is now called "special education," the possible etiology of alcoholism currently is most typically discussed in terms that imply sympathy rather than condemnation. Nevertheless, the argument to be made here is that this has not necessarily been the result of a more "enlightened" or sympathetic view of the problem. Rather, the moral model may be out of fashion partly because one of its central aspects—its attribution of blame to the afflicted individual—generally makes social control of the deviant more difficult.

THE PSYCHOLOGICAL MODEL

Various explanations of the etiology of alcoholism view it as originating from certain personality characteristics. In some cases, the analysis is a deduction from a broader theoretical perspective, such as the Freudian interpretation of alcoholism as rooted in a pattern of oral dependency (Bertrand and Masling 1969; Fenichel 1945). However, most empirical investigations of the psychological model have been somewhat atheoretical analyses of responses to paper-and-pencil inventories, conducted in the hope of finding a pattern to be labeled "the alcoholic personality."

A literature review reported by Barnes (1979) cited 234 studies on the relationships of personality traits to alcoholism. Unfortunately, virtually all of these studies obtained data from subjects only after they had been diagnosed or treated for alcoholism. This fact confounds the interpretation of the most consistent finding in this literature, that alcoholics have higher scores on the MMPI depression scale than do nonalcoholics (e.g., Hoffman 1970; Kristianson 1970; Speigel, Hadley, and Hadley 1970).That is, it is not surprising to find that individuals who have been admitted to a hospital for treatment of alcoholism tend to be depressed. The fact that posttreatment administration of the MMPI finds subjects less depressed (Ends and Page 1959; Rohan 1972; Rohan, Tatro, and Rotman 1969; Shaffer et al. 1962; Wilkinson et al. 1971) further reduces the likelihood that this is a stable personality trait of those who will go on to become alcoholic. With respect to other personality traits, Barnes (1979) noted that there is evidence that individuals about to embark on treatment for alcoholism tend to be characterized by neuroticism, weak ego, stimulus augmenting, and field dependence, but concluded that "direct evidence is not available to support the connection between any of these traits and a prealcoholic personality" (p. 621).

Longitudinal research, which would be necessary to demonstrate that a personality trait has a specifically causal role in the development of alcoholism, has generally been lacking. The available evidence from the few such studies (Hoffman, Loper, and Kammeier 1974; Kammeier, Hoffman, and Loper 1973; Loper, Kammeier, and Hoffman 1973; Vaillant 1983) provides mild support for a conclusion that prealcoholics tend to be characterized by a lack of psychological control. In general, however, the intuitively appealing idea that a certain type of personality will lead to alcoholism has sparse scientific support.

Despite the lack of scientific evidence favoring the psychological model, it is the one with which survey respondents have been found most likely to express agreement (Tolor and Tamerin 1975; Weiss 1980). This may be attributable to the general population's attraction to an explanation of alcohol problems that neither places total blame on individual alcoholics, nor completely absolves them of responsibility for their dilemma. Whereas active promotion of the moral model might most likely be associated with the clergy, the secularization of society appears to have lessened reliance on members of the clergy for assistance with personal problems. Their place seems to have been taken by large numbers of mental health "professionals," carrying a variety of credentials and competing to sell services for which there apparently is a relatively inelastic demand.Thus, it would appear to be in their interests to define as broad as possible a range of behaviors as within their competence to treat. Defining behavior that fails to comply with normative expectations as evidence of weak moral character places it in the province of the clergy, and calling it a medical disease puts it in the realm of physicians; it is perhaps for these reasons that mental health professionals have promoted an often-vague explanation of many behaviors (including alcoholism) as psychological or mental "problems" or "illnesses" (see Wilensky 1964). It is possible that this frequent vagueness in the psychological model constitutes much of its appeal to the public. Referring to alcoholism as mental illness suggests sympathy and absolution of responsibility (for having acquired the condition). Yet it does not require the concession, which many seem to resist, that alcoholism is a normal medical debility.*

Nevertheless, although referring to someone as having a mental problem or a mental illness is clearly assigning that individual to a stigmatized social status, it is not nearly as harsh as an accusation of degeneracy or weak moral character. The specific behavior described by proponents of the moral and the psychological models may be identical— an apparent inability to cease a pattern of drinking that has clearly negative consequences. However, whereas the moral model blames individuals for not taking responsibility for their weaknesses, the psychological model attributes the behavior to a personality trait, something that one presumably did not wish on oneself, and that is highly resistant to change—without the help of a professional therapist.

THE SOCIOLOGICAL MODEL

The one general view of the etiology of alcoholism that has considerable empirical support is the sociological model. Although it certainly does not provide a complete explanation of the phenomenon, numerous social and cultural variables have been shown to have clear associations with the incidence of alcohol addiction and overconsumption. Not only have associations been shown, but the nature of the factors investigated often facilitate clearer interpretations of causal direction than is possible in investigations of psychological or medical links with drinking problems. Whereas mental depression or the presence of certain chemicals in the brain may be effects rather than causes of alcoholism, it is more difficult to argue that alcoholism causes one to have a particular ethnicity.

The preeminent body of research literature on social and epidemiological factors in alcohol abuse has been that of Cahalan and his associates (e.g., Cahalan 1970; Cahalan and Room 1974). Importantly, this group has specifically disavowed having any information on *alcoholism;* their focus has been on the social patterning of alcohol consumption and

---

*Hawkins and Tiedeman have presented the difference between mental and "real" illness as follows: "'Mental illness' differs from all other illness in that it refers not to organic malfunctioning but to *behavior*. When a physician diagnoses an organic ailment, he tries to base his decision upon objective characteristics that indicate departure from a state of bodily health—e.g., fever, elevated blood pressure, lesions, growths, abnormal cell count. Similarly, when a psychiatrist (or lesser psychiatric agent) diagnoses a psychiatric ailment, he purports to indicate a departure from a state of mental health. But his decision has an inherent *subjective* base because of its linkage to behavior rather than to physiological malfunctioning. Thus, the psychiatric decision constitutes a more obvious value judgment" (1975, p. 154).

attendant problems. Despite their specific disclaimers (e.g., Cahalan and Cisin 1976), however, their findings concerning the incidence of problem drinking have constituted the basis for the federal government's assertions about the incidence of alcoholism (e.g., U.S. Department of Health, Education and Welfare 1974), which in turn have become the official reference for others.

In these data socioeconomic status (SES), ethnicity, and age consistently appear as predictors of problem drinking (Cahalan 1970; Cahalan and Room 1974). The evidence on drinking and SES indicates that, although a greater proportion of higher SES respondents are drinkers, it is among low SES individuals that problem drinking is more likely to occur. Research on the links between ethnicity and drinking patterns (e.g., Bales 1944; Glassner and Berg 1980; Snyder 1978) has indicated that Jews are less likely than other groups to be either teetotalers or problem drinkers; Irish, Blacks, and Hispanics, conversely, are more likely to become problem drinkers. Those in the 20- to 24-year-old age category are more likely than those in other age groups to develop drinking problems; this finding has been validated longitudinally (Clark and Cahalan 1976), suggesting that it is age, rather than particular cohort characteristics, that explains the drinking behavior.

In addition to demographic characteristics, other factors at the sociological level have been linked to alcohol problems. A report from the U.S. Office of Vital Statistics (1961) listed the following occupations as having unusually high age-adjusted standard mortality ratios of death due to cirrhosis of the liver (the most frequent medical indication of alcoholism, according to Schuckit 1985): authors, editors and reporters, waiters, bartenders, longshoremen, transportation laborers, cooks, musicians, meatcutters, and bakers. Although the statistical association between alcohol problems and certain occupations is fairly clear, an understanding of why these relationships exist is far from established, in part because the majority of investigations of this topic have been merely descriptive case studies (e.g., Carman 1971; Dennis, Henriques, and Slaughter 1956; Rose and Glatt 1961).

The major empirical investigation of the reasons for the links between alcoholism and certain occupations has been that of Hitz (1973), who concluded that her findings supported selection theory, the view that individuals disposed toward alcoholism choose occupations conducive to a drinking career. Cosper's reanalysis (1979) of Hitz's data, however, seriously questions her conclusions. Noting that the overarching problem in the interpretation of the connection between occupation and alcoholism is that of causal direction, he argued that Hitz's data do not permit the support of the selection perspective over the other major interpretive framework, structural strain theory (see Hirschi 1969). According to this latter perspective, work role characteristics, particularly those inducing stress, contribute to the development of alcohol dependence. Confirmation or disconfirmation of selection theory would require a sophisticated longitudinal analysis, which to this date has not been reported. Evidence bearing on the structural strain perspective, however, is more readily obtained. That is, although individuals may have selected to engage in particular occupations, it is less likely that they chose particular job characteristics, such as role overload. The available evidence, however, provides only the most minimal support for the general view that alcoholism results from job stresses (Fennell, Rodin, and Kantor 1981; Parker and Brody 1982).

Nevertheless, as Cosper (1979) noted, stress theories of drinking "have become part of popular culture." However, it has not been only popular culture that has promoted this viewpoint. Its prominence has been abetted as well by the work of academics, such as the sociologists Trice and Roman who, in numerous writings (Roman and Trice 1970, 1976; Trice and Roman 1972, 1978), have argued that "occupational risk factors" such as role stress contribute significantly to the development of alcoholism. Unfortunately, they have never provided data in support of their contentions, and empirical research designed to test their specific hypotheses (Schollaert 1977) has been disconfirming.

More success has been met by research relating alcoholism to stressful life events and sources of chronically stressful conditions. Although studies at the individual level have not successfully established such an association, an investigation at the macro-social level has yielded remarkable findings. Linsky, Straus and Colby's (1985) analysis employed independent variables such as state-by-state measures of divorces per 1,000 population, mortgage loans foreclosed per 100,000 population, and fetal deaths per 1,000 live births. Additional predictors included indices of status integration (measured as the proportion of citizens occupying unusual combinations of marital, occupational, age and sex statuses [e.g., a young widower]) and relative opportunity (measured by dividing the number of citizens in managerial, professional, and kindred positions by the number of adults with college educations). Using these and other measures they were able to explain more than one-quarter of the state-to-state variation in cirhossis death rates, and almost one-half of the variation in average alcohol consumption.

Studies at the individual level have been more successful in analyzing remission from alcohol dependence and alcohol problems, rather than their development. Reviewing the literature on spontaneous remission from alcoholism (which Smart [1976] contended accounts for between 10 and 42 percent of recoveries from alcoholism), Ludwig (1985) stated that "the most frequent reasons given for the initiation of remission pertain to changes in life circumstances, such as marriage, job or residence." He found that all forms of "treatment," combined, were far less frequently cited by respondents as the reason they stopped their abusive drinking.

The sociological model lays the blame for the development of alcoholism on elements of the social environment that are substantially beyond the control of the individual. From this perspective alcoholics are relatively innocent victims of society. Although at first glance it might seem that alcoholics themselves would wish to advance this interpretation of their problem, for them to do so could well be viewed by the larger society as merely an alibi propounded by individuals who are unwilling to take responsibility for themselves. Indeed, Parsons (1951), in his analysis of the "sick role" in society, argued that individuals whose behavior does not conform to normative expectations strike a deal with society, in which they are absolved of personal responsibility for acquiring their condition in return for their commitment to take responsibility for removing it. Not only is the sociological model of little ideological value to alcoholics, but the solutions implicit in its findings, such as reducing the number of mortgage foreclosures or increasing the number of professional job opportunities, are not readily accomplished. Indeed, it is difficult to imagine whose interests, other than those of a few social scientists, would be served by supporting this interpretation of alcohol problems. Although Linsky (1970) found that a general population sample gave a high ranking to social and economic stress as possible etiological factors in alcoholism, such sentiments would not appear to represent any major group or institutional interest. Consequently, this perspective persists as an academic theory and as a fairly popular view among the general public but rarely has formed the basis for specific social action.

THE MEDICAL MODEL

The conceptualization of alcoholism as a medical disease state has many variants, all of which share the view that the problem's origin in some way involves human physiology. There is a large body of research literature that has investigated the possible organic etiology of alcoholism. However, the nonresearch literature addressing the concept of "alcoholism as a disease" may be even more significant in its implications for dealing with individuals labeled as alcoholics, and will also be reviewed here.

A number of biophysiological explanations of alcoholism have been advanced, each suffering from a paucity of supportive evidence. For example, Lemere (1956) posited that alcoholism results from heavy drinking, which, he suggested, causes cerebral damage, destroying "willpower" and "judgment" brain cells. Tintera and Lovell (1949) argued that in some cases alcohol ingestion leads to deficiencies in adrenocortical hormones, a stressful condition that leads to further drinking. Randolph (1956) viewed alcoholism as resulting from a sensitivity to nutrients in alcohol, leading to addiction.

The hypothesis that genetic transmission underlies the development of alcoholism in an individual has been subjected to a number of tests. To circumvent the confounding effects of "nurture" as opposed to "nature," investigations have focused on either twins or adopted children. Kaij (1960) found that patterns of alcohol use and abuse were more concordant for monozygotic (identical) than for dizygotic (fraternal) twins, supporting the hypothesis of a genetic link. Jonsson and Nilsson (1968) and Partanen, Bruun, and Markkanen (1966) found patterns of alcohol consumption to be more concordant for monozygotic male twins, but found no difference between identical and fraternal twins on criteria used to diagnose actual addiction to alcohol.

Investigations that have studied the offspring of alcoholic parents, using adopted children separated at infancy and raised by nonrelative parents, have also been interpreted as supporting the view of alcoholism as genetically transmitted. The frequently-cited studies reported by Goodwin and his associates (Schuckit, Goodwin, and Winokur 1972; Goodwin et al. 1974) concluded that alcoholism among biological parents does, and that alcoholism among adopted parents does not, predict alcoholism among these children. Regrettably, these studies, conducted by medical doctors, leave much to be desired methodologically. In one case (Schuckit, Goodwin, and Winokur 1972), hypothesis testing was limited to simple t-tests and, in the other (Goodwin et al. 1974), to one chi-squared test. Given the clearly warranted assumption that alcoholism is a complex phenomenon, multivariate analyses would have been far more appropriate, and appear not only to have been feasible with the data available, but necessary in light of some of their incidental findings. For example, Goodwin et al. (1974) merely noted that their alcoholic subjects had a divorce rate three times higher than that of the controls, yet provided no empirical analysis to eliminate the possibility that divorce rather than genes was the cause of the alcohol problems (a possibility that seems worth investigating in light of Ludwig's findings on the role of marital stability in alcohol abuse).

The major obstacle, however, to determining whether alcoholism is genetically transmitted is the inability of twin or adoptee studies to distinguish whether the inherited characteristic is an inability to consume alcohol without adverse consequences or a tolerance for consuming large quantities of alcohol. The twin studies do seem adequate to establish the second alternative, that a particular level of tolerance to alcohol is heritable, but do not demonstrate adequately a genetic link to alcohol addiction or chronic abuse. Although the studies of adoptees claim that it is alcoholism (i.e., uncontrollable overconsumption associated with adverse consequences) that is inherited, Vaillant's (1983) 30-year longitudinal panel study of the development of drinking patterns among over 400 individuals found that the craving for alcohol and loss of control over drinking that are said to be among the disease's symptoms were never exhibited in the absence of a lengthy history of overconsumption of alcohol. Thus individuals who have had the misfortune to be born with the ability to drink their peers under the table appear to be at risk to develop a pattern of addictive and uncontrollable alcohol abuse.

Whatever the nature of the debates in the research literature over the significance of organic factors in the development of alcoholism, such discussions constitute the least problematic aspect of the medical model. Far more widely and vigorously diffused than any research-based conception of alcoholism is a model of the "physical, moral, and spiritual disease of alcoholism," advocated primarily by members of Alcoholics Anonymous, but by many clinicians as well. Pattison (1976) has abstracted the following traditional medical disease model of alcoholism, noting that the key is the fourth proposition, for which the first three serve as justification and explanation:

Proposition I. The alcoholic is essentially different from the non-alcoholic.

Corollary a. There are inborn genetic differences or developmental genetic differences.

Corollary b. These genetic differences lead to fundamental changes in the biochemical, endocrine, or physiologic systems of the alcoholic.

Proposition II. Because of an organic difference, the alcoholic experiences a different reaction to alcohol than does the non-alcoholic.

Corollary a. The alcoholic develops an allergy to alcohol.

Corollary b. The allergic reaction creates untoward responses to alcohol, including a craving for alcohol, an inability to stop drinking, and a loss of control over the use of alcohol.

Proposition III. The alcoholic has no control over these inexorable processes, which is a disease process.

Corollary a. The disease process will proceed in inexorable progression to ultimate deterioration and death.

Corollary b. The disease process is irreversible.

Corollary c. The disease process can be arrested but not cured.

Proposition IV. The alcoholic is not personally responsible for his alcoholism, since the disease process is an impersonal illness with which the alcoholic is afflicted.

Corollary a. The alcoholic is relieved of social stigma for moral failure.

Corollary b. The alcoholic is relieved of personal guilt for his alcoholism.

Corollary c. The alcoholic is not to be blamed and
punished for his alcoholism.

Corollary d. Society has a responsibility to rehabilitate
sick members of society, including the sick
alcoholic (1976, pp. 410–11).

The allergy theory of alcoholism, which provides a key explanatory
mechanism in this traditional disease model, seems to have been a
product of the medical *zeitgeist* of the 1930s, when Alcoholics Anonymous
was founded. This was a period during which doctors were positing
allergy etiologies for a great many common illnesses (Pattison 1976). The
theory's direct source is clearly a Dr. Silkworth, a New York allergist who
was an early supporter of A.A. and who provided "The Doctor's Opinion"
for A.A.'s book, *Alcoholics Anonymous* (1939) (referred to as the "Big
Book" by A.A. members), in which he made claims for the validity of the
theory. Beyond opinion, however, no evidence exists to support it (Lester
1966).

The second corollary of the proposition that alcoholics have a
different reaction to alcohol than do others is the idea that the disease of
alcoholism is characterized by a "craving" for alcohol. Mello (1972) has
pointed out that postulation of such a need state presents a problem of
circularity, by confusing description with explanation: alcoholics are said
to drink because they crave alcohol, which is demonstrated by the fact that
they drink. Two studies have investigated the phenomenon of craving,
using retrospective self-reports from alcoholics as to why they resumed
drinking after a period of abstinence (Ludwig 1972; Marlatt 1973). In both
studies the proportion of respondents reporting subjective feelings even
akin to craving was extremely low—only 1 percent in the Ludwig study. In
Marlatt's research 21 percent of the relapses were coded into a category he
labeled "inability to resist intrapersonal temptation to drink"; this category included "craving" but was so broad as to also include such factors as
"social temptation." The methodology used in these two studies certainly
has limitations, and Ludwig, Wikler, and Stark (1974) have argued that
self-reports about drinking resumption may be merely the assignment of
labels to physical states that are conditioned responses to alcohol withdrawal. They presented evidence to support their own view that a clas-
sically conditioned craving may exist. This approach differs considerably
from the traditional medical disease model, however, in that craving, as a
conditioned response, presumably can be extinguished through behavior
therapy rather than medical therapy.

The third proposition, that alcoholism is characterized by loss of
control over alcohol consumption—that for the alcoholic "one drink is
too many, and a thousand are not enough"—has been broadly examined
and in over 70 studies (cited in Pattison, Sobell, and Sobell 1977) has been
refuted. For example, placebo control studies (e.g., Engle and Williams

1972; Marlatt, Demming, and Reid 1973) have shown that whether beverages actually contain any alcohol has no effect on alcoholic patients' reactions to them; rather, alcoholics exhibit a loss of control over alcoholic and nonalcoholic beverages that they are *told* contain alcohol.

The disconfirmation of this proposition also calls into question the corollaries that alcoholism is an irreversible disease and can be arrested but never cured. Proponents of the traditional medical model believe that "once an alcoholic, always an alcoholic" and that the only means of salvation is to arrest the incurable process through total abstinence. Over the past decade, however, the weight of evidence opposing this perspective has accumulated dramatically. There are now more than 70 studies (see Armor, Polich, and Stambul 1978; Pattison, Sobell, and Sobell 1977) showing that some alcoholics (albeit a small proportion of them— perhaps 1 in 12) have been able to return to "social drinking." This general conclusion has held up: whether the subjects were merely problem drinkers or were chronic alcoholics; whether the treatment program had a goal of controlled drinking or abstention; across a broad range of treatment modalities (indeed, Edwards et al. [1977] reported controlled drinking among untreated alcoholics); and across individuals in various cultures.

For the purposes of the present study, the most crucial element of the traditional medical model is the corollary of Proposition III stating that, if unarrested, the disease moves through an inexorable progression of phases and symptoms, leading eventually to death. The primary source of this idea is the influential writing of E. M. Jellinek (1952, 1960) who proposed that a sequence consisting of 43 symptoms and three major phases (called the prodromal, crucial, and chronic phases) is characteristic of the problem's progression among "the great majority of alcohol addicts" (1952, p. 676). The data on which these conclusions were based consisted of 98 responses to a distribution of 1,600 questionnaires to members of Alcoholics Anonymous, who provided retrospective reconstructions of their drinking careers. Subsequent studies, with response rates greater than Jellinek's 6 percent and with samples more broadly representative than only those alcoholics affiliated with A.A., have failed to find Jellinek's (or any alternative) ordering of stages for "the great majority of alcohol addicts" (Orford and Hawker 1974; Park 1962, 1973; Polich and Kaelber 1985).

Nevertheless, one of the most frequently seen accouterments on the walls of alcohol treatment facilities is the "Glatt Chart" (Glatt 1958), which presents what is essentially a synthesis of Jellinek's stages of disease progression with Glatt's view of the stages of recovery. His chart shows a U-shaped line along which the disease progresses, from the left-side peak of the U, to the U's bottom, and (with the benefits of treatment and abstinence) back up the right side toward recovery. Some of the highlights along this journey to dipsomania and back are as follows (listed here in the order shown on the chart): "occasional relief drinking," "feeling of guilt," "unable to discuss problem," "persistent remorse," "moral deterioration," "impaired thinking," "drinking with inferiors," "vague spiritual desires," and "obsessive drinking continues in vicious circles" (the bottom of the U, illustrated with little, presumably vicious, circles). The progressive stages to recovery include "right thinking begins," "realistic thinking," "re-birth of ideals," "facts faced with courage," "appreciation of real values," and finally "enlightened and interesting way of life opens up with road ahead to higher levels than ever before."

As colorful as the language in Glatt's chart is, it may be presumed to be only illustrative. Certainly he has never provided data indicating that the "appreciation of real values" is preceded by facing facts with courage, which in turn had been preceded by a "re-birth of ideals." Of greater relevance than Glatt's work for evaluating the accuracy of the notion of the inexorable progression of alcoholism is the longitudinal research on drinking behavior conducted by Cahalan and his associates (Clark and Cahalan 1976). Analyzing the incidence of symptoms of alcoholism in the general population, they found that a great many individuals move out of, as well as into, a variety of problems with alcohol. Thus they demonstrated frequent remission, rather than progression of the disease.

With all of the evidence disconfirming the medical disease model of alcoholism, why, and by whom, is it defended? That its defense is fervent is illustrated by the reaction to an evaluation study of federally sponsored alcoholism treatment facilities conducted by social scientists at the Rand Corporation. They had suggested, in what came to be known, notoriously, as the Rand Report:

> Many researchers faced with results similar to our own have raised questions about whether total abstention is a necessary goal for all alcoholics. Obviously, alcoholics who have suffered irreversible physical damage or who have repeatedly failed to maintain normal drinking should be advised to abstain. But our findings that some alcoholics appear to return to moderate drinking without serious impairment and without relapse, and that permanent abstention is relatively rare, suggest the possibility that normal drinking might be a realistic and effective goal for some alcoholics.
>
> However, it would be premature to endorse or advocate a policy of normal drinking for alcoholics. The data from this study and similar studies are simply not adequate to establish, beyond question, the long-term feasibility of normal or "controlled" drinking among alcoholics; nor do the data enable us to identify those specific individuals for whom normal drinking might be appropriate. On the other hand, we have found no solid scientific evidence—only non-rigorous clinical or personal experience—for the belief that abstention is a more effective remedy than normal drinking. The conclusion, therefore, must be that existing scientific knowledge establishes neither an abstention theory nor a normal drinking theory of recovery from alcoholism. Thus, we do

not make any policy recommendations at all about therapeutic goals either for alcoholics in general or for any individual alcoholic (Armor, Polich, and Stambul 1978, p. 171).

In response to this cautiously phrased statement, which simply repeated what had been shown in dozens of previous studies, the medical director of the National Council on Alcoholism (NCA) said, "It takes little subtlety to read between the lines in this paper and see a slanted polemic advocating the return to normal drinking as a goal" (Hodgson 1979). Apparently, his associate, the vice-chairman of the NCA board, did have sufficient subtlety to do so and *he* attacked the Rand Report by stating, "This [controlled drinking] could mean death or brain damage for these individuals unless they return to abstinence" (Hodgson 1979).

The outcry against the Rand Report did come from sources in addition to the NCA, but it was this group that brought itself to the fore in the extremely vociferous reaction that the Rand Report engendered. The National Council on Alcoholism, the major voluntary organization in the alcoholism field, had been founded in 1944 by Marty Mann, who explained in her book *Marty Mann's New Primer on Alcoholism* (1958) (a major manifesto of the traditional disease ideology) that "the N.C.A. was designed to do those things for alcoholism which A.A. could not, and did not wish to do." Specifically, the "twelve traditions" of A.A. created impediments to the advancement of A.A.'s views with their injunctions against a variety of activities generally engaged in by interest groups: "Alcoholics Anonymous has no opinion on outside issues; hence the name A.A. ought never be drawn into public controversy," "Every A.A. group ought never endorse, finance, or lend the A.A. name to any related facility or outside enterprise," "A.A. should remain forever nonprofessional," "A.A. . . . ought never be organized," and "Our public relations policy is based on attraction rather than promotion." All of these activities, which are proscribed for A.A., are engaged in by the NCA.

That the vanguard of critical rhetoricians assaulting the Rand Report should consist of officers of this organization is illustrative of the social and ideological basis of the traditional medical disease model. Perhaps the most central ideological thrust of the NCA's activities is the promotion of the idea that alcoholism is a disease, rather than a personal moral failing. A pamphlet soliciting contributions for the NCA (1976a) listed a number of "Facts on Alcoholism" that, for the most part, consist of unsupported assertions of the medical disease ideology. For example, "10 million" alcoholics in the United States are said to be suffering from a "progressive disease," which "untreated . . . results in physical incapacity, permanent mental damage and/or premature death." In what would appear to be an attempt to refute the psychological and sociocultural models, they stated that "there is no 'typical' person with alcoholism."

Some of the assertions made in their literature take the form of creative expansions of public surmise, such as the statement that "Less than 3% of the people with alcoholism are found on Skid Row." In truth, no available evidence either supports or disconfirms this figure (or the more typical figure of 5 percent). The closest that this author could get to a source for this "fact" was the following description by Straus (1979) of a talk he gave in which he suggested that skid row alcoholics were a relatively small percentage of the alcoholic population:

> In the question period, somebody said, Well just what percent of the population is Skid Row people? I remember very distinctly, I said: I have no idea—maybe 20 percent? The next day the *New York Times* printed 20%. Fortunately, they didn't print my name. But that figure got into the literature. I dare you to find the source for that figure, but it got into the literature, and for years, until Morrie Chafetz [director of the NIAAA] changed it to 5%, it was the figure (1979, p. 302).

Connecting alcohol problems to problems that are highly salient to the general public, the NCA literature asserts that "Violent behavior attributed to alcohol misuse accounts for 64% of murders, 41% of assaults, [etc.]. . . . When alcoholism is treated, associated violent behavior is known to decrease" (1976a, p. 1). Although it is likely that treated alcoholics are less prone to violence than they might have been prior to being treated, the NCA probably would not want the credibility of their ideology to rest on such implausible putative "facts" as an assertion that 64 percent of murders are committed by what they claim is the small portion of the population who are victims of "the disease of alcoholism." The ideological dilemma confronted by the NCA is that although it would seem to be in their interest to make as broad as possible a definition of alcoholism, stretching it to include people who have been intoxicated prior to committing violent crimes threatens the credibility of the disease concept. Thus a careful reading of their brochure notes that they did not associate criminal behavior with "alcoholism," but with "alcohol misuse," a substitution that may not have reflected merely a pamphlet writer's stylistic concern with avoiding repetitiveness. The medical model of alcoholism promoted by the NCA holds that nonalcoholics can choose to either misuse or not misuse alcohol, but that victims of this disease have no choice and can *only* misuse alcohol. The distinction between "real alcoholics" and nonalcoholics who overindulge is crucial in defining the NCA's domain. Without clearly distinguishing victims of an unusual and virulent disease from individuals of normal constitution who have over-indulged, the NCA undercuts the basis of its supposed distinctive competence. The more closely associated alcoholism is with behaviors that are obviously clear-cut matters of discipline, the less appropriate is any role for the NCA.

The National Council on Alcoholism represents, in the main, people who had problems with alcohol and were helped by Alcoholics Anonymous. Many of these individuals are employed in the alcoholism field (as Wiseman [1970] has observed, a frequent social mobility pattern of former alcoholics is to become alcoholism counselors). This involvement often entails the admission (sometimes tacitly, often overtly) that one is a "recovering" alcoholic (according to A.A. ideology one is never cured finally; the disease is merely "arrested" as long as one abstains). Whereas an emphasis on anonymity reduces the salience of a face-saving ideology, "coming out of the closet" makes the condition's respectability more crucial. As Pattison (1976) noted, a key to the medical disease model is that it absolves the alcoholic of responsibility for having developed the problem. The argument is that we do not condemn diabetics, whose bodies cannot tolerate sugar, so why should we condemn alcoholics, whose bodies cannot tolerate alcohol?

The fervor with which the disease model is defended suggests that it is directed at influencing not just public attitudes, but the ego esteem of alcoholics as well. According to the best evidence now available, it is not yet scientifically justifiable to reject the idea that alcoholics are those individuals who, because of a lack of "will power," cannot limit their consumption of alcohol, despite its deleterious effects. Corollaries of such a perspective might be that those able to strengthen their "will" might be able to return to normal drinking and that only those individuals with the least "moral fiber" would require total abstinence to avoid negative consequences. Admitting to the validity of the Rand Report and its many predecessors would be corroborative of such an embarrassing conclusion and seems to be strongly opposed by those many former alcoholics who appear to maintain sobriety (and avoid temptation) by believing that anything other than abstention is inconsistent with their body chemistry.

Whatever the scientific validity or psychological virtue of the medical disease model of alcoholism, its acceptance has been aided not only by individuals who themselves have had alcohol problems. In the mid-1950s a relatively small group within the American Medical Association succeeded in convincing the AMA to classify alcoholism as a disease (Rorabaugh 1979). They accomplished this in spite of the fact that many physicians had experienced unpleasant and unsuccessful clinical work with alcoholics and were less than anxious to strengthen a connection with such a stigmatized condition. In fact, the AMA, despite having awarded alcoholism classification as a disease, seems to betray a somewhat cavalier attitude in its *Manual on Alcoholism* (1967), in which it states that specialists in internal medicine should consider themselves competent to engage alcoholics in long-term psychotherapy.

Of course, support for the disease model has also come from individuals who recognize that many people have serious alcohol-related problems in their lives and that a perspective on the problem that is able to elicit greater sympathy and help for such persons could serve a constructive purpose. A prime example of this is Jellinek's monograph *The Disease Concept of Alcoholism* (1960), which, contrary to its frequent misunderstanding as an explication of established fact, was intended primarily to address the implications of the observation that the alcohol addiction patterns of some individuals had disease-like characteristics.

Cahalan (1979) proposed another social mechanism that would favor the disease model over one that emphasizes the social and epidemiological causes and cures of the problem:

> The liquor industry naturally would like to stave off all attempts to constrain the sale of alcoholic beverages, so they try to focus public attention on the individual-person "disease" aspects of alcoholism intimating that those not born with the disease may drink "moderately" (undefined) without risk of alcoholism. Thus they make common cause with the leaders of the NCA and related associations, who would like to see practically all of the available public funds spent on treatment of the unfortunate crop of present alcoholics probably because most of these agency leaders come from the ranks of Alcoholics Anonymous. They are understandably preoccupied with the lack of funds to treat all of the present alcoholics, and thus resent the expenditure of public funds on prevention programmes over which they have little or no control. Further, there is a hard vein of anti-intellectualism within the Alcoholics Anonymous movement which ridicules most research and long range prevention planning with such remarks as, K.I.S.S.—which means, "Keep it Simple, Stupid!" And since much prevention planning is far from simple and runs counter to powerful economic and political interests, it is no wonder that treatment of alcoholics consumes about 80 percent of the NIAAA budget, whereas preventive efforts probably account for no more than 1 or 2 percent (1979, p. 236).

COMPARING THE MODELS

Discussing the relationship between culture and alcoholism, Stivers (1976) suggested that all of the models considered in this chapter are essentially equivalent.

> The concepts of illness, maladjustment, social problems, and deviant behavior are the modern counterparts to those of sin and immorality. Both the former and latter are concepts of evil. The concept of illness when applied to moral, political, and social behavior is an expression of a technological morality which demands the normal, the successful, and the efficient. This morality deals exclusively with means; the end tends to disappear as the distinction between ends and means is blurred. The real problem with the alcoholic from the point of view of this morality is that he is inefficient on the job, and, secondarily, a failure at home. In short he is a real problem and an embarrassment to a technical system. Thus the alcoholic's illness is an illness of the system as well. Alcoholics

"screw up the works" and the company loses time and money. Hence the alcoholism becomes business and industry's problem. It is not surprising then to find alcoholism broadly defined and widely applied. The more alcoholic behavior increases or becomes visible, the greater the need to enforce the definition; likewise, the more therapeutic culture becomes the broader the definition of alcoholism will become (1976, pp. 597–98).

Even accepting Stivers' argument that these models all carry the same message, it is still possible that they are not equally useful for controlling deviants. Organizations interested in controlling deviant behavior among their employees would presumably not wish to promote the idea that alcoholism is a social problem resulting from such factors as stress; such a view might well inculpate organizations themselves for creating stressful work roles. Calling alcoholism a moral deficiency is unlikely to inspire very many individuals to step forward and admit to having that problem, or very many supervisors to expose a subordinate to the consequences of being identified as immoral. Updating the terminology to reduce the low social desirability of expressions such as "moral" by labeling alcoholism a personality, rather than a moral, defect may be somewhat useful. However, euphemistic strategies of this sort may turn out to be fairly transparent and thus might vitiate only slightly the problems of identifying employees engaged in deviant behavior, the process that is at the core of the social control mechanisms to be discussed in this book.

Uniquely, the medical disease ideology of alcoholism says that neither employers, employees, nor any other individual or institutional actors in society are to blame for the development of alcoholism. Contracting this illness is said to be merely a matter of bad luck, about which no one need feel ashamed.

This chapter has reviewed four perspectives on the etiology and nature of problems associated with the ingestion of alcohol, considering both the scientific evidence and the political interests arrayed for and against each. The focus has been on the medical disease model of alcoholism as being particularly suited to facilitating social control in the workplace. Using both qualitative and quantitative data, the chapters that follow examine whether the social control potential of the disease ideology is, in actual organizational practice, realized.

5

Alcoholism Programs in Industry

One manifestation of the greater credence given to perspectives on alcohol dependence that construe it as something other than the consequence of moral turpitude has been increased attention to rehabilitative efforts. For reasons that this book will elaborate upon, in recent decades the workplace has become an important site for establishing programs that purport to initiate treatment for alcoholics. This chapter begins with a discussion of the historical background against which contemporary "occupational programming" has emerged. Subsequent sections explicate the structure and operating policies of these programs. First, advice on how to run a program, offered by individuals and agencies that claim status as experts, will be considered. That will be followed by descriptions of individual company programs, which, because the descriptions are invariably laudatory, generally include implicit if not explicit advice. Finally, research on the structure and operation of programs will be reviewed.

ORIGINS OF OCCUPATIONAL PROGRAMMING

Beauchamp (1980) has argued that the modern concept of alcoholism as a disease, promoted by an ideologically concerted alcoholism movement, resulted from basic cultural changes in the United States and as a reaction to Prohibition:

> The alcoholism movement's central ideas cannot be understood apart
> from the transformations occurring in American Society during the first
> 50 years of this century. Paradoxically, even as the drive for national
> Prohibition succeeded and seemed to thrive, the very forces of rising
> prosperity—urbanization, mass media, advertising, and the automo-

66

bile—were undermining the cultural fundamentalism that sustained
Prohibition. These forces for change set the stage for the "discovery" of a
new theory of alcoholism problems, one that would conform to a central
tenet of modernism, the freedom of the individual from community
controls of personal conduct. Thus, the idea that the vast majority of
drinkers possessed the personal ability to control their drinking was a
theory that perfectly matched the triumph of modernity.... In this view,
after Prohibition any social movement concerned with alcoholism that
still emphasized alcohol control was doomed. The widespread perception of Prohibition as a failure, according to this view, directly
transformed our collective definition of alcoholism problems from
being a threat to the entire community to being a threat only to a
minority of drinkers. The need was to construct a definition or explanation of alcohol problems that relegated alcohol as a substance to a
relatively minor role (1980, p. 6).

Thus the appealing idea was promoted that there are two kinds of
people: that small minority among us who, for whatever reasons, cannot
consume alcohol without disastrous consequences (a group to be known
as "alcoholics," who are said to have the disease of "alcoholism") and the
majority of us, for whom the results of alcohol consumption (although, by
definition, not overconsumption) are essentially benign. Alcoholics
Anonymous is the most obvious outgrowth of that perspective: a group of,
by, and for that minority of individuals having what they characterize as a
constitutional inability to consume alcohol safely. Consistent with this
interpretation is the fact that A.A. historically has avoided being associated with temperance or Prohibitionist ideas (Beauchamp 1980);
although A.A. members clearly proselytize for the abstemious life, such
efforts are only directed toward other "alcoholics."

Another result of this perspective, building directly on the growth of
A.A., was the development of alcoholism programs in industry. As
Brandes (1976) noted, industrial medical departments have long been
viewed as helping to control drunkenness among workers; in some plants
medical diagnosis was useful for disqualifying drunkards from disability
benefits, which were reserved for what a Procter and Gamble manager
(cited in Brandes 1976) called "bona fide Sickness." But such an approach
was not in keeping with the general themes of welfare capitalism, for
which, in contrast, the disease concept of alcoholism was amiably suited.
That is, the medical disease model of alcoholism transforms a company's
attention to employee drinking problems from a paternalistic intrusion
into employees' personal affairs into an ostensibly legitimate medical
concern.

What is generally considered to have been the first corporate alcoholism program was founded by the DuPont Company in 1942. The
program operated out of the corporate medical department and company
physicians were aided by employees who had recovered from their own

drinking problems through A.A.* In succeeding years, similar programs were adopted at Eastman Kodak, Consolidated Edison, Illinois Bell, Allis Chalmers, and Western Electric, among others. The main elements of these programs generally included supervisory training sessions to explain the new, medical approach to the problem and to emphasize the importance of the supervisor's role in getting the afflicted employee into the company's program. Typically, the programs also involved assigning the company's medical department the formal responsibility for diagnosis, counseling, and treatment referral for alcoholics. These programs were simple and inexpensive for companies to establish and the corporations mentioned above have frequently reported their programs as successful.

Nevertheless, through the 1950s the growth in the number of companies with alcoholism programs was much less than explosive. There is reason to believe that the use of the medical disease model had some unanticipated and undesirable consequences. The central problem seems to have been that supervisors, who had the key role in finding alcoholics, were reluctant to apply such a stigmatizing label to one of their subordinates. Efforts by companies to dispel the stigmatic nature of the label—perhaps the central focus of training programs—could not, of course, be completely successful. Indeed, in at least one of these programs, that of DuPont, the disease model was so closely intertwined with the moral model that whatever destigmatizing effect the medical perspective might provide presumably would be lost. DuPont's medical director explained their perspective on this disease in the following testimony to a Senate hearing on alcohol problems:

> Our concept of alcoholism as a disease is, contrary to many diseases, alcoholism is self-induced. We must assume that one who cannot drink does not have to, or at least he should not. The cause of alcoholism is known. That one has the power to refrain from drinking whenever he develops the will to do so in spite of the compulsion to drink is firmly attested by the thousands and thousands of the number of Alcoholics Anonymous. Thus, the disease is preventable (U.S. Senate, Committee on Labor and Public Welfare 1970).

In addition to the reluctance of supervisors to stigmatize their subordinates, there may have been an even more important reason for the slow growth in the number of these early industrial alcoholism programs.

---

*The utilization of A.A. members in company alcoholism programs is an extremely common practice. For the A.A. member/company employee, it is an opportunity to fulfill the twelfth (and final) step of the A.A. program, that of bringing other sufferers into the fold. The value of proselytizing others for maintaining one's own faith is a familiar theme in the social sciences, derived from the work of Festinger, Riecken, and Schachter (1956).

Supervisors apparently objected to being told that their role in the program would include watching for overt physical symptoms of this illness, such as bleary eyes and hand tremors; they were work supervisors, they argued, not medical diagnosticians.

The solution to this dilemma took the form of a subtle, yet radical reconceptualization of job-based alcoholism programs. Occurring during the late 1960s, it shifted the emphasis from the corporate medical department to the personnel department. Yet paradoxically, it depended even more heavily on the medical disease ideology of alcoholism. Although more than one person has attempted to take credit for this innovation, one claimant, Ross Von Wiegand, was probably the most influential in the idea's dissemination (see Follmann 1976). Von Wiegand, the late director of labor-management services for the National Council on Alcoholism, wrote:

> The new methodology consists of a system which focuses exclusively on monitoring job performance. Under this system all employees whose performance drops below acceptable standards, and where regular corrective procedures fail to restore acceptable performance, are referred to professional counseling and diagnostic services for identification of the employee's problem, followed by treatment appropriate to whatever the employee's problem is (1974, pp. 83–84).

What, one might ask, has such a system to do with alcoholism? According to Von Wiegand, the problem with the old programs was that, by emphasizing the stereotypical physical symptomatology of alcoholism such as bloodshot eyes, companies would be able to identify only the "late-stage alcoholics." More favorable prognoses, he argued, would result from earlier interventions. Von Wiegand provided a set of symptoms of early-stage alcoholism, and explained that his "breakthrough"

> was the result of many surveys of employee personnel records of a number of large national multi-plant corporations conducted by the Labor-Management Services Department of the National Council on Alcoholism.
> The conclusion warranted by the data developed in these surveys was:
> every employee who is suffering from alcoholism, even in its early stages, will have a deteriorating pattern of job performance which is readily observable by any reasonably alert supervisor.
> This pattern is manifested through such objective factors as absenteeism, poor judgment, erratic performance, excessive material spoilage, decrease in productivity, poor interpersonal relationships, lateness and early departures, customer complaints, failure to meet schedules, and countless other instances of poor performance (1974, p. 83).

What has been especially consequential about this list of symptoms of "the disease of alcoholism" is that not one of them is a problem for which an industrial physician or nurse would have relevant skills or expertise. Rather, although Von Wiegand made no specific statement to this effect, all of these "symptoms" are clearly the province of the supervisor and the personnel department.

As remarkably broad-ranging and formidable as this statement of findings is, Von Wiegand did not present them as hypotheses but averred that these observations had been "validated by the studies conducted by the National Council on Alcoholism." Certainly, validation of findings that "every employee" having this problem will exhibit a pattern of deteriorating job performance must presumably have been based on a very detailed and extensive research program. However, beyond the excerpt quoted above, mentioning that employee personnel records were "surveyed," neither sample characteristics, instrumentation, analysis procedures, nor specific findings have ever been reported. In a footnote Von Wiegand (1974) provided what may have been the implicit explanation for this lack of disclosure, referring to the basis for his assertions as "confidential studies in the files of the National Council on Alcoholism."

The sanctity of the confidential relationship between alcoholics and the "professionals" treating them is often invoked as a reason for not revealing information about clients' participation in the program. Many of the program administrators interviewed for the study to be reported here were unable to provide even aggregated data, such as the proportion of employees who referred themselves into the program, insisting that collecting and maintaining any information compromised clients' confidentiality. In a lengthy interview with Von Wiegand the present author attempted to learn more about the methods and specific findings of his research. Not responding to questions about the study's methods, Von Wiegand boasted that he could pick out almost all of a company's alcoholics from an examination of their personnel records, stating that employees whose records indicated a pattern of sickness absenteeism with vague symptoms (such as upset stomach) and of absences on Mondays and Fridays were alcoholics. Beyond having perused personnel records, Von Wiegand offered no indication of having conducted any research to justify his claim that these behaviors are indicative of alcoholism. Little systematic evidence addresses the appropriateness of these diagnostic criteria, but Trice (1962) reported that, among a sample of 200 A.A. members, although absenteeism had often been one of their job-related symptoms, it did not occur disproportionately on Mondays and Fridays.

Historically, the development of this new "job performance" approach to diagnosing individuals as alcoholics coincided with an increased national interest in nontraditional health problems, exemplified by legislation such as the Community Mental Health Act of 1963. In 1966 the National Center for the Control and Prevention of Alcoholism was established as a small unit within the National Institute of Mental Health.

On December 31, 1970, President Nixon signed the Comprehensive Alcohol Abuse and Alcoholism Prevention, Treatment, and Rehabilitation Act (The Hughes Act, named after the formerly alcoholic senator who sponsored the legislation). This act established the National Institute on Alcohol Abuse and Alcoholism (NIAAA) as a separate agency under the Public Health Service. In the decade after its founding, the NIAAA's budget increased tenfold.

Presumably, at least some of this measurable success that the alcoholism field has experienced is attributable to having convinced relevant publics that alcoholism is a major problem. Indeed, efforts to convey that message have been extensive and have generally emphasized two assertions: that alcoholism is widely prevalent and that its costs to various sectors of society are very high. The National Council on Alcoholism has been prominent in this campaign and, in a great many cases, promotional literature from the government's alcoholism agency has closely paralleled that of the NCA.

Both groups present statistics whose impact depends somewhat on the reader more or less equating alcoholism with any misuse of alcohol. For example, the National Institute on Alcohol Abuse and Alcoholism stated (1972) that "half of all homicides and 1/4 of all suicides are alcohol-related" and "almost half of the 5-1/2 million arrests yearly in the United States are related to the misuse of alcohol."

Similarly, in government publications concerning the number of alcoholics in the United States the usual figure has been nine million (although more recently it has increased to ten million, reflecting general population growth, and thus a presumed commensurate growth in the number of alcoholics). As a scientific basis for this assertion, Cahalan's (1970) research is cited. However, as noted earlier, Cahalan has been abundantly clear in stating that this figure represents not the number of persons addicted to or dependent upon alcohol (that is, the symptoms that typically might be considered to indicate "alcoholism"), but rather just the number of those who have had some problem associated with drinking (Cahalan and Cisin 1976).

Not only is alcoholism said to be rampant in our society and closely related to the crime rate, but purported to be among the enormous costs of alcoholism to society are its effects on industrial productivity. In the mid-1960s a book labeled this problem "The Billion Dollar Hangover" (Coppolino and Coppolino 1965). Inflation soon took over; in a 1970 Congressional hearing (U. S. Senate, Committee on Labor and Public Welfare 1970) Senator Dominick stated that "losses to industry from absenteeism and other problems associated with alcoholism are about $2 billion annually." Only two witnesses later that figure had again doubled—to $4 billion! By 1974, in NIAAA's second report to Congress (U.S. Department of Health, Education and Welfare 1974), the figure had been raised to $10 billion. In that agency's fifth report to Congress (U.S.

Department of Health and Human Services 1983), not quite a decade later, the annual losses to industrial productivity attributable to alcoholism were stated to be $26 billion.

From where have these figures on the cost of alcoholism come? It appears that they are not quite plucked out of thin air but have generally been the product of simple calculations based on some simple assumptions. For example, if one proceeds from the assumptions that: there are nine million adult alcoholics; their participation in the labor force is proportional to that of the nonalcoholic population; and they are at least 25 percent less productive than nonalcoholic workers, then these extraordinary figures can be derived merely by multiplying one-quarter of the national average salary by the number of alcoholics in the workforce. Unfortunately, not only is there inadequate support for this estimate of the number of alcoholics, but the other assumptions are equally unjustified: labor force participation of alcoholics is not known, but is very likely to be lower than that of nonalcoholics (due to associations between alcoholism and old age, frequent hospitalization, and so on); and, as the following chapter will detail, the impact of alcohol addiction on job performance is by no means clear.

Perhaps the most sophisticated attempt to determine the cost of alcoholism to productivity has been a study by a Harvard economics professor and his associate. Working under a grant from the NIAAA, Berry and Boland developed a new means of estimating these costs and, in *The Economic Cost of Alcohol Abuse* (1977), concluded that the losses to all of society were over $30 billion a year and that lost industrial productivity alone cost at least $11.4 billion (in 1971 dollars). These figures, corrected for inflation, have often been the basis for NIAAA's assertions, but their acceptance has not been limited to the agency that funded this study. Their book's dust jacket features the following comments from Professor Harrison Trice of Cornell University, probably the most widely known researcher on occupational alcoholism programs:

> No prior effort to deal with the cost dimension has used the sophistication they have in this book. If those of us interested in improving alcohol abuse programming in the workplace can encourage the level of scholarship represented here, we will have contributed substantially to realizing our goals (in Berry and Boland 1977).

Because of the imprimatur of legitimacy Berry and Boland's study has provided for claims of extraordinarily high productivity losses caused by the disease of alcoholism, the level of scholarship represented by this study deserves examination. Reviewing the extant research literature, the authors noted Winslow et al.'s statement (1966, p. 217), concerning one company's evaluation of their alcoholism problems, that "apparently the company was already paying a higher base daily wage rate to the problem-free employees than to the suspected problem drinking employees." Making the assumption that alcoholics *are* less productive, Berry and Boland interpreted this finding as indicating that "the market corrects for lower productivity in the form of lower wages." They interpreted Pell and D'Alonzo's study of the alcoholism program at DuPont (1970), in which identified alcoholics were found to come disproportionally from among the hourly wage earners (whose incomes are lower than salaried employees), as an additional demonstration of the market's ability to correct efficiently for lower productivity. Asserting that wage differentials are a good measure of productivity differentials, Berry and Boland argued that the lower wages of alcohol abusers compared to nonabusers is a good measure of lost productivity due to alcohol abuse. As further corroboration they cited the finding, from Cahalan's (1970) national probability sample of households, that those that included an adult male problem drinker had substantially lower incomes than did those without such a member.

They did not, however, simply multiply this gross difference in income by the number of households with alcoholics. They were aware that additional variables might help explain some of the difference between the incomes of alcoholics and nonalcoholics, but regretted that they were not able to control for other factors with the data available to them. However, they cited a study by Luft (1975) of the earnings differential between those in poor health and those in good health, which ascertained that factors such as education and family structure accounted for 23.9 percent of the variation in earnings. Reasoning that both Cahalan and Luft had studied national samples, and that both studies were of health problems (although not explaining why these simple parallels would allow for the interchangeability of their findings), they used 23.9 percent as a correction factor in arriving at the net effect of alcohol abuse on income. They then multiplied the net earnings differential ($1,734 in 1971 dollars) by the number of households with adult male abusers (they chose the figure of 6.5 million) to arrive at $11.4 billion as, in their view, a conservative estimate of the productivity lost to the U.S. economy due to alcohol abuse.

In interpreting the data, Berry and Boland failed to consider an alternative hypothesis, which may be compared to theirs on logical and empirical grounds: low income and its correlates drive some people to drink. For example, interpreting the differential between alcohol-abusing hourly workers and nonabusing salaried employees at DuPont as a function of market responsiveness to differing marginal productivity implies that the cessation of alcohol abuse would *cause* an improvement in income and occupational status. It is logically possible that DuPont could find better-paying jobs for its recovered alcoholics (in reward, perhaps, for their success in overcoming this difficult problem). However, it seems unlikely that, if tomorrow all alcohol abusers were relieved of their affliction, the occupational structure of the United States would suddenly have 6.5 million additional jobs paying about $1,700 a year more (in 1971 dollars) than those held yesterday by those same individuals. There are simply not enough opportunities for promotion nor enough jobs in which remuneration is tied directly to levels of productivity for anything approaching that level of income mobility to occur, after one day or after five years of a totally sober population.

Studies investigating whether socioeconomic status (SES) causes alcohol problems or alcohol problems cause SES (referred to as the social causation and drift hypotheses, respectively) have come to differing conclusions. Cahalan (1970) and Cahalan and Room (1974) have argued for the social causation hypothesis, whereas Roebuck and Kessler (1972) and Ortega and Rushing (1983) have favored the drift hypothesis. In light of the methodological weaknesses of each of these studies, none of them could be considered definitive. It would therefore appear that the causal argument advanced by Berry and Boland has no more support than the opposite view, that alcohol problems result from, rather than cause, low socioeconomic status. Most probably, Ortega and Rushing suggest, "the relationship between occupational performance/stability and excessive drinking . . . is circular, with poor occupational performance and downward mobility contributing to excessive drinking and excessive drinking contributing to poor occupational performance, and so forth" (1983, p. 168).

Despite the tenuous link with reality of not only Berry and Boland's assessment of the productivity lost to alcoholism, but of the purported facts concerning the prevalence of the problem and the availability of symptoms by which alcoholics can be identified, these ideas seem to have been major contributions to the rapid proliferation of alcoholism and employee assistance programs starting in the mid-1960s. The following sections consider principles that have guided the development of these programs.

EXPERT ADVICE ON PROGRAM STRUCTURE

From the time of the rapid growth of occupational alcoholism programs in the late 1960s, the two most influential sources of advice on implementing them have been the National Council on Alcoholism and the National Institute on Alcohol Abuse and Alcoholism. As discussed earlier, advice provided by the NCA has been based, to a great extent, on what they claim were the findings from their confidential and unpublished studies. The NIAAA's recommendations have been based largely on those of the NCA, but have included additional themes.

The National Council's broad principles for program development and operation were presented in their widely distributed 12-page brochure, *A Joint Labor-Management Approach to Alcoholism Recovery Programs* (National Council on Alcoholism 1976b). The brochure addresses the seeming paradox of the job performance approach: How does one know that actual alcoholics are being identified if the only diagnostic criterion is deteriorating work performance? The reader is assured that, of course, not all employees exhibiting lateness, absenteeism, and poor performance will be alcoholics. Nevertheless, the NCA maintains that "60–80% of cases of persistent job performance problems are directly attributable to alcoholism" (p. 1). The brochure then details the reasons that these programs are needed, stating that the disease of alcoholism is the nation's number one health problem and has among its various unique aspects the dilemma that its victims deny the problem and resist treatment. Additionally, in what appears to be an attempt to blunt criticism that these programs have been directed disproportionately toward blue-collar employees (see Trice and Roman 1978), the NCA asserts that alcoholism is a democratic, classless disease: "No employee or class of employees enjoys special immunity from the disease of alcoholism. It is as prevalent in the executive suite as it is in all other job categories including middle management, office, clerical and production workers" (1976b, p. 3).

According to the NCA, the solid foundation of program development is a written policy statement acquainting all employees with the central features of the program. They recommend that the policy statement include the idea that the company considers alcoholism to be a treatable illness that will be handled just as any other employee illness—including equivalent benefits and insurance coverages. They suggest that the policy statement should encourage employees who suspect themselves to have an alcoholism problem to seek diagnosis and treatment, but that it should also make employees aware that supervisors have been trained to identify the job performance symptoms of alcoholism and will make referrals strictly on the basis of such symptoms. However, no matter what the means of entering the program, according to the NCA, employees should be assured that participation in the program will be held in confidence and that neither job security nor opportunities for promotions will be jeopardized by participation. They also recommend the inclusion of a passage such as the following: "Refusal to accept referral for diagnosis or follow prescribed treatment will be handled in accordance with existing contractual agreements and union-management understandings with respect to job performance" (1976b, p. 5).

The NCA pamphlet goes on to emphasize that "treatment for alcoholism (as for many other diseases) is not the function of managements or unions. Rather, referrals are made to ... qualified agencies" (p. 9). Their view is that the function of the company program should be limited to the effort to "achieve the objectives of earliest possible identification and motivation to accept treatment" (p. 9). They see the role of the company and its union partners in the treatment process as identifying and building close working relationships with local treatment resources, such as A.A. groups and alcoholism detoxification units of hospitals.

The pamphlet does concede that, because one of the symptoms of alcoholism is denial, many program clients will be nonvoluntary, having been referred by their supervisors, who have identified them as in need of the company's help on the basis of careful observation to detect signs of deteriorating job performance. Consequently, the National Council views the process of creating motivation to accept treatment as a key issue, and suggests the following procedures for dealing with poor performers who don't voluntarily enter the alcoholism program:

> The focus of the first interview should be restricted to the issue of job performance. Opinions or judgments on alcoholism should be avoided.
>
> After the job performance has been reviewed by the supervisor and the union representative, if desired, the worker should be informed of the professional services available on an absolutely confidential basis, including diagnosis and counseling.
>
> The worker may choose to accept or reject the offer of confidential help and services. If the worker chooses to accept, referral should be made directly to a qualified professional counseling and diagnostic facility that has been approved by the committee [of union and management representatives who jointly oversee the program] for determination as to whether or not the problem is alcoholism.
>
> If the worker rejects the offer and the job performance problems do not reoccur after the interview there is no longer a problem. If the job performance problems reoccur, then the union representative(s) and the supervisor may agree that the worker's performance is not acceptable and that the next appropriate step is to offer the worker a firm choice between either accepting the assistance offered by the program or accepting whatever action is appropriate within the framework of existing union-management agreements.
>
> In the majority of cases, when confronted with this clear choice, the worker will choose to utilize the program services and thus may be referred directly to the committee-approved resource ... to determine whether or not alcoholism is the problem.
>
> If the worker still refuses the offer of help, then appropriate action should be taken within the framework of the existing union-management agreements (p. 8).

Finally, the NCA pamphlet provides a checklist of "key program elements ... which have been found to be essential in maximizing program effectiveness" (p. 10). In addition to a written policy, these recommended provisions include training of supervisory and union personnel, education of all employees, program procedures that are specific, program personnel who are qualified, access to treatment facilities that are appropriate, and medical recordkeeping that is confidential and effective. Although they provided no empirical confirmation that these features are indeed predictive of effectiveness, it seems an exceptionally good bet that an evaluation that found a program to have been successful would also conclude that the personnel had been qualified, the treatment appropriate, and the recordkeeping effective.

NIAAA's advice on program design is very similar to that of the NCA; the former acknowledges the NCA as one of the two sources that provided the basis for their recommendations. The other major source appears to have been the work sponsored by the Christopher Smithers Foundation and directed by Harrison Trice, for many years retained by Smithers as a consultant. Trice's view, expressed most fully in *Spirits and Demons at Work* (Trice and Roman 1972, 1978), one of the most influential books on alcoholism programs in industry, is that the most crucial component of a program is motivating employees who perform poorly to do something about their inadequate performance. Certainly this concern is evident in the NCA's approach, but the difference is that Trice casts actual treatment for alcoholism as potentially irrelevant, counterproductive, and even immoral.

In his earlier research on Alcoholics Anonymous, Trice (1966) had observed that many individuals who eventually affiliated successfully with A.A. had not become serious about controlling their addiction until spurred by some crisis in their lives, and he applied this principle to motivating alcoholics on the job. First, Trice (1969) suggests, employees who perform poorly should be confronted with the documented evidence of their deficient job performance and told that the company considers continued performance at that level unacceptable. In a great many cases, he argues, merely confronting an employee in this manner will result in improvements in absenteeism, lateness, and productivity (that is to say, in a remission of the "symptoms" of alcoholism). With employees who do not respond to this treatment, the supervisor should engage in "crisis precipitation" through use of the "job threat." In simple terms, Trice recommends that employees who have been diagnosed as alcoholics on the basis of poor performance, who do not improve their performance and, secondarily, who refuse to accept treatment for alcoholism, should be told that either they will "shape up" or they will be fired. Trice and his graduate students originally referred to this process as "constructive coercion" (Ritzer and Belasco 1969; Trice 1969) but later changed it to "constructive confrontation" (Trice 1972).

Because of this emphasis on threat as therapy, Trice discourages the use of actual treatment for alcoholism. In the preface to the second edition of *Spirits and Demons at Work* (actually, the only part of the book revised from the first edition), Trice and Roman (1978) reaffirmed their earlier recommendations, but regretted that some of their basic ideas had not been heeded. Apparently displeased that many organizations' programs were inclined to refer employees diagnosed as alcoholic to treatment rather than just threaten them, they observed that "we have noticed disturbing trends toward bypassing confrontation with referral" (p. xvi). They went on to deplore "the rush to treatment," in part because they viewed referral to treatment as vitiating the potential of confrontation strategies. Additionally, however, they argued for the moral and ethical superiority of coercion over treatment on the grounds that the latter procedure "may deny the employee the right to choose how to bring his or her performance back into line" (1978, p. xvi).

In addition to adopting Trice's emphasis on motivating rather than treating alcoholics, the NIAAA's set of recommendations differ from the NCA's in its view of the implications of using the job performance diagnostic technique. Rather than saying that 60 to 80 percent of employees identified in this manner will be victims of the disease of alcoholism, it says that "the bulk" of such employees "have problems with alcohol in addition to their other difficulties" (U.S. Department of Health, Education, and Welfare 1974). Consequently, the NIAAA maintains that programs should be equally concerned with the manifold personal problems that lead to deteriorating job performance—with alcoholism first among these equals, however. This perspective, which was the basis for the shift from alcoholism-only to broader, "employee assistance" programs, is referred to as the "troubled-employee" or "broad-brush" approach.

Following are the NIAAA's "five essentials of program design":

I. *A written policy* which specifies the procedures for identifying and confronting employees who may have drinking problems, and includes explicit recognition by the organization that alcoholism—more usefully called "problem drinking" in the work setting—is a health problem, and that employees with such problems will not be penalized for seeking such help;

II. *Specific channels* within the work organization, including designation of a program coordinator, through which identified problem-drinker employees are confronted, counseled, and, if necessary, referred to appropriate resources in the community for help in dealing with their problems;

III. *Training of managerial and supervisory personnel* regarding their responsibilities for identifying poor work performance as the basis for confrontation and referral;

IV. *Education of the entire workforce* concerning policy, procedures, and the provision of help-without-penalty for problem-drinking;

V. *Cooperation by management and labor unions* and other employee organizations in providing support for the program, its implementation and its continuity.

This list closely resembles that of the NCA, with the very notable exception, in Principle II, that referral of problem-drinkers to treatment resources is advised only "if necessary." Similarly, the NIAAA's recommendations on case handling, given below, deemphasize treatment and emphasize constructive coercion/confrontation in comparison to those of the NCA:

I. *Recognition.* In most instances, problem-drinking by an employee will become manifest in (a) impaired job performance, and (b) absenteeism, before the appearance of the severe classical symptoms of alcohol dependence. When supervision is competent, these early but repeated signs—poor work, or patterned or suspicious absenteeism, or both—are easily recognized in spite of the efforts of the employee to conceal them.

II. *Documentation* of impaired performance sets the stage for intervention. Unlike most other social relationships, the link between the employer and the employee is contractual. Repeated instances of inadequate job performance constitute a breach of the contract. Where employees are represented by a labor union, such documentation is in accordance with procedure established by the labor contract.

III. *Confrontation.* Problem drinking accompanied by impaired performance often occurs in employees who, having worked for years in one organization, have intense psychological as well as economic investments in their jobs. Confrontation of such an employee is a momentous event when fortified by evidence of inadequate job performance that is documented jointly by labor and management, and is coupled with the clear possibility that disciplinary action will be taken if he does not take steps to return his performance to an acceptable level.

This confrontation usually precipitates a crisis which can motivate the employee to do something about his problem. Often he responds by accepting the help offered by the organization rather than face possible adverse action that may shatter his central life role. In many instances the confrontation undermines the basic rationalization which enabled the employee to avoid recognizing his problem—the notion that his drinking did not affect his work. ("If I'm doing my job, I can't be one of those . . . ")

IV. *Offer of assistance.* The amount and kind of assistance offered depend on the capability and circumstances of the employer. Implementing a program to identify and help the problem drinking employee recover his health may necessitate an investment in specialized personnel and procedures, additional supervisory training, and employee education. If the program is correctly viewed as a means of regaining the productivity of skilled employees in whom the organization already has considerable investment, it is simply an addendum to typical company goals and assigned supervisory responsibilities. In many cases the program can be located in existing personnel or medical departments.

DESCRIPTIONS OF COMPANY PROGRAMS

The manner in which the broad guidelines discussed above have been specifically operationalized may be illustrated by descriptions of individual company programs.

The Bethlehem Steel Corporation has been a strong supporter of the National Council on Alcoholism and its executives have served on NCA advisory boards. Therefore, the operation of its occupational programs should illuminate the practical application of the NCA's recommendations. The training and follow-up procedures used by the alcoholism program at Bethlehem's huge Sparrow's Point plant have been described in an article coauthored by the plant's medical director and alcoholism counselor (Salazar and Doyle 1978). According to this description their supervisory training program opens with a videotaped message from the plant's general manager, who emphasizes the importance of supervisors learning the symptoms of alcoholism and referring employees exhibiting those symptoms to the program. This is followed by a speech by the plant's medical director, who describes the types of drinkers and the symptoms of alcoholism. He then reemphasizes the importance of supervisors learning the symptoms of alcoholism and referring their subordinates to the program. Next, a film strip entitled "Open Your Eyes" is shown, followed by a discussion led by the alcoholism counselor, who explains how to confront problem employees. A booklet describing program procedures is distributed, and a question and answer period is held.*

The authors reported that referrals to the program increased by over one-third after the workshops were held, but that far fewer than the "seven percent of any industrial workforce" who, according to "national figures," should have been in the program had yet been enrolled. Nevertheless, due to the "anticipated influx of new patients, 15 new employees now enrolled in the plant's alcoholism program were selected to help handle the increased workload." All members of A.A., "they were chosen for their ability to work with alcoholics, their dedication to maintaining their own sobriety, and their desire to help other alcoholics to achieve sobriety." The authors added that these 15 current program clients "have attended two college-level courses in sociological and related fields" and "in the near future, these 15 employees will be fully qualified to serve as lay counselors" (Salazar and Doyle 1978, p. 81).

---

*Although Bethlehem's program may reflect the influence of the NCA, this corporation does not necessarily share the National Council's view of the ubiquity of alcoholism problems in the workplace. The NCA's Von Wiegand told me that alcoholism problems accounted for 80 percent of the grievances at Sparrow's Point. Recounting this assertion to Bethlehem's vice-president for personnel, he expressed surprise and promised to have his staff check into that figure. Their own examination of their personnel records indicated that the grievances attributable to alcohol problems were not exactly four out of each five; rather, they turned out to be four out of 1,900.

The program at Arizona Public Service (APS) should also reflect the NCA's orientation; it was described in a monograph (Habbe 1969) that was substantially influenced by the staff of the NCA, who directed its author to examples and information (and who were sufficiently in agreement with the finished volume that they distributed 2,000 copies of it). The implementation of an alcoholism program at APS was said to have been spurred by the concern of a top executive: "knowing that alcoholism was a major health problem in all parts of the nation, he saw no reason for thinking that the problem would be any less in Arizona or at APS." In cooperation with the local affiliate of the National Council on Alcoholism, APS conducted a survey of company documents and employee personnel records to see if behavior patterns symptomatic of alcoholism could be detected. The following findings were reported:

1. That Arizona Public Service had no written policy with regard to alcoholism and/or behavioral medical problems of its employees;
2. That APS unwittingly allowed concealment of such problems through uninformed supervisory practices;
3. That APS employee records were kept in a manner that made problem drinking hard to detect; however, the patterns of a number of employees suggested they were heading toward *some kind* [emphasis in original] of a medical-behavioral problem;
4. That APS tended to practice punitive rather than corrective measures when actually faced with the drinking employee (in Habbe 1969, p. 74).

Although three of these four conclusions have no relevance to the stated purpose of investigating whether symptoms of alcoholism could be detected from personnel records, and although the one relevant conclusion indicated that company records could at best hint that some employees might be "heading toward *some kind*" of problem, this study was said to have motivated the implementation of the APS program. Its policy statement asserted that alcoholism is a treatable illness for which the company has a sympathetic concern, and it laid out the following procedural steps for supervisors to follow:

(A) recognize and understand the symptoms of alcoholism;
(B) refer an employee to *experts* on alcoholism (not try to be an expert on alcoholism himself);
(C) apply the same supervisory standards to declining job performance because of alcoholism as to any other health problem;
(D) apply disciplinary measures (including termination, if necessary) only if the employee is not demonstrably cooperative in making a conscientious effort to rehabilitate himself (in Habbe 1969, p. 74).

At the same time that the above procedures were being distributed to supervisors, the following letter, making no mention of the connection of the alcoholism program to discipline and job performance, was being sent to the homes of all employees:

Dear Fellow Employees,

Arizona Public Service Company has demonstrated its concern for the personal well-being of its employees by continually improving their health and medical program. In keeping with this philosophy the company has established a policy on alcoholism.

Alcoholism is a controversial subject. Any statement of policy runs the risk of being misunderstood. The best way to avoid misunderstanding is to clarify the reason for the policy.

Adoption of this policy is recognition of the fact that "problem drinking" or alcoholism is a public health problem of major concern to all communities and industries. There are 6,000,000 alcoholics in the United States and the problem is growing rapidly. We are concerned only with problem drinking. There is no interest in social drinking and no wish to intrude upon your private life.

By bringing the problem of alcoholism out in the open it can be fully discussed. Through early detection and referral for treatment, rehabilitation can be most profitably undertaken. This is the approach defined in our new policy. We do not know the extent of our problem or even if we now have one. Our only purpose in sending you this letter is to inform you that this new policy exists and assistance is available for those who need it. We encourage you to think of alcoholism as a health problem that can be treated and often solved (in Habbe 1969, pp. 74–75).

After the plans for the program were developed, company management discussed them with union leaders and gained their consent. Supervisory training was conducted and reported as very well received. No specific data on referrals into the program, or on outcomes from the program, were presented.

The medical director of the Boston Edison Company, in developing their alcoholism program, reviewed writings on other company's efforts in this area. He wrote that the company

studied the pros and cons of the different approaches as they applied to our individual situation at Boston Edison, and we made our own evaluation of the "best" methods. This is where Professor Trice's manual assisted us so very much, in particular, the principle of "constructive coercion" which he expounds (Ravin 1975, pp. 199–200).

According to Ravin, the company's medical director, "even though we readily admit that A.A. is the only effective method for almost all alcoholics to personally recover from the sickness," A.A. principles alone are "not satisfactory or effective because they primarily exclude the 'coercive' features, and only focus on the constructive aspects of dealing with alcoholism" (1975, p. 195).

The company held a full-day orientation conference, "primarily designed to inform union officials on the subject." Ravin admitted, however, that "complete recognition and endorsement...from all the parties involved" were not achieved. Sessions to train managerial personnel included an explanation of the program, a film, and a discussion period; and Ravin reported that, as in the case of the union leaders, many being trained had reservations about the program:

> Many of these supervisors had been promoted from the union ranks and felt a close kinship with the men. They felt a strong emotional reaction from "suspensions" and "firing"; and it was, and still is, most difficult to convince them that "early treatment" for alcoholism is the humane and effective approach just as early treatment of cancer or tuberculosis or any other sickness.
>
> There were some few management people who took a different view. They felt we were "coddling the drunks" and we're going to let them "get away with murder." They just could not see this "hospitalization" and "special treatment" for "these people."
>
> The reaction of the union officials and stewards was quite similar to management, but just the opposite. Some expressed the feeling we were "starting a purge" to rid the company of "loafers" and "trouble makers" under the guise of medical treatment. The majority, however, were in agreement with the general concept of rehabilitating the alcoholic but were hung-up emotionally when it came to specific cases of suspensions and firing. They had extreme difficulty in reconciling this new approach to alcoholism with the traditional "protective" role (1975, pp. 207–208).

The program's procedures were distributed and explained at these sessions. They emphasized that rehabilitation might or might not include a physical examination, hospitalization, psychiatric counseling, or counseling with clergy. The two imperatives of the rehabilitation process, however, were participation in A.A. and sessions with the company's rehabilitation counselor. Attendance at A.A. meetings was required "three to four times weekly, but more frequently in the beginning." Rehabilitation counseling was to be given weekly for the first two months, biweekly for the next three months, and monthly for the next seven months. Clearly, the counselor is at the center of the company's efforts to help employees victimized by what they refer to as a "sickness." Thus, it is surprising that the detailed criteria listed by Ravin for choosing the person for this job did not include any qualifications in therapy or rehabilitation. Rather, the rehabilitation counselor was selected from among the company's employees, according to the following criteria:

The job specifications call for a male, a minimum age 35, someone willing to work (or be on call) 24 hours a day, someone who had been an alcoholic himself, someone who had been a union leader (officer, steward, on bargaining committee, etc.) but who would be willing to give up his union membership and relinquish all claims to overtime pay, someone who could work harmoniously and effectively with problem drinkers and with members of their families, someone capable of speaking in public, and someone approved to operate a company-owned auto (Habbe 1969, p. 79).

The alcoholism program at the Boeing Company's Vertol Division has been described by the company's medical director (Mellon 1969), who seemed less concerned than was Boston Edison about the A.A. approach having too little an emphasis on coercion. Stressing the importance of the alcoholism program by noting that "most people today will agree upon the two to three percent figure of any plant population as having some problem with alcoholism," he stated that the results of Boeing's program had been gratifying. He claimed that the key to this success had been the reliance on recovered alcoholics as counselors; referring to Boeing's counselor at that time, Mellon wrote, "He knows all the rationalizations the alcoholic himself is using. He is able to get down on the ground, so to speak, and talk bluntly with the alcoholic employee" (p. 319). The A.A. philosophy, however, did not seem to Mellon necessarily to eliminate the possibility of using constructive coercion; indeed, he described firing employees as a part of the therapeutic process. Stating that progressive discipline should be the key in any program, he explained that to mean

that if the alcoholic fails to get the proper motivation to do anything about his drinking, that he may be treated as any other employee would be treated in any company violation: that he be given progressive days off in the various steps of arbitration until such time as he realizes that his continued drinking is going to mean termination. In the eyes of the alcoholic counselor at Vertol, Dave M., it sometimes takes termination for an employee to get such motivation. Indeed, in some cases it is only through termination that the man has stopped drinking (1969, p. 319).

Boeing's "alcoholic counselor" also gives presentations to managerial personnel. Similar to the training sessions at Boston Edison and Arizona Public Service, they typically include a film, a talk entitled "What is alcoholism?," and a question and answer period. Also similar to the other two programs described here, the procedures are characterized as having been quite successful, although no specific measures of success or failure were mentioned.

Measures of program success (although never failure, of course) have appeared in some descriptions of company programs. Wagner (1982) described his organization's EAP, called Project Concern, as having achieved "a 50 percent success ratio, resulting in returning about 565 [of the 1,130] participants to full productivity," and thereby having saved the organization $2,447,000 annually. He then explained the formula he used to arrive at this estimation of savings and described how readers could apply it to their own organizations, advising them to

> simply divide the average total number of employees into your annual payroll to derive the average employee wage. Multiply the average annual wage by 17 percent of your total employees (statistical average of troubled employees) to obtain the payroll for troubled employees. Next, take 25 percent of the troubled employee payroll to obtain your present loss due to troubled employees. Finally, take 50 percent of this loss to identify the amount you could save through an EAP (1982, pp. 59-60).

Explaining how Project Concern works, Wagner stated that "In a typical situation an employee is referred to counseling by his supervisor [this was the type of referral for roughly 60 percent of his clients] because of a Friday-Monday absence pattern coupled with tardies and a poor production record" (1982, p. 61). If the problem is determined to be alcoholism, the counselor gives the employee a 45-minute talk explaining that alcoholism is a disease. If the employee answers affirmatively to the question "Do you want to do something about your alcoholism," "the concept of Alcoholics Anonymous is explained." Stating that "the next step is crucial and determines the success of [clients'] rehabilitation," Wagner explained the significance of "matching the employee to the most compatible A.A. group" in terms of "the client's social, ethnic, and economic background" (1982, p. 62). This type of segregation appears to be a fairly common practice among alcoholism counselors and means, for example, that they would not expect a white manager to go to an A.A. meeting at which black manual laborers were in attendance. Clients are required to attend five A.A. meetings per week and a weekly session with the Project Concern counselor.

RESEARCH ON PROGRAM STRUCTURE

Many studies have attempted to assess the prevalence of the various elements that might be included in an occupational alcoholism or employee assistance program. Somewhat puzzlingly, most of these have made no attempt to determine whether the inclusion of any of these structural features are associated with any aspect of program effectiveness. Rather, they have looked simply at how many programs have each feature. A possible interpretation of the reasoning behind conducting such studies might be that most of these programs are believed to be successful, and information on how most programs operate would allow others to copy their procedures and thus their success. A more parsimonious (if less charitable) interpretation of the lack of sophistication of these studies is that their authors have generally not had adequate sophistication in research methods to be aware that it is possible and valuable to assess the relationships among variables.

In July 1974 NIAAA awarded a grant to the Association of Labor-Management Administrators and Consultants on Alcoholism (ALMACA), the fledgling occupational association in industrial alcoholism, to develop information useful to the field. One report produced under this grant (Wilder 1976) was prepared by ALMACA itself, and a series of other studies (Hayward, Schlenger, and Hallan 1975; Matthews 1976; Schlenger, Hallan, and Hayward 1976; Schlenger and Hayward 1975; Schlenger, Hayward, and Hallan 1976; Threatt 1976) were produced under a subcontract from ALMACA to The Human Ecology Institute (THEI).*

Wilder's report (1976) under this contract focused on the programs' "information systems." To identify programs for his study, Wilder contacted the federally-funded Occupational Programming Consultants (OPCs) located in each state, asking them to provide a list of all the organizations in their state having programs. Emerging from their collective training program as the "Thunderin' Hundred," the OPCs appeared, from the present writer's contacts with many of them, to have had enthusiasm for their jobs, a high level of *esprit de corps,* and good relations with NIAAA. For a NIAAA-funded study to gain the cooperation of the OPCs in collecting this information would have seemed to have been relatively easy. Nevertheless, after receiving responses from only 38 of 50 states, Wilder reported that "this effort required several months." He identified over 1,000 organizations operating occupational programs and mailed surveys to 350 of them, from whom 130 usable responses were received. Analysis of his responses was limited to the listing of frequency counts. One finding that is pertinent to the differences between the National Council's emphasis on programs to deal specifically with alcoholism, as opposed to NIAAA's "broad-brush" approach, was that 26

---

*In an interview, James Baxter, the Executive Director of ALMACA, explained to me that the NIAAA grant had been intended as a means of getting financial support to ALMACA to assist in its general development (personal communication 1979). Baxter, a retired Navy captain, hired William Wilder, another retired Navy captain, to conduct the research. Baxter reported that they had great difficulty in conducting surveys and eventually subcontracted the work to THEI. He summarized the experience as more trouble than it was worth and vowed never again to seek federal funding. This experience was somewhat parallel to the history of Alcoholics Anonymous (to which many "Almacans" happen to belong), whose early leaders, before deciding on their low profile policies of anonymity and refusal of outside financial support, strove mightily, but without success, to attract large grants from major corporations (Beauchamp 1980).

percent of the respondents had alcoholism-only programs, and 71 percent had "broad-brush" programs. This study also investigated the distribution of operational responsibility for the program between management and the union. As noted earlier, the NCA is an advocate of full union-management cooperation and collaboration, and they have been joined in this recommendation by Follmann (1976), Habbe (1973), Trice and Belasco (1966), Trice, Hunt, and Beyer (1977), and Trice and Roman (1972, 1978). In Wilder's study, 44 percent of the respondents reported theirs to be management-run programs, and 53 percent reported joint programs. He provided considerable detail about the recordkeeping procedures used in these programs, but did not report any attempt to relate these various practices to differences in program results.

Schlenger, Hallan, and Hayward's report (1976), "Characteristics of Selected Occupational Programs," provided an analysis of a much broader range of program structural elements, but on a sample of only 15 companies' programs. Five pages of their report were taken up with the argument that their use of geographic region, alcoholism-only versus broad-brush approach, and organizational size as stratification dimensions for their sample ensured that these 15 programs were representative of all existing programs in the United States. The data they provided to support this unusual contention seem, rather, to refute it. For example, attempting to demonstrate that their sampling had done a reasonable job of matching the actual incidence of programs in large and small firms, they presented a table indicating that whereas 37 percent of the programs in their sampling frame were in companies with fewer than 1,000 employees, 7 percent of the programs actually studied—that is, 1 out of the 15—was in that size category. Attempting to demonstrate that their sample accurately represented the prevalence of alcoholism-only programs versus broad-brush programs, they presented rather contrary data. Whereas their universe consisted of 58 percent alcoholism and 38 percent broad-brush programs, their sample included 27 percent alcoholism and 73 percent broad-brush programs—a clear reversal. Nonetheless, the authors concluded that "none of these deviations appears serious."

As with Wilder's report, data analyses were limited to frequency counts. Their tabulations indicated that 13 of the 15 programs had written policy statements, union involvement, and organizationwide distribution of program information. However, it is not discernible from their report whether the same 13 had all of these features. All 15 programs were reported to have included some form of supervisory training and to have conducted follow-ups on patients. Clients entered the program through supervisory referrals in 54 percent of the cases, through self-referrals in 32 percent, through medical department referrals in 8 percent, and through union referrals in one percent of the cases. A.A. was used as a treatment resource by 13 of the programs; inpatient alcoholism rehabilitation facilities were used by 12; and mental health clinics, general hospitals, and financial counselors were each used by 8 programs. None of the companies' insurance policies covered total outpatient costs, although 4 covered partial costs of such treatment. Inpatient treatment was covered in full by 5 of the companies and partially by 7; 2 companies were reported to have no insurance coverage for alcoholism treatment. Despite the numerous factors on which data were gathered, no attempt was made to relate these practices to programs' results.

A survey of 21 programs (in 18 different organizations) was conducted by Erfurt and Foote (1977) in cooperation with the Detroit Chapter of ALMACA. Some of the characteristics they examined (again, analyzed by merely using frequency counts) were addressed in the studies already reviewed here and invite comparison. Their findings on sources of referral into programs are consistent with those of Schlenger, Hallan, and Hayward: 41 percent of the referrals were made by supervisors, 32 percent were self-referrals, 10 percent came from the medical department, and 8 percent from the union. Whereas 53 percent of Wilder's respondents had reported their program to be joint union-management efforts, Erfurt and Foote found that 57 percent characterized their programs as jointly operated. In addition, Erfurt and Foote examined the backgrounds of the individuals who directed these programs and described their training and expertise as "very high"; there were 7 with master's degrees in either social work, education, psychology, or counseling, 5 social workers with bachelor's degrees, 4 recovered alcoholics, 3 nurses, and 2 members of the clergy. The authors specifically stated that their study did not involve any attempt to measure program effectiveness. Nevertheless, despite the admitted absence of any facts on what features are related to effectiveness, they frequently provided advice as to what elements should be included in a program in order for it to be successful.

In *Employee-Assistance Programs* (1980), Shain and Groeneveld presented a number of studies they had conducted on occupational programs. Their book represents a significant improvement in methodological sophistication over the studies reviewed so far, as the authors presented some of the data in cross-tabulation tables and made some relational statements based on these analyses. Tests of statistical significance, however, were not reported.

Shain and Groeneveld's major empirical study of program structure involved a search for "hypothetical key elements," that is, program components that are especially important for success. Their sample consisted of 12 "successful" programs that were selected, not because they were shown to have successfully helped alcoholics, but because they had all identified high proportions of their employee populations as alcoholics. Shain and Groenveld investigated whether the program structural elements that had been discussed by others as important for program success were present in these 12 programs. Their reasoning was that, if all 12 had certain structural features in common, then those features must be responsible for the programs' success; the possibility that these same features might also be present in some unsuccessful programs was not addressed. Information about each of the programs was obtained from interviews with a total of 46 respondents from the 12 organizations. Shain and Groeneveld's data indicate, however, that not only was there little consistency in structural features among organizations, but there was little consistency among respondents within the same organizations in their reports of the presence of various program elements.

Undeterred by the lack of structural consistency among "successful" programs, they searched for a variable that seemed to influence program structure, concluding that organizational size was the only one with such an effect. Presenting cross-tabulations of size (divided into three categories) with structural features, they concluded that greater organizational size is associated with older programs, formal promotion of the program, written policy statements, and coverage of wage losses during treatment. Their cross-tabulation tables, however, contained some statistical impossibilities: 92.9 percent of the four large organizations and 61.5 percent of the four medium-sized organizations were claimed to have a written policy. Of the four medium-sized firms, 63.6 percent promoted their programs; of the four small programs, 37.5 percent provided wage coverage. Because none of these figures is derivable from taking a percentage of four, it seems clear that Shain and Groeneveld have confused levels of aggregation. Rather than studying 12 companies and their programs, they appear to have analyzed individual respondents' varying perceptions of their companies' programs. The data do suggest that there is considerable disagreement among respondents within the same organization and, given that some of the issues are matters of fact rather than of opinion, it appears that many of their respondents provided them with misinformation. Further, in analyzing these data they inexplicably reduced continuous level data (company size) to categorical data (small versus medium versus large companies), a strategy that greatly weakens potential statistical inference. These problems, of the accuracy of respondents' information and of the reduction of continuous level data to categorical data, limit the usefulness of this study, as well as that of the study described next.

In 1972, 1974, 1976, and 1979, NIAAA contracted with the Opinion Research Corporation (ORC) to include questions about company alcoholism programs in their omnibus "Executive Caravan" surveys of executives in Fortune 500 firms (Opinion Research Corporation 1972, 1974, 1976, 1979). The samples for the four surveys were drawn independently, so that this was not a panel study. Nevertheless, it was, in certain ways, the most extensive study among those discussed so far. The contracts with ORC called for them only to gather the data, and their responsibility ended with their presentation of marginal frequency listings of responses. For further analyses of these data, NIAAA contracted with Professor Paul Roman of Tulane University. His analysis of the 1972 and 1974 surveys (Roman, n.d.) consisted of a verbal discussion of the contents of the frequency listings. His published reports on the more recent surveys represent a considerable increase in sophistication over the research reviewed so far, including not only cross-tabulations but tests of statistical significance.

In an article published in the National Council's *Labor-Management Alcoholism Journal,* Roman and Thomas (1978) listed the prevalence of program components, based on responses to the 1976 Executive Caravan survey. Approximately half of the survey's respondents, 270 of 536, indicated that their companies had alcoholism programs. Very unfortunately, however, it is not clear how many corporations (or alcoholism programs) this number represents. This issue was not addressed by Roman and Thomas, and the only information that the Opinion Research Corporation was willing to volunteer (Thomas, personal communication 1980) was that they requested 15 interviews in each corporation in which they conducted interviewing, but might complete as few as 7 in any one company (this writer was told that if he wanted to know precisely how many different corporations were in fact studied, he would have to try and figure it out for himself). From this sparse information a rough estimate may be attempted: if an average of 11 interviews were conducted in each company, the accumulation of 536 interviews would require contact with 49 companies. Given that half of the respondents reported having alcoholism programs in their firms, Roman's sample might actually consist of roughly two dozen organizations. Further, if the 270 respondents who stated that their companies had alcoholism programs came from companies in which all 15 interviews had been completed, Roman's sample would consist of only 18 programs.

Among the findings from the 270 respondents who indicated that their companies did have programs were that 94.2 percent stated that their programs included an assurance of client confidentiality, 76.8 percent said that they included written procedures, and 57.9 percent said that management orientation sessions had been conducted. Insurance coverage for inpatient alcoholism treatment was claimed to be a program feature by 84.1 percent of the respondents, and 63 percent said that outpatient alcoholism treatment was covered.

Roman and Thomas did attempt to relate these and other features to two outcome measures, whether an executive had ever dealt with a problem-drinking subordinate and whether the case's outcome had been successful (success was defined as the employee returning to adequate job performance). To do so, they analyzed the responses of the 227 executives who stated that they had dealt with a problem-drinking subordinate, despite the fact (not mentioned by Roman and Thomas, but indicated in ORC's frequency listings) that 41 percent of these 227 respondents were from companies that apparently had no program. Roman and Thomas found that only three program ingredients were significantly related to successful versus unsuccessful outcomes: written procedures for identification and referral, training of all supervisors, and, similar to training, orientation sessions for management. Not one of the program elements was related to having dealt with a problem-drinking subordinate. Nonetheless, Roman and Thomas summarized their findings by stating that "these data confirm what have been believed to be key program ingredients" (1978, p. 40).

The same article also reported on a separate set of data collected by Roman's Tulane Center for the Monitoring of Occupational Alcoholism Programming. Having gathered data from the administrators of 564 programs, they presented frequencies showing the prevalence of program components for the 140 respondents in two of the five original company size categories, small and large; the 424 respondents in the "very small," "medium-sized," and "very large" categories were, inexplicably, left out of all analyses. They reported that the large organizations were more likely to have each of those components studied in the ORC survey and that the presence of these features was more variable among the smaller companies. In addition to company size, the associations of program features with rates of referral into the program were investigated. Trichotomizing referral rates and using only the two extreme categories, Roman and Thomas presented two-by-two contingency tables of high versus low referral rates, tabulated against the presence versus absence of each of ten program elements. Three of the tables yielded significant chi-squares, showing that employee education, access to the program for employees' dependents, and a 24-hour hotline were related to higher referrals.

Overall, Roman and Thomas found that the programs in their own sample generally had more features than those in the ORC's sample of Fortune 500 companies. They speculated that this discrepancy might have occurred because their own listing consisted of programs that NIAAA had targeted to receive developmental support and that, as a result, might have been more complete than those not receiving this guidance. An examination of the ORC data, however, suggests a more parsimonious explanation. The Executive Caravan survey included respondents engaged in a wide variety of corporate functions, and ORC provided a breakdown by functional area in their marginal frequency listings of responses for each question. Executives from all corporate functions gave very similar answers, with the notable exception of those from personnel departments. As examples, 78 percent of personnel functionaries reported that their programs had written policy statements, in contrast to 62 percent of all other respondents; in addition, 78 percent of respondents in personnel said that their programs included written program procedures, in contrast to only 57 percent of the others. Similarly, insurance coverages were reported differently by personnel functionaries and others; of those in personnel, 83 percent claimed that their companies provided coverage for inpatient treatment of alcoholism, versus 47 percent of other respondents, and 50 percent of personnel functionaries claimed coverage for outpatient treatment, versus 29 percent of all others. Indeed, when responses on the Executive Caravan from just the personnel functionaries are compared to the results of the analyses of Roman's own data from program administrators, program structures in the two samples are rather similar.

A possible, albeit unlikely, explanation for the discrepancies between the ORC's and Roman's data is that the personnel department respondents in the Executive Caravan happened to have come from organizations with more elaborate programs. A second possibility is that personnel functionaries, typically responsible for these programs, will make exaggerated claims concerning their completeness. However, in the ORC surveys respondents from personnel departments were not always more likely to claim the inclusion of a program element; for example, whereas 40 percent of other respondents claimed that all employees had been educated about the alcoholism program, only 33 percent of those in personnel so stated. The most likely interpretation of the discrepancies between personnel and other respondents would therefore seem to be that personnel functionaries are simply (and understandably) better informed about the structures and operating policies of their companies' alcoholism programs.

Under a contract with the Federal Railway Administration, University Research Corporation produced a monograph entitled *Problem Drinking among Railroad Workers: Extent, Impact and Solutions* (Mannello 1979). The major focus of the study was the drinking behavior of railroad employees and the impact of their drinking on work performance. This project surveyed a large and representative sample of workers on seven major railroads and analyzed the survey data with correlational and partial correlational procedures. Although more sophisticated than the studies reviewed so far, this survey did not collect any data pertinent to the railroads' alcoholism programs. Nevertheless, consistent with the monograph title's promise of a consideration of "solutions," Mannello concluded with a discussion of company programs that were implemented to help solve problems with employee alcohol abuse. Eschewing partial correlations, cross-tabulations, and even frequency counts, Mannello drew conclusions about the relationships of program features to outcomes. On the basis, apparently, of conversations with a number of employees from each of the seven railroads, who presumably had stated their opinions as to which program components they felt were crucial for success, Mannello provided a list of recommendations. Many of these recommendations are difficult to disagree with. As examples, Mannello recommended a "program director with sufficient time and proven competence" rather than one with "insufficient time or ability"; "competent personnel who assess and refer" rather than "unqualified counselors"; "adequate referral agents" rather than "unactivated, untrained, unmotivated referral agents"; "use of high quality treatment agencies" rather than "over-reliance on ... treatment modalities that do not fit in with client's situation"; and "adequate program promotion" concentrating "on high payoff channels" rather than "haphazard," "little, or no program promotion," or "promotion through relatively ineffective channels" (1979, pp. 44–77). These recommendations were not empirically tested, but unless "effectiveness," "competent," and so on, are operationalized independently of program success, they are merely circular and a test would be neither possible nor necessary. That is, these characterizations seem most likely to be applied as post hoc explanations of a program's outcomes.

Another study funded by the Federal Railway Administration was conducted by Hitchcock and Sanders (1976). Of the 20 railroads' alcoholism programs included in the study, 13 were primarily management-run with union cooperation, six were joint union-management efforts, and one had little union input. Only five of the programs were limited strictly to alcoholism, with four covering alcohol and drug abuse and the remainder structured as "broad-brush" programs. Seven of the programs were located in personnel departments, four in medical departments, four in labor relations, and the others in safety, casualty prevention, or independent offices. Supervisors referred 34.4 percent of clients, 31.7 percent of the programs' clients were self-referrals, 12.8 percent of referrals were based on "Rule G" violations (an industrywide rule proscribing alcohol use while at work or on call), 9.6 percent entered through union referrals, and 7.2 percent were referred through the medical department.

This study differed from those reviewed here so far on a number of dimensions, one of which was the incisiveness of the questions asked. For example, rather than merely asking "Do you assure confidentiality?"—a question likely to elicit social desirability bias—the researchers inquired into specific details of that question, such as who determines what information about participation in the program will be released and whether a signed release statement must be obtained. Moreover, to analyze the relationships of program design elements to a variety of clearly operationalized outcome measures and to each other, a variety of relatively sophisticated statistical techniques were employed. In a series of stepwise multiple regression analyses, approximately 50 independent variables were used to predict dependent measures such as the proportion of company employees identified as alcoholics (the "penetration rate") and the proportion of program clients reported as having recovered from their drinking problems.

The prediction equations for the dependent variables were stunningly impressive, with no less than 95 percent of the variability in each outcome explained by the measured variables. Regrettably, however, the fact that these analyses were run on a set of data consisting of only 15 organizations (5 of the original 20 respondents were omitted from these analyses because of missing data) makes the findings a mere statistical artifact, and entirely invalid. Any multiple regression in which there are as many predictors as cases will automatically yield these high predictions— even if the predictors consist of randomly generated data (Cohen and Cohen 1983). In this study there would appear to have been at least three times as many predictors as cases. Although Hitchcock and Sanders' final equations used only about half a dozen predictors, in a multiple regression with few cases and many predictors, the likelihood is great that some of these predictors will, purely by chance, appear closely correlated with the outcome (Cohen and Cohen 1983). By capitalizing on chance in this manner, a small number of independent variables can give the impression that they provide a strong prediction of the dependent measure.

One of the most influential discussions of program design has been Habbe's study for the National Industrial Conference Board (now known simply as the Conference Board), *Company Controls for Drinking Problems* (1969). Although it is among the weakest of the research studies reviewed here, the very high prestige of the Conference Board (an independent, nonprofit, business research institution) and the report's wide circulation made it a basic reference source on occupational alcoholism programs. Based on a survey that was mailed to 520 corporations, 160 of which responded, the report presented relatively little information from those data. Of the 160 respondents, 27 indicated that "we have what we consider to be a fairly good control program" for alcoholism, and 40 stated that "we have at least the beginnings of a control program." Eight of these respondents described their programs as joint union-management operations, and 14 said that theirs were "partly so." One hundred forty-nine firms (obviously, those without, as well as with, programs) responded to the question "How successful do you feel your supervisors and foremen have been in identifying those with drinking problems and in counseling with them?" Eleven said they were "quite successful," 32 indicated that they were "fairly successful," 43 said "not very successful," and 63 responded that it was "hard to estimate." No attempt was made, however, to relate these outcomes to program structure. Nor, for that matter, was there even an effort to relate these measures of effectiveness in dealing with alcoholics to whether the company had a program.

Habbe's report for the Conference Board was the second such report from that organization (*The Alcoholic Worker* had appeared in 1958). A decade later the Conference Board published a third monograph on occupational alcoholism and employee assistance programs, *Dealing with Alcoholism in the Workplace,* written by the present author (Weiss 1980). In addressing many of the same questions that were examined by studies already reviewed here, it provided descriptive statistics on program features and used multivariate statistical techniques to assess how elements of program structure were related to various program outcomes. The survey on which the analyses were based, the methodological details of which will be presented in Chapter 7, provided information from 346 large U.S. corporations that stated that they had functioning alcoholism programs (thus, this study was based on responses to 346 independent programs, in contrast to other studies in which a number of the surveyed programs have operated within the same corporation).

Using this comparatively large sample, the Conference Board report examined a number of program characteristics studied by some of the research projects previously discussed. For example, other studies observed self-referral rates of 32 percent (Erfurt and Foote 1977; Schlenger, Hayward, and Hallan 1976) and 31.7 percent (Hitchcock and Sanders 1976). These fairly consistent findings concerning the percentage of program clients who refer themselves into the program were again corroborated by the data from the Conference Board report, which found that 30 percent of the clients in the programs it studied were self-referrals. The findings of earlier research on supervisory referral rates, however, are less consistent, with reported figures of 60 percent (Wagner 1982), 54 percent (Schlenger, Hayward, and Hallan 1976), 41 percent (Erfurt and Foote 1977), and 34.4 percent (Hitchcock and Sanders 1976). The Conference Board's finding of a 65 percent supervisory referral rate is higher than earlier estimates.

Other studies have investigated the extent of insurance coverage for alcoholism treatment carried by companies with programs. The Conference Board study, however, inquired about the availability of a substantially wider range of financial supports for program clients. The 326 corporations responding to this set of items in the survey did not report only on the availability of insurance for inpatient and outpatient alcoholism treatment, and for stays at residential alcoholism treatment facilities; in addition, the survey inquired about various provisions to help remove the financial disincentives to receive treatment for alcoholism. The study found that 73 percent of the responding corporations provided paid leave for employees to attend treatment, and 45 percent had provisions for long-term disability benefits for alcoholic employees who could not be restored to good health.

The Conference Board study provided, in general, more finely detailed descriptions of many aspects of program design than did earlier studies. For example, whereas other studies asked whether companies engaged in any training or orientation activities for the program, the Conference Board study sought to identify the specific company personnel to whom training was given. Two-thirds of the responding corporations were found to train their first-level supervisory personnel and middle managers, but only 53 percent extended training to top management and only 17 percent trained all their employees. The staffs of the medical departments were trained in 44 percent of the cases, and 64 percent of the respondents trained their personnel functionaries.

These and many other structural and processual aspects of program design were presented, first in simple marginal frequency tables, and then in terms of their relationships to a number of dependent measures. For example, the Conference Board study found that 78 percent of the surveyed corporations had written policy statements on alcoholism (a widely recommended program feature). Moreover, statistically controlling for the effects of other program features, the presence of a written policy statement was found to be associated with a higher proportion of program clients being reported as abstaining from drinking. Other analyses, however, did not support the importance of a written policy for a successful program; existence of a policy statement was not associated with the proportion of employees who were identified as alcoholics and entered the program, nor with the proportion of program clients who kept their jobs. Indeed, it was found to be related to a decrease in the proportion of clients who entered the program voluntarily (that is, through self-referral).

These analyses of the relationships between written policy and program outcomes illustrate the general thrust of the Conference Board report, that of uncovering associations between what programs do and what results they achieve. However, because the design and operation of alcoholism and employee assistance programs is not the subject of the present study, the reader is referred to the Conference Board report for further details of its findings concerning relationships among program features and outcomes.

Reports on at least half a dozen surveys of alcoholism and employee assistance programs have appeared since the widely-publicized issuance of the Conference Board report. Unfortunately, in each case they have been based on far smaller samples than the Conference Board's, have analyzed their data at no higher a level than that of relative frequency listings, and have generally addressed the same questions addressed by the Conference Board report (which none of them cited).

Ford and McLaughlin (1981) explained that the reason for their study was the absence of information on the structure and effectiveness of EAPs. Working in cooperation with the Personnel Research Committee of the American Society for Personnel Administration (ASPA), they sent out questionnaires about EAPs to 1,000 ASPA members, of whom 106 responded with data concerning their companies' programs. Ford and McLaughlin's results, reported as relative frequencies, included information on a number of aspects of program structure. For example, they found that 69 percent of the program directors report to the company's senior personnel executive. The survey also collected data on respondents' perceptions of their programs' effectiveness (most respondents indicated that they were satisfied with their programs). However, despite the availability of both predictor and outcome variables, Ford and McLaughlin reported no attempt to investigate any relationships between program characteristics and results.

Also reporting their findings in *Personnel Administrator*, ASPA's publication, LaVan, Mathys, and Drehmer (1983) analyzed survey responses from the 97 respondents to a mailing of 500 questionnaires to a sample of half of the Fortune 1000. They found that 62 percent of referrals into alcoholism and drug abuse programs came from clients' immediate supervisors, and that counseling on other issues, such as "personal problems," was less likely to have been initiated by clients' supervisors. They reported their most significant finding to be that only 15 percent of their respondents indicated that they have the means to evaluate the program's effectiveness, and suggested that reduced absenteeism, fewer accidents, and increased productivity might be good indicators of the effectiveness of alcoholism programs.

Writing in *Personnel*, published by the American Management Association, Levine (1985) presented findings from a survey on EAPs. The 66 respondents, 39 of whom reported that their firms had EAPs, included an unreported number who completed and returned a questionnaire included in the pages of a previous issue of *Personnel*, as well as an unreported number who responded to a mailing to 100 human resource managers. Among her contributions to the research literature on occupational programs were her findings that 35 of the 39 programs had insurance that covers "some or all" of the costs of treatment for alcoholism and that 24 of the programs conducted training sessions. More difficult to understand was her finding that in 23 of the 39 programs, referrals may come from supervisors, and that in 21 programs they may come from employees themselves. From these figures, it would appear that Levine believes, for example, that 18 of these 39 EAPs do not permit self-referrals. This contrasts rather sharply with the finding in the Conference Board study that, of the 191 corporations providing information on referral sources, not one excluded self-referrals. Concerning program outcomes, Levine reported that 35 of the 39 responding firms "rated their programs successful," but did not investigate any possible relationships between program features and success.

Lewis (1981), in a doctoral dissertation conducted at Northwestern University, presented frequency listings of program features from questionnaire responses of 68 corporate alcoholism and employee assistance programs. Leaving little doubt as to the purpose of her study, she stated that "only minimal information has been disseminated about these programs. The amount of available information on employee assistance programs appears to be inadequate. Very little detailed data has been provided; thus the literature is sketchy, at best" (pp. 2-3). Lewis' own findings suggest that she may have confused detail with redundancy. For example, she reported that "in 60 of the organizations (88.2%), supervisors and/or union personnel are trained to identify troubled employees and to make referrals to the program. In 8 organizations (11.8%), these persons do not receive training" (p. 49). Her study did not include any measures of effectiveness.

Dorfman (1982), working in consultation with Walter Reichman, chairman of the ALMACA research committee, surveyed ALMACA members in order to assess the use of features included in a proposed set of standards for program design. Surveys were mailed to 330 individual members of that association, and 151 completed instruments were received. She presented two "highlights" of her findings as "92 percent of ALMACANs surveyed had a written policy statement," and "written consent [for release of clients' records] is required in 98.6 percent of the locations surveyed." However, individuals—not locations—were surveyed, and programs—not ALMACANs—have policy statements. Although a number of her respondents were consultants, who each worked with many programs, she repeated the errors of Roman (1981) and Shain and Groeneveld (1980), by treating each individual's response as information about one particular program. Repeating the errors of Erfurt and Foote (1977) and Mannello (1979), she concluded, without benefit of any relational statistics or even any measure of effectiveness, that features used by many programs must be those that lead to effectiveness. The logic of her conclusion is also of similar quality to that of these other studies: If programs almost all have certain elements (such as written policy statements and requirements for written consent), but differ at least somewhat in their levels of effectiveness, the presence of these elements cannot be considered to cause greater success. To justify such a conclusion, research would have to demonstrate that those programs not having, for example, a written policy and guarantees of confidentiality are less successful than those that do.

Also researching ALMACA's standards for program design, Myers and Myers (1985) wrote to 299 corporations asking if they had an alcoholism or employee assistance program and requesting those that did to send them a copy of their program's policy statement. Responses were received from 158 companies, 70 of which indicated that they had an EAP, and the policy statements were used as the source of information on what features the programs did or did not include. This study was somewhat different from those that have been discussed so far. Whereas most all of the others seem to have been concerned with determining what constitutes effective program practice (even if their research methods were not especially amenable to addressing that issue), Myers and Myers took the ALMACA standards as prescriptions that needed no further substantiation. Indeed, a year before this survey the second author had published a 335-page book, *Establishing and Building Employee Assistance Programs* (Myers 1984), providing emphatic prescriptions on how a program should be designed and operated for peak effectiveness. Analyzing the policy statements sent by their respondents, Myers and Myers were appalled to find that 29 percent of the policies did not include a specific statement of the program's objectives, stating that "a program without an objective is analogous to taking a trip without deciding where to go" (1985, p. 58). Gravely disappointed that only 23 percent of the policies were signed by the corporation's chief executive officer, they explained that "we cannot expect to motivate employees to use the EAP" without such a signature, which they asserted is "more than a symbol. It is credible evidence that the EAP is important" (p. 58). Finding that a mere 14 percent of the policies stated that no management feedback will occur in self-referral cases, they wondered, "How are employees expected to know that anonymity is assured unless the policy states it?" (p. 62).

One might wonder, however, why Myers and Myers expected every program feature to be discussed in the policy statement. Many companies responding to the Conference Board study's questionnaire enclosed their program's policy statement, and in general these statements discussed policy rather than the details of implementation. For example, they might declare concern for confidentiality, but not spell out all of the details of who gets to know what under various conditions. Myers and Myers emphasized the importance of the policy statement as an indication to employees of the legitimate intentions of the program, but, as noted above, the Conference Board study found that, although most programs have such a document, the existence of a written policy statement was irrelevant to how many employees entered the program, and its presence was associated with a lower level of voluntary referrals.

SUMMARY

This chapter has reviewed quantitative research, case studies, and advice from sources claiming expertise, to provide a description of corporate alcoholism and employee assistance programs. From these data, at least a rough sketch of a typical program can be drawn. It is likely to be based on a written policy statement professing the company's interest in rehabilitating rather than punishing individuals whose work performance is affected by alcohol abuse or other problems. The company is likely to assign responsibility for the program to a staff department in the general area of human resources, which will be expected to disseminate information about the program and serve as a point of entry for clients. These clients may be referred into the program from a variety of sources, but most probably will be referred by their immediate supervisors. The programs usually are not considered to be engaged in conducting therapy, but as providing referrals to appropriate treatment, for which the company typically provides some financial coverage. Although there appears to be a very general consensus that programs adopting these procedures will be successful, systematic evidence is not available to support that belief. The chapter that follows examines the structural and ideological mechanisms by which many companies have used these programs as a means of social control.

6

The Social Control Functions of Alcoholism Programs in Industry

The research on program structure, descriptions of individual programs, and experts' prescriptions reviewed in the previous chapter indicate that there is a great deal of enthusiasm for a variety of unvalidated notions concerning alcoholism and how to deal with it. That discussion also intimated, however, that EAPs may serve as social control measures, for example, by promoting the notion that poor job performance constitutes evidence for a diagnosis of alcoholism. Moreover, the suggestion was made that the coercive potential of these programs has been recognized by at least some individuals, such as the union personnel at Boston Edison who were reticent to accept the firing of employees who refuse treatment mandated by the program.

The assertion that these programs may be helping to ensure that employees comply with management's norms has been made very directly on a number of occasions, and this chapter begins with a review of such assertions. Next, quantitative research on the reasons stated by management for instituting occupational programs is reviewed. The literature distributed by companies to explain their programs is then examined to identify the mechanisms by which many companies may have been using these programs to effect social control.

A major focus of this chapter will be to investigate whether the use of the medical disease model of alcoholism functions as a managerial ideology. In Chapter 3 it was argued that for a set of ideas to serve as an ideology, it should be consistent with broadly held values and have a factual basis that is difficult to disconfirm. Chapter 4 indicated that the medical disease concept of alcoholism does appeal to broad values and that, although the scientific evidence pertaining to its validity has been overwhelmingly negative, persistent and emotional advocacy of the concept has helped to obfuscate this empirical reality. Thus the medical disease concept of alcoholism, in particular, is argued to be the essential key—through the redefinition of many behaviors as symptoms of alcoholism—to the identification and sanctioning of a wide range of deviance.

MOTIVES FOR PROGRAM IMPLEMENTATION

Critical Assessments of Program Motives

As discussed in the previous chapter, Ravin's description of the alcoholism program at Boston Edison noted union officials' concerns that the alcoholism program might be a purge "to rid the company of 'loafers' and 'troublemakers' under the guise of medical treatment." This view appears not to be restricted to unionists at the Boston Edison Company. Trice and Roman described this skepticism as a rather general phenomenon:

> Union leaders who are especially aware of the social class differences between the union and management may feel very negative toward deviant-drinking and drug-use programs. In other words, there may be a suspicion that norms defining deviance will be more strictly enforced among blue-collar and lower-status workers. Furthermore, it is possible that "deviant behavior" may appear to union leaders as a vague and mysterious concept; their reaction to this ambiguity may be rejection and retreat. Support of an alcohol and drug program may appear to give management a blank check to label union members. Instead of taking an active interest in a particular management-based program, unions may adopt an attitude of apathy and disinterest, coupled with a vague threat to disrupt any program which might "injure" a union member (1978, pp. 199–200).

Trice and Roman, as well as Ravin (the medical director of Boston Edison), prescribed increased union awareness of the program's intentions and operations as the cure for this fear that the program "might 'injure' a union member." Trice and Roman wrote confidently that increased understanding of these programs would lead to union support, quoting Leo Perlis, the director of the AFL-CIO's Department of Community Services, as stating that "Industrial programs for the rehabilitation of alcoholic employees are neither pro-management nor pro-labor, but simply pro-people" (1978, p. 199). Similarly, Shostak, claiming that unionists used to be opposed to these programs, but no longer are, wrote that "even the union leaders' suspicions that these are only 'productivity scams' seems to be decreasing, and certain major labor unions are ... implementing ... programs of their own!" (1980, p. 130).

However, not all observers have viewed such problems as mere past history or present failures in communication. Shain and Groeneveld (1980) contended that conceiving of alcoholism and employee assistance programs as simply health benefits might not be appropriate. Starting from the premise that "industry is interested in public health only insofar as it serves some economic goal" (pp. 15-16), they considered occupational programs as a part of the "human relations" movement in industry (a theoretical link made in the present book as well). Citing Bartell's argument (1976) that the human relations ideology was a self-serving response to managements' problems of maintaining social control in the workplace and a favorable image in the community, they suggested that occupational programs be considered "in the same light as corporate involvement in urban renewal, equal opportunity hiring and community programs for the disadvantaged" (p. 31). Beyond their skeptical view that programs are adopted to give the appearance of "corporate social responsibility," Shain and Groeneveld also made note of "the social control value of occupational programs" (p. 31):

> Essentially, when employers opt for an EAP they are often opting for a method of job performance control which is expected to deal with certain kinds of problems for which alternative solutions (discipline, dismissal, retiring, or retraining) are becoming increasingly impractical (1980, p. 29).

A report from the International Study of Alcohol Control Experiences, in collaboration with the World Health Organization (Makela et al. 1981), traced the rise of occupational alcoholism programs to "a revival of health moralism," and to shifts "in the allocation of welfare resources, from marginal groups and the elderly (i.e., non-productive groups) to those who are more apt to contribute to the national economy" (p. 105). Arguing that there is an ongoing redefinition of health as an individual responsibility and a public duty, they noted that "industrial alcoholism programmes are very much in line with the overall trends in social control mentioned above; notwithstanding the medical vocabulary adopted by the programmes, they usually also imply a more continuous surveillance and control by the employer" (p. 105).

That possibility was also suggested by Hingson, Lederman, and Chapman (1985), who examined the relationship between drinking and accidents. They noted that although a number of evaluations of EAPs reported that clients had fewer accidents than prior to entering the program, no studies connected that improvement to any change in alcohol consumption; they suggested, therefore, that the salutary effect of the programs on safety might have less to do with rehabilitation from alcoholism than with increased "disciplinary oversight." Additionally, they found that in their own sample of 879 employees "employee assistance programs are reaching a miniscule proportion (4%) of employees with self-reported drinking problems" (p. 303). They had no specific explanation for this finding other than to wonder whether these programs "are in some way too unpalatable for the vast majority of these employees to use" (p. 303).

An unexpected source of criticism of the intent of occupational programs is an article by Professor Paul Roman, who is widely viewed as a leading researcher and advocate of employee alcoholism programs. Writing in the *Journal of Applied Behavioral Science* (an academic journal generally not read by individuals in the occupational programming field) he argued that employee assistance programs constitute a subtle, insidious form of social control over the workforce:

> At first blush these programs appear both constructive and benign. . . . A closer look at these programs, however, raises important concerns. For example, the programs have the potential for a considerable transformation of social control in the workplace. This transformation is based on the nature and consequence of medicalization and the extent to which medicalized frames of reference and procedures seem impervious either to criticism or to alternative approaches (1980, p. 409).

Roman (1980) argued that through the process of the medicalization of deviance "employee assistance programs have remarkably open possibilities for expanding the definitions of problems that require medical attention" (1980, p. 419). In his view, not only does this perspective offer "infinite possibilities" for intervention into employees' lives, but "a second consequence of medicalization is the extent to which it locates problems in the individual with the latent consequence of 'blaming the victim'" (p. 419). He predicted that the result of this will be

> that job dissatisfaction and job role stress come to be defined as individual mental health problems rather than as consequences of the work environment itself. Thus employee grievances about the nature and conditions of jobs may be neutralized by redefinition as individual mental health problems (1980, p. 419).

Additionally, Roman argued that these programs function as a mechanism of social class domination, asserting that "as has happened with other seemingly democratic systems of social control, employee assistance programs are most easily implemented among the lower socio-economic classes" (p. 420).

Also writing in the *Journal of Applied Behavioral Science* Sonnenstuhl offered another critical commentary on the motives of EAPs, stating:

> Management and labor have always fought over the right to establish work norms. Into this fray management has introduced, under the guise of science, a number of policies designed to set work standards, motivate workers, and control deviants. Among the best known of these experimental policies are social welfarism, scientific management, company

unions, and human relations. Employee assistance policies ought to be
seen within this historical context (1980, p. 123).*

Quantitative empirical research that questions the motives of occupational programs has been reported by Weiss (1985). He contended that
under certain conditions these programs serve to assist employers in
establishing a justification for terminating poorly performing employees.
Arguing that firing an employee is an awkward and unpleasant interpersonal situation, he suggested that the difficulty of terminating an
individual is greater to the extent that the person responsible for making
that decision is close, organizationally, to the person being fired. He
hypothesized that this inconvenient propinquity would be greater in
organizations that are decentralized or not highly differentiated vertically,
and that in such circumstances the potential of an occupational program
for facilitating the removal of unwanted employees is more likely to be
realized if an outside agency helps in the firing (perhaps through a
"medical" diagnosis that legitimates the company's intentions). Operationalizing his hypotheses by examining, for 90 large corporations, the
relationships among measures of organizational structure, executives'
assessments of community support in the functioning of the program, and
termination rates of employees referred into the programs, he was able to
support his hypotheses. Moderated regression analyses indicated that
when organizations had low levels of centralization and vertical differentiation, the perception that community support had helped the program
was associated with higher termination rates. When organizations had
high levels of centralization or vertical differentiation, community support was not correlated with the rate of terminations.

A very extreme indictment of occupational programs was expressed
in a handbill distributed by members of the U.S. Labor Party outside a
union meeting in Schenectady, New York, in November 1974. Titled
"Have Martucci and Mongin Fingered YOU Yet?" it read, in part:

> The Labor Party has gotten direct documentation from workers: so-
> and-so used to be in a caucus, used to bitch against management and
> union alike. But he was forced in this Alcoholic's program, and he just
> came back; he doesn't bitch anymore. Get the picture? Brainwashing!
>
> The SCHENECTADY CONNECTION
>
> Across the country, CIA agents Woodcock and IW Abel are
> pushing slave-labor relocation and brainwashing. *Right here*, IUE 301

---

*Writing in the *EAP Digest* (Trice and Sonnenstuhl 1985a) and in the *Employee Assistance
Quarterly* (Trice and Sonnenstuhl 1985b), however, Sonnenstuhl has been totally supportive
of these programs, professing that by cutting through alcoholics' denial of their illness with
constructive confrontation they successfully have been leading alcoholic employees to
sobriety.

Martucci and GE's Mongin sit together on the Board of Directors of the Alcoholic Council. Also Russell Sage College - Cornell School of Labor Relations hold brainwashing group classes for the local labor leaders.

   These labor KAPOS are acting as Rocky's cops inside the factory to insure that slaves stay slaves. That you don't get angry about speed-up, wage cuts, pension cuts, or layoffs.

The Labor Party's notion of a conscious conspiracy among Nelson Rockefeller (vice-presidential nominee and living symbol of monopoly capitalism), Leonard Woodcock (president of the United Auto Workers, and, in their view, a CIA agent), I. W. Abel (president of the Steelworker's Union, and also alleged by them to be a CIA agent), General Electric's president, a local leader of the electrical worker's union, and Harrison Trice of Cornell (instructor for the "brainwashing group classes") certainly has not been documented. However, the substantive issue addressed in the handbill, the use of alcoholism and employee assistance programs to control workers, echoes that of the other writers discussed above. It adds, however, a nuance not considered by these other commentators, the idea that occupational programs may serve as mechanisms by which management and unions collude to control workers who deviate from the norms of the leaders of both of those groups.

Organizations' Expressed Reasons for Program Implementation

Presumably, few if any companies would openly express agreement with the skeptical views of the reasons for program implementation offered above by some scholars and political radicals. This section reviews a number of studies that have asked corporate executives why their companies adopted alcoholism and employee assistance programs.

   Schlenger, Hallan, and Hayward (1976), in their previously discussed study of a sample consisting of 15 programs, asked, "How did the program get started (i.e., what were the factors that entered into the decision to begin a program?)?" The responses, to what were apparently open-coded items, reported in cryptically-stated categories, indicated that 8 of the 15 companies answered "large number of troubled employees," 3 answered "cost-benefit factors," 2 answered "conservation of long-term employees," and 1 each said "expansion of benefits" and "high termination rate."

   The 1976 ORC Executive Caravan survey asked a sample of executives from, as noted previously, perhaps two dozen Fortune 500 firms with occupational programs, "What was the main reason or event that led this company to start a program to identify and provide assistance to problem drinking employees?" Responses to this item were reported in 12 categories, although it cannot be determined whether this had been a closed-coded item or the categories had been developed post hoc. A general awareness of employee alcohol problems and an interest in employee well-being were the two most popular responses. "Poor job performance" and "recognition of alcoholism as a medical problem" were the third and fourth most frequent responses. No other categories contained more than 4 percent of the responses, and all 12 categories accounted for only 62 percent of the total number of responses.

ORC again asked this question in their 1979 Executive Caravan survey, and Roman (1982), working under an NIAAA contract to analyze and interpret the ORC data, and writing in an NIAAA publication, reported the results of this later polling. His tabulations, however, are difficult to reconcile with ORC's own presentation of its results. In particular, comparing the 1979 to the 1976 results, Roman stated that "corporate social responsibility remains the single, most prominent reason for program adoption" (pp. 181–82). According to ORC's frequency listings of their data (1976), however, in the 1976 survey corporate social responsibility was given as the main reason for program adoption not by the 21.3 percent that Roman claimed they had found, but by 3 percent. Rather than being the highest ranked of the 12 reasons for program adoption, it was tied for seventh. Continuing his interpretation of the data, he stated that "job-related consequences such as poor performance . . . remain relatively minor reasons for program adoption." In fact, however, his table showed poor performance to have maintained its status as the third-ranking reason for program adoption.

It seems reasonable to conjecture that program implementation is usually based on a combination of the motives that these studies have noted. Thus, asking for, or reporting only, the one "main reason" for

TABLE 6.1. Executives' Reasons for Program Implementation
($n = 350$)

Reason	Mean*	Standard Deviation
Recognition of alcoholism as a medical problem affecting the well-being of our employees	3.735	.502
Concern over poor job performance	3.455	.661
Assumption of an increased social responsibility	2.902	.784
Problem brought to company's attention by highly visible cases of problem drinking	2.860	.948
Concern over high absenteeism	2.605	.918
Spurred by efforts of an employee with personal contact with the problem	2.319	1.027
Concern over high turnover	1.823	.779

*"very unimportant" = 1; "very important" = 4

program implementation would seem to lose a great deal of information. Additionally, it would seem likely to induce an unnecessarily high level of social desirability response bias. The Conference Board survey, therefore, was designed to permit independent responses concerning the salience of each of seven possible motives for program implementation. Corporate senior personnel executives were asked to rate the importance of each of these reasons on a scale in which 1 = "very unimportant" and 4 = "very important." The means for each item, along with their rank ordering, are shown in Table 6.1. "We recognized alcoholism as a medical problem affecting the well-being of our employees" was the highest ranked response, although it is also probably the highest on social desirability. Ranking a close second was "We were concerned about poor job performance," a response that is less patently altruistic and presumably less socially desirable. These high averages, however, might reflect merely their low variability, as few respondents rated either of these reasons as very unimportant.

Respondents had also been asked to check the two of these seven reasons that had been the most important reasons for starting the program, and the two that had been the least important. Table 6.2, which presents the rank ordering and number of responses for each motive as either the least or most important reason for program adoption, reconfirms the importance of recognition of alcoholism as an employee medical problem and of concerns about poor job performance. These two

TABLE 6.2. Items Chosen as One of Executives' Two Most or Two Least Important Reasons for Program Implementation (n = 350)

Reason	Most Important	Least Important
Recognition of alcoholism as a medical problem affecting the well-being of our employees	220	6
Concern over poor job performance	147	11
Problem brought to company's attention by highly visible cases of problem drinking	63	64
Assumption of an increased social responsibility	55	57
Concern over high absenteeism	28	87
Spurred by efforts of an employee with personal contact with the problem	34	119
Concern over high turnover	1	110

Note: Items ranked by net of choices for most important reason minus choices for least important reason.

categories were clearly the two most important reasons for program implementation.

These data strongly suggest that altruism is not the only reason behind the implementation of occupational programs. Starting a program because of concern over poor work performance certainly does not prove any conspiratorial hypotheses about the hidden motives of these programs; many alcoholics, after all, *are* somewhat less productive than others (Borthwick 1977). Nonetheless, the data indicate that, along with the "motherhood and apple pie" explanation from personnel executives that they started their programs because of a recognition of alcoholism as a health problem for their employees, the other preeminent reason for program implementation was clearly a "bottom line" concern about how hard employees are working. And, given the cynical view expressed by various writers that these programs may be operating to increase the productivity of the general workforce, the high salience of the second of these dual motives suggests that research should focus more attention on the precise ways in which alcoholism programs operate to help managements concerned about poor job performance.

THE SOCIAL RECONSTRUCTION OF DEVIANCE
INTO ALCOHOLISM

The argument that occupational programs function as instruments of social control requires more than reference to the views of a few skeptical writers or to surveys showing that executives intend to improve employee productivity with these programs. In addition, it is necessary to describe the specific mechanisms through which alcoholism and employee assistance programs effect social control. This book has contended that the social control potential of these programs, whether designed to deal only with alcohol problems or taking a "broad-brush" approach, is greatly enhanced by the medical disease model of alcoholism, a perspective that has failed to receive support from systematic research. The remainder of this chapter will examine how this explanation of alcohol problems, which argues that alcoholism is a pervasive and tragic problem whose victims can be diagnosed on the basis of absenteeism and poor work performance, and treated through constructive coercion, facilitates the identification and sanctioning of employees who cause difficulties for management. Evidence that management often promotes a set of ideas about alcohol problems that on the one hand is absolutely untrue and, on the other, facilitates management control is offered as support for this study's contention that promotion of this perspective is not simply accidental, but constitutes a specific usage of a managerial ideology to facilitate social control of the workforce.

Constructing a Crisis

In implementing alcoholism and employee assistance programs, companies issue a variety of written materials, including inserts for policy and procedure manuals and special brochures and pamphlets. Not only do these writings provide instructions in the operation of the program; they usually attempt to convey the company's philosophy about alcohol problems. Many respondents to the Conference Board survey, in addition to completing questionnaires, included copies of such materials in their responses. Excerpts from these documents are presented below. Because of the confidentiality promised to the survey's respondents, the companies whose materials are quoted here cannot be identified by name.

As serious and as recalcitrant as are the problems associated with alcohol abuse, it would seem that little promotion of the problem's significance would be necessary, beyond merely reporting the facts. Nevertheless, discussions of its prevalence sometimes border on histrionics. Writing in the *EAP Digest* Dwyer (1984) prophesied that unless the national crisis of alcoholism is dealt with—and quickly—"the U.S. is doomed to become a second rate power!" (His article happened not to address the geopolitical status of the Soviet Union, whose alcohol problems are immensely more severe than are those of the United States). The medical director of General Motors' executive offices, who has been a key member of the National Council on Alcoholism, offered the familiar figure of nine million as the number of adult alcoholics in the United States, and then stated (Pace 1981, p. 24): "some experts indicate that there are now 3.4 million teenage alcoholics in the United States, and their ranks are expanding at an alarming rate." In light of the fact that there were approximately 27 million teenagers and 160 million adults in the United States (U. S. Bureau of the Census 1983) at the time of his writing, his experts (who were not cited) apparently believe that the incidence of the disease of alcoholism is more than twice as great among teenagers as among adults. This distressing warning is especially surprising given the clear evidence (Vaillant 1983) that alcoholism is a disease that only strikes those who have been heavy drinkers for many years.

Although typically not as dramatically, company program literature often begins by making the point that alcoholism is a problem of the highest magnitude. These pamphlets often state that the United States has a serious and widespread problem—called alcoholism—and that the company's employees are no less susceptible to this problem than anyone else. A major chemical firm writes that alcoholism "is the nation's fourth leading killer, outranked only by cardiovascular diseases, cancer, and mental disorders" and "that about 500,000 new victims join the ranks each year" because "alcohol is a poison for some ten percent of the drinking population." As discussed earlier, however, there is no factual basis for the idea that some individuals are unable, by dint of some physiological difference, to control their alcohol consumption. Similarly, there is no accurate count of how many of alcoholism's "new victims join the ranks each year," especially in the absence of a clear consensus on a definition of alcoholism and of systematic data on how many alcoholics there are.

Nevertheless, companies' program literature frequently cites as factual information figures that are no more than alarmingly high "guesstimates" of the severity of many aspects of alcohol's impact on the workplace. An oil corporation states that "there are approximately ten million alcoholics in this country and their behavior directly affects another 40 million persons. Alcoholism costs industry $25 billion a year in absenteeism, disability payments and poor performance."

A somewhat lower national cost figure is found in the program literature of a metal producer, in which it is then connected directly to costs for that particular company:

> Alcoholism is a health problem that affects from six to ten percent of industry work forces. According to the National Council on Alcoholism, problem drinking costs the economy $10 billion in lost work time; $2 billion for health and welfare services; and $3 billion in property damage, medical expenses, and insurance claims.
>
> Naturally [this company] pays its share of this $15 billion annual hangover. It is estimated that, in lost time and poor job performance alone, alcoholism costs the company more than $9 million each year!

Hyperbole such as this may well serve to impress upon employees the putatively calamitous dimensions of this problem. Further, this company's literature demonstrates the use of the NCA's subtle differentiation between alcoholism and problem drinking, as discussed in Chapter 4. The health problem said to affect six to ten percent of workforces is "alcoholism," a term that is likely to be interpreted by most readers as referring to a long-term uncontrollable addiction to alcohol. The NCA's claims about costs to the economy, however, refer to the costs of problem drinking—alcohol consumption by *anyone,* alcohol addict or not, that creates some sort of problem. Attributing these enormous expenses to individuals engaged in a wide range of drinking behavior, rather than to those relatively few addicts, increases the credibility of the NCA's figures. However, in the statement cited above, the national figures on the costs of *problem drinking* are scaled down to the size of the company and labeled as their losses due to *alcoholism.* This company's choice of words may reflect pure chance; however, it fits a pattern of definitions, explanations, and authoritatively-stated assertions that, together, construct a situation of crisis proportions. By doing so, and capturing the attention and sympathy of employees and supervisory pesonnel, the stage is set for an explication of a solution to the crisis.

Another element of that pattern is evidenced in an interview carried in the house organ of another major corporation in the same metal industry. Asked about the seriousness of the company's alcoholism problem the director of their "Health Assistance Program" (90 percent of whose clients were diagnosed as alcoholics) stated that "the statistics indicate that between five and ten percent of the U.S. workforce are alcoholics," and although he believed the company's problem to be about average, he added that "we've only reached the tip of the iceberg so far."

As discussed earlier, these "statistics" on the prevalence of the problem, although frequently cited, lack a factual basis. Nonetheless, for the program director interviewed here they may provide a justification for his continuing employment. From his comments, it is clear that far fewer than five percent of the workforce had been referred into his alcoholism program. Rather than considering the possibility that alcoholism is not nearly as prevalent in this organization as the national "statistics" claim should be the case, he simply asserts that the prevalence of alcoholism within "the plant is about average"; by explaining that, "so far," "we've only reached the tip of the iceberg," he implies that more complete success is a matter simply of continued vigorous effort.

These putative facts about the prevalence of alcohol problems are echoed, but with some added creativity, by a communications company: "Most people can drink socially without becoming alcoholics, but about five percent to ten percent cannot. Therefore, in our company, about five percent to ten percent of employees will have a drinking problem." The inference of these statements, that the percentage of employees who become alcoholic is the same as the proportion of drinkers who become alcoholic, rests on the assumption that all of the company's employees do indeed drink. However, given the best evidence on this question (Cahalan, Cisin, and Crossley 1969), indicating that only 68 percent of the adult population drinks, this would appear to be highly unlikely.

Of all the program literature supplied to the Conference Board, the least exaggerated pronouncement on the prevalence of alcohol problems was provided by a large New York bank that stated, "Our employees are no more immune to this disease than any other (national estimates place the average incidence at five percent in any corporation)."

The function of the hyperbole and apparently misleading information sampled here may be to convince those with supervisory responsibilities that some of their very own subordinates (indeed, 1 out of each 10 or 20) are likely to have this serious problem. Although the statement that 5 to 10 percent of a company's employees are alcoholics is a major component of that thrust, such a claim has a problematic corollary. The fact that virtually none of these programs comes close to identifying that high a percentage of the company's employees as alcoholics (Weiss 1980) would seem to imply that they are failing. However, the assertion that 1 in every 10 or 20 of the firm's employees is an alcoholic is useful not only to justify the program's continued vigorous efforts, but also as a social control strategy; claiming that alcoholism is a very prevalent problem and that the company has "only reached the tip of the iceberg" counsels greatly increased vigilance on the part of supervisors. Perhaps as importantly, it also justifies labeling up to 10 percent of the employee population as alcoholics—even if that diagnosis does not seem to fit some "alcoholic" employees all that well—because that, supposedly, is the national prevalence and, as a major petroleum company put it, "We believe national statistics on the incidence of alcoholism can be applied to us."

To explain why programs fail even to approach full "penetration" into the supposed population of alcoholics, companies assert that it is a result of the tragic ignorance surrounding the "true" nature of alcoholism. At least in part to account for this seeming failure, much of the literature that companies distribute to introduce these programs frequently is directed to dispelling this "ignorance" with the explanation that alcoholism is a medical disease. Apparently a major objective in this general strategy is to disavow the validity of the moral model of alcoholism. For example, a mineral company's brochure makes the blanket statement that "the social stigma often associated with this illness has no basis in fact," although it provides no substantiation of this assertion. Another firm does attempt a more detailed explanation of this position (which they broaden into a disclaimer of the moral model's relevance for drug abuse as well) with the somewhat confusing declaration that "the social stigma often attached to alcoholism and drug abuse has no basis in fact since these are medical illnesses which are either physical and/or medical in nature."

Some company literature opposes the moral model not only on the grounds that it is invalid, but also because they view the consequences of that belief as counterproductive. A major oil corporation asserts that it "recognizes that the social stigma often associated with alcoholism and other medical/behavioral illnesses is erroneous and destructive." A metal producer writes, "The moral stigma often associated with alcoholism is out-of-date and unproductive." A public utility company does not bother to claim that the moral model is incorrect, but simply that its consequences for changing the problem drinker are undesirable: "The social stigma associated with behavioral-medical disorders often discourages a person from accepting proper consultation and treatment." The purpose that can be served by the disavowal of the moral model's accuracy is made most clearly in this particular quote; calling the alcoholic a sinner or a weakling decreases the likelihoods that employees will voluntarily identify themselves to the program and that their supervisors will be willing to refer them.

Defining "Alcoholism"

After refuting what might be more "common sense" understandings of alcohol problems, literature on alcoholism distributed through corporate programs usually proceeds to a description of the nature of this problem that is claimed to affect 5 to 10 percent of the workforce. Defining the phenomenon of alcoholism, however, has always posed a considerable dilemma. For example, in 1951 the World Health Organization (WHO) arrived at the following definition of alcoholism:

> Any form of drinking which in its extent goes beyond the traditional and customary "dietary" use, or the ordinary compliance with the social drinking customs of the whole community concerned, irrespective of the etiological factors leading to such behaviour and irrespective also of the extent to which such etiological factors are dependent upon heredity, constitution, or acquired physiopathological and metabolic influences (in Davies 1976, p. 56).

However, less than a year later this group decided that the statement above should be a definition only of "excessive drinking". The following conditions were added as those that would qualify an individual as alcoholic:

> Alcoholics are those excessive drinkers whose dependence upon alcohol has attained such a degree that it shows a noticeable mental disturbance or an interference with their bodily and mental health, their interpersonal relations, and their smooth social and economic functioning, or who show the prodromal signs of such developments, they therefore require treatment (in Davies 1976, p. 57).

A more recent and influential definition of alcoholism has been offered by Keller, a leading (and self-styled) "alcohologist," in *A Dictionary of Words about Alcohol* (Keller and McCormick 1968):

> A chronic and usually progressive disease, or a symptom of an underlying psychological or physical disorder, characterized by dependence on alcohol (manifested by *loss of control over drinking*) for relief from psychological or physical distress or for gratification from alcohol intoxication itself, and by a consumption of alcoholic beverages sufficiently great and consistent to cause physical or mental or social or economic disability. Or a learned (or conditioned) dependence on alcohol which irresistibly activates resort to alcohol whenever a critical internal or environmental stimulus occurs (p. 14).

Keller's definition would seem to include the conditions identified by Davies as those that are at the core of the WHO definition: "(a) excessive drinking, (b) dependence, (c) harmful drinking, leading to the established state" (1976, p. 60). However, by employing the word *or* ten times, it would also seem to greatly broaden the range of behavior appropriately considered indicative of "the disease of alcoholism."

Yet, Jellinek (1952), who is most frequently cited as the source of the disease concept, cautioned against broad definitions of the disease of alcoholism (in a passage that is *not* frequently cited):

> The lay public uses the term alcoholism as a designation for any form of excessive drinking, instead of as a label for a *limited* and well-defined area of excessive drinking behavior. Automatically, the disease conception of alcoholism becomes extended to all excessive drinking, irrespective of whether or not there is any physical or psychological pathology involved in the drinking behavior. Such an unwarranted extension of the disease conception can only be harmful (pp. 673–74).

For most corporate alcoholism and employee assistance programs, however, the complexities of defining alcoholism appear to be largely an irrelevancy. A few go through the medical disease ideology in some detail, such as this dramatic presentation from a chemical firm's program literature:

> Alcoholism is a chronic, progressive disease that occurs in a person who has developed a morbid and uncontrollable craving for alcohol. It affects the nervous system, beclouding judgment and destroying the brain so that the brain loses control of bodily functions, gradually resulting in death. Alcoholism is a *chronic* disease because, like diabetes, it is a permanent disability that demands constant attention to keep it under control. It is *addictive* because the patient has a compulsive, irrational need to drink, as a narcotics addict craves dope. The "alcohol addict" drinks even when he knows that liquor has wrecked his health and perhaps cost him his family, his friends, his job, and his self-respect.
>
> It is *progressive* in that, like cancer, the ravages of the disease will steadily increase in severity and the degenerative process cannot be reversed.

Having argued forcefully that a serious disease is being dealt with in their program, the next page of their pamphlet imputes disease characteristics not only to the alcohol addict but to the "problem drinker" as well, stating that "a problem drinker or an alcoholic drinks because he *has to*."

An even broader usage of the disease ideology is evident in a brochure, distributed by a number of EAPs, that was written by a clergyman who has organized a private treatment facility. Appearing to be a description simply of alcoholism, this brochure starts out with the typical contention that in the past "the alcoholic was looked upon as a weak-willed individual." It continues, stating that "today, of course, medical doctors, clergymen and other professionals have come to realize that alcoholism is a disease," and then goes on to assert that recognition of alcoholism as a disease has a number of specific corollaries:

1. The illness can be described.
2. The course of the illness is predictable and progressive.
3. The disease is primary—that is, it is not just a symptom of some other underlying disorder.
4. It is permanent.
5. It is terminal—if left untreated, it inevitably results in premature death.

Although the American Medical Association and other medical professional groups have labeled alcoholism a disease, none have defined it as including this list of characteristics. Rather, the research literature, as reviewed in Chapter 4, suggests that the list is highly inaccurate. What may be most significant about the list, however, is that in the brochure's later pages, it is referred to as having been not simply an enumeration of the characteristics of the "disease of alcoholism," but of the characteristics of the "disease" of "chemical dependency" as well. Undeniably, society's view of individuals having problems with alcohol is more sympathetic than in the past, and the opening paragraphs of this brochure play on that sympathy with the plausible view of "alcoholism as a disease." It is also undeniable that alcohol is a chemical and that addiction to it would therefore constitute a "chemical dependency." Perhaps it is in the hope that the sympathy-arousing disease concept will be extended to the reader's attitude toward "junkies" and other poorly regarded deviants that this more general term is inserted.

These examples illustrate how the disease concept of alcoholism serves the broad purposes of justifying the vigorous search for not only alcohol addicts, but for those with other putative chemical dependencies, as well as for individuals whose nonaddicted, relatively controllable alcohol use is deemed a problem. Creative extensions of the disease concept, they also illustrate the typical inattention to Jellinek's injunction that the concept of alcoholism as a disease should be applied to only a strictly delimited group of excessive drinkers. One possible explanation of this confusing usage is that for corporate programs to be effective instruments of social control, able to identify many employees as in need of their watchful "assistance," alcoholism may need to be defined as broadly as possible. Interspersing terms such as chemical dependency, problem drinking or alcohol abuse in discussions of alcoholism may help to increase the credibility both of claims of the magnitude and ubiquity of alcoholism, and of claims of the chronicity of "chemical dependency" and "problem drinking."

The definitions given above, even with their questionable logic, actually may underutilize the possibilities of the disease ideology of alcoholism for social control. Most companies go into much less detail in defining or describing alcoholism, yet their definitions allow for even greater opportunities for the medicalization of deviance. Generally, companies state that they consider alcoholism to be a "treatable disease" or a "treatable illness" that they regard sympathetically, and for which they wish to provide the same treatment as for any other disease or illness. They then typically offer a simple operational definition of alcoholism. An influential source for such a definition has been a widely distributed pamphlet from the Kemper Insurance Companies entitled *What to Do about the Employee with a Drinking Problem* (Rouse n.d.). It quotes Harrison Trice as observing: "Recurrent poor job performance due to the use of alcohol becomes a simple, direct and clear definition of alcoholism. . . . Alcoholism is simply repeated poor work because of the way the employee uses alcohol" [ellipses in original].

To some this definition might read like a Marxist's caricature of occupational medicine in capitalist society—constructing a pernicious disease whose only symptom is a loss of productivity and profits for the corporation. Nevertheless, it has considerable currency. A chemical company's manual on alcoholism states: "A definition [of alcoholism] that has found good acceptance in industry is: continued or repeated drinking in an amount or manner that interferes with the efficient performance of one's duties." Similarly, a magazine well known for an editorial policy upholding "traditional American values" and a personnel policy emphasizing welfarist measures writes: "For the purpose of this policy, alcoholism exists when the employee's consumption of any alcoholic beverage repeatedly interferes with job performance."

Pronouncements such as these, however, have the potential to strain the credulousness of the uninitiated, who are first told that this is a ruinous disease and shortly thereafter informed that its direst consequence is a hampering of work efficiency. Perhaps because of this problem, some companies' literature makes semantic adjustments to provide a smoother logical fit. For example, a public utility company, although using the term *alcoholism* everywhere else in its pamphlet, writes, "The Company defines *problem drinking* [emphasis added] as drinking to the extent that it affects job performance." Certainly, there is an adequate internal logic to such a statement; drinking that (adversely) affects job performance is obviously a problem (for the employer, if not for others).

More commonly, however, company policy statements acknowledge that the disease of alcoholism may have something to do, at least secondarily, with peoples' health. The following is the most common operational definition of alcoholism among the company policies available to this writer: "For the purpose of this policy, alcoholism is defined as the consumption of alcoholic beverages which definitely and repeatedly interferes with an employee's job performance and/or health." Also quite common are amendments of the above statement that add on other "illnesses," perhaps hoping to gain the coattails of alcoholism's moderate credibility as an illness. This is illustrated by the statement of a farm equipment manufacturer: "For the purposes of this policy, alcoholism, drug abuse and emotional problems are defined as illnesses which repeatedly interfere with an employee's job performance and/or his health."

In the case of one automobile manufacturer, the definition is so broadened that it borders on doubletalk: "For purposes of this policy, behavioral-medical problems are defined as illnesses in which the employee's behavior definitely and repeatedly interferes with his or her job performance and/or health." The internal logic of this perspective, which considers those whose behavior is interfering with their job performance to be victims of the illness of "behavioral-medical problems," is also compelling. It is difficult to imagine what about an employee, other than his or her behavior, would cause job performance problems. A major consequence of such a definition, it would appear, is to justify the labeling of any employee deviating from company standards as an appropriate client for the employee assistance program.

Many of the other operational definitions, stating that the disease condition exists when, for example, consumption of alcohol impairs job performance, would appear to have a much narrower license for the impressment of clients into the program. However, such a narrow and seemingly self-interested specification of what constitutes alcoholism would seem to leave companies open to the charge that they are not genuinely concerned about employee welfare. To reduce exposure to such charges, program literature frequently includes the explanation that this narrowness is proof that the company is not guilty of any inappropriate paternalism. This strategy is illustrated in a mineral company's statement that: "The company's concern is strictly limited to its [alcohol's] effects on the employee's performance on the job. It is not concerned with social drinking. Whether an employee who is not an alcoholic chooses to drink or not to drink is of concern only to the individual."

At first glance, using job performance as the criterion for diagnosing employees as alcoholics would seem to provide an appropriate justification for the company's intervention. Nonetheless, the practical implementation of programs using the job performance diagnostic criteria confront two major dilemmas. The first and more readily addressed is that of establishing that individuals whose job problems can clearly be connected to misuse of alcohol are "alcoholics" rather than simply "drunk." The second and far more complex dilemma is determining that alcohol is in fact the specific cause of a particular work problem.

The research evidence indicating that alcohol problems are often viewed sympathetically, reviewed in Chapter 4, suggests that the alcoholism movement has had at least some impact on the extent to which alcoholism is seen as a condition that is not necessarily under an individual's control. The term drunkenness, it would appear, is now reserved for alcohol abuse that is engaged in voluntarily. Thus, although occupational alcoholism and employee assistance programs generally broaden the definition of alcoholism to cover a wide range of behaviors, program literature does not employ the specific term "drunk." These programs profess a sympathetic understanding of, and concern for, what they justifiably characterize as a grave health problem; without such a premise, it seems unlikely that many employees would voluntarily enter the program. Perhaps more importantly, it also seems unlikely that many supervisors would refer their subordinates. A claim of such sympathy for employees who, by choice, frequently overindulge on weekends and are hung over on Mondays would have little credibility. The problem confronted by programs using the definitions given here is that alcohol clearly can be responsible for adversely affecting the job performance of individuals who are neither "alcoholics" (with the supposedly attendant symptoms, such as craving, loss of control, and dependence), nor even problem drinkers (except in a very short-term sense), but simply drunk or hung over.

Research evidence corroborating the difficulty of disentangling the effects of alcoholism from those of drunkenness has been reported by Mannello (1979), who found that among railroad workers the 28 percent of the nonabstinent workforce who are problem drinkers account for one-third of drinking rule violations, while the remaining 72 percent, who are not considered to be problem drinkers, account for the remaining two-thirds of these violations. These data suggest that the preponderance of drinking rule violations are not attributable to those employees who have fallen victim to a treatable illness; rather, these data indicate that the number of problems caused by "problem drinkers" are not all that disproportionate to their prevalence in the nonabstinent population.

Thus, the operational definition of alcoholism as alcohol consumption that interferes with job performance allows for labeling as alcoholic those employees whose work has been impaired as a result of even one or two episodes of drunkenness. For example, in a conversation with a former director of the alcoholism program for one of the United States' armed forces, this author expressed surprise in response to his statement that he believed that one-quarter of the people in that service were alcoholics. The question was posed as to whether he included in that estimate, for example, the 19-year-old recruit, away from home for the first time, who returns from a weekend pass with a hangover and has a minor accident. The response was that such a person is an alcoholic and should be mandatorily referred into the alcoholism program and made to attend meetings of Alcoholics Anonymous.

In a sense, this estimate of the extent of drinking problems in the armed forces may not be too far off. Gray et al. (1983) found that approximately 18 percent of the personnel in the Canadian armed forces had very high levels of alcohol consumption, a conclusion that is similar to that of a number of studies, conducted a decade earlier, of drinking patterns in the U.S. military (e.g., Greden, Frenkel, and Morgan 1975; Ruben 1974). Another convergence among the findings of various studies of drinking patterns in the military is that the highest rate of alcohol consumption is among personnel who are male, unmarried, and roughly 17 to 23 years of age. These correlates of drinking patterns provide some difficulties for the medical disease model and its proponents, particularly the consistent finding over the years that consumption is highest between the ages of 17 and 23, and decreases substantially thereafter. Data indicating that a decade after 23-year-olds were found to have deviant drinking patterns those patterns are not found in 33-year-olds suggest that either the disease ideology's contention that alcoholism invariably becomes progressively worse (without treatment) is incorrect, that effective treatment is widely available and fully utilized, or that these young heavy drinkers are not alcoholics. The first of these alternatives is obviously unacceptable to advocates of the disease model, as is the second for those committed to the expansion of the alcoholism treatment "industry." The implication of the last explanation, however, is that these young soldiers and sailors are not victims of the disease of alcoholism, but are merely choosing to get drunk, in which case it would be inappropriate to place them into a program designed to rehabilitate individuals with a serious medical problem.

Some programs seem to be aware of the threats to the program's credibility entailed in imposing a label of alcoholic on individuals who may merely have come to work while suffering the aftereffects of a socially active weekend. Wagner (1982), for example, described a program in which "the employee rates whether he has an alcohol problem and to what extent, not the counselor" (p. 61). Explaining how this is accomplished, he wrote that "a short 26 yes-no quiz is read to the employee and the results indicate if alcohol is a problem and to what degree" (p. 61). What he did not mention, however, was that this widely-used quiz includes such relatively innocuous items as "Do you drink because you are shy with other people?" and that answering yes to one item is interpreted as a definite warning of alcoholism, yes to two is said to indicate a probability of alcoholism, and answering yes to three is taken as confirmation of the presence of alcoholism. Individuals responding to a counselor administering this quiz (but who are unaware of the scoring system) might wish to make it clear that they were not denying a problem and therefore might be inclined to admit, for example, that they mix themselves one martini when they come home from work every day, and drink it whether or not their spouse is home. But the result of providing candid, affirmative responses to questions about having a drink the same time every day and drinking alone would be that, according to the test's criteria, they had diagnosed themselves as alcoholic.

Also attempting to avoid the appearance of imposing the label of alcoholic on employees, an insurance company whose medical director has been an active member of the NCA's board makes use of the disease model. In an interview, the medical director explained to this author how supervisors are trained to make referrals to the program on the basis of job performance, and how program counselors attempt to determine the source of an employee's difficulties. In cases where employees disagree with an initial diagnosis of alcoholism, they are entirely free to decline participation in the program. However, if their poor work performance (supposedly symptomatic of alcoholism) recurs, and if they still refuse to accept the company's help, the medical director stated that he felt obligated to mandate such employees' participation in the program, as their continued poor job performance, "denial," and obvious "loss of control" confirmed not only the accuracy of the original diagnosis but the advanced stage of the disease's progression.

The legitimacy of alcoholism and employee assistance programs among a company's workforce rests, substantially, on convincing the organization's members that it is rehabilitating individuals who are suffering from an illness, not just sanctioning employees who misbehave. Labeling as alcoholic an employee whose deviant behavior is associated with overconsumption of alcohol adds some "face validity" to the diagnosis. Nevertheless, it is an inaccurate basis for diagnosing alcoholism, and these examples suggest that programs have attempted to develop procedures to avoid the appearance of overlabeling.

Linking Poor Performance to Alcoholism

Probably the more significant difficulty with defining alcoholism as consumption that affects job performance is that the actual cause of the deficient behavior is not always apparent. This dilemma is made especially problematic by the perspective, in many modern occupational programs, that alcohol abuse has subtle yet pervasive effects on individuals' behavior. That is, the concerns of most programs are not limited merely to obviously drunk or hung over employees. Whereas the old-fashioned alcoholism programs of the 1940s counseled supervisors to be vigilant for evidence of employees with alcohol on the breath, bloodshot eyes, and an unsteady gait, modern programs pointedly eschew such tactics. Nor are searches conducted, in modern occupational programs, for liquor bottles hidden in desks or lockers or for any concrete evidence (or even an oral statement in many cases) that an employee has been engaged in inappropriate consumption of alcohol. In general, there need be no evidence of drinking on the job, before coming to work, or at lunch to conclude that the disease of alcoholism is the proximate cause of deficient job performance. Rather, it is argued that employees may be moody, uncooperative, and in general unproductive because of alcohol problems that do not necessarily manifest themselves in overt physical symptoms.

The question, then, is how the company determines that employees' use of alcohol is what has caused their deficient job performance. For a great many corporate alcoholism programs, the medical disease ideology provides the answer. As discussed previously, the disease ideology argues that alcoholism is progressive and fatal unless there is a therapeutic intervention, that the prognosis is more favorable if the disease can be arrested in its early stage, and that the symptoms by which one can identify an individual as being in this early stage of alcoholism are various manifestations of deteriorating job performance. The elegance of this viewpoint (for social control purposes) is that it virtually eliminates the problem of demonstrating the connection between work performance deficiencies and alcoholism. By definition, employees are in the early stage of the disease of alcoholism if they exhibit "absenteeism, poor judgment, erratic performance, excessive material spoilage, decreasing productivity, departures, customer complaints, failure to meet schedules, and countless other instances of poor performance" (Von Wiegand 1974, p. 83). As outlandish as this idea would appear, companies do promote it. Indeed, Von Wiegand's list appears, usually with just a deletion or two, in many companies' program procedure manuals.

Also frequently reproduced in such company documents is a chart that purports to show the "Behavioral Pattern of Employee with Drinking Problem." In the early stage of the disease, the alcoholic is shown as functioning at 75 percent of job performance, with such observable signs as "absenteeism," "lowered job efficiency," "errors due to inattention or poor judgment," "misses deadlines," and "makes untrue statements." By the middle stage the alcoholic employee is claimed to be at 50 percent of job performance standards, as indicated by, for example, "spasmodic work pace," "repeated minor injuries on and off job," and "unreasonable resentments." The "late middle stage" alcoholic employee is supposed to be functioning at 25 percent of appropriate job performance, with observable signs such as "seems to lose ethical values" and "will not discuss problems."

Companies whose literature does not include this chart frequently provide a description of a behavioral pattern to watch out for, as in this excerpt from the program guidelines of an aircraft manufacturer:

> The employee was seldom absent or tardy—now his absences and tardies are increasing in frequency, especially Friday p.m., Monday a.m., and the day before and after a holiday. You see a pattern developing. Employee was safety conscious—now he is careless and has needless accidents or near accidents on the job with which he is familar.

As discussed in Chapter 4, the view of alcoholism as a progressive disease, moving inexorably through set stages, is inaccurate. Nonetheless, a great many employed people do develop serious difficulties with overconsumption of alcohol, and an understanding of the behavioral syndromes, if any, that are common along the path of development of such problems could prove useful in treating and preventing this problem. There is not much evidence, however, that the symptoms listed in the aforementioned company literature are those that characterize the early alcoholic.

Shirley (1985), director of industrial programs for the New York City affiliate of the A.A.-oriented National Council, has reported survey data on the work experiences of 62 business executives who were formerly active alcoholics and continued to be members of A.A. His respondents averaged almost 20 years between the first onset of their drinking problems and their eventual recovery, and he admitted that "all 62 of our subjects had progressed to a state of debilitation typical of late stage alcoholism before seeking the help that brought them to recovery." Concerning the effects of their long-term addiction on their work performance, he also admitted that "it's true that 43% of our subjects did advance in their careers during their drinking years." Apparently searching for evidence that would be at least somewhat consistent with views such as the claim, noted above, that "late middle stage" alcoholics function at only 25 percent efficiency, Shirley described the effects of his subjects' drinking on work performance in their last days before finally seeking treatment. He wrote that "ninety-two percent of our subjects were driven, finally, to come in early, stay late and to work on weekends in a desperate effort to compensate for their growing inability to accomplish their work during normal hours" (p. 26). Although this experience was undoubtedly a very painful one for these addicted executives, evidence that employees in the late stages of this virulent disease come in early, stay late, and work on weekends is not consistent with contentions that late-stage alcoholics are only one-fourth as productive as nonalcoholics.

The most detailed and useful published research on the work performance of employees with alcohol problems is that of Maxwell (1960), who analyzed survey responses from 406 recovered alcoholics—who had been employed during the period of their misuse of alcohol—concerning the on-the-job signs of their drinking. From a list, obtained through interviews, of 44 signs of drinking problems, those reported most frequently as serious or moderately serious problems were hangovers on the job (84 percent of respondents), increased nervousness/jitteriness (83 percent), and edginess/irritability (75 percent). In a rank-ordering of the signs from the most- to the least-frequently occurring, those discussed in company alcoholism program literature as the major symptoms of alcoholism did not appear until nearly the middle of the list. A lower quantity of work was the first such sign to appear on the list; it was ranked fifteenth, with 60 percent of the respondents having stated that this was a serious or moderately serious problem associated with their drinking. Lower quality of work was eighteenth, with 58 percent of respondents having reported it as a serious or moderate problem. Half-day or full-day absenteeism ranked twenty-fourth as a serious or moderately serious problem attributable to alcoholism, reported by 52 percent of the respondents. Minor accidents on the job were rated a serious or moderate problem by only 9 percent of the respondents, and accidents on the job in which work time was lost, presumably the more significant of these two aspects of accident-proneness, was the lowest ranked of all 44 signs, with only 5 percent of the respondents considering it to have been a serious or even a moderate problem.

The list discussed above was not, however, a measure of the *early* signs of alcoholism on the job, but simply of *any* signs that appeared prior to recovery. Roughly 40 percent of the respondents had reported that more than five years (and, for some, as many as 31 years) had passed between the first signs of drinking problems and the seeking of help; consequently, many of the signs that they reported may have occurred late in the development of the problem. To identify the early symptoms, Maxwell asked his respondents which of the 44 signs had been among the 5 earliest-occurring indicators of their drinking problems. Twenty-seven percent of the respondents stated that absenteeism was one of these early signs, 9 percent admitted to lower quantity of work, and 8 percent to lower quality of work. Finally, less than 1 percent of the respondents stated that accidents on the job were among the first 5 signs of their problem drinking. Thus, of the behaviors listed in company program literature as symptoms indicative of "early-stage alcoholism," only one (absenteeism) was reported by as many as one-quarter of these recovering alcoholics to have occurred in the early stages of the problem.

The most prolific writer on the topic of the job behavior of alcoholics has been Trice. Unfortunately, although he has apparently conducted survey research on indicators of drinking problems, his writings have provided only general verbal descriptions of the findings, rather than detailed reports. The first of his publications on this topic (Trice 1957) was apparently based on 200 case histories of A.A. members, with data "secured by means of interviews and questionnaires." The respondents were asked "*What job-related clues would have indicated to an observer that you were developing a drinking problem?*" (p. 529). Trice reported, as had Maxwell, that the incipient alcoholic employee has a more spasmodic work pace than others, apparently as a result of lost time due to drinking and its consequences, along with a desire to compensate for such problems. Two of his major findings, however, were somewhat contradictory to the pronouncements found in the literature distributed by occupational programs. First, although his subjects' "increased absenteeism was a prominent feature of their work histories," it did not occur disproportionately on Mondays and Fridays, as is often said to be the case. Also, lateness was *not* a characteristic feature of their work histories.

In a later publication, Trice (1962) described some findings of two additional studies on this topic. One study consisted of roughly 200 survey and interview responses from A.A. members. The second study, employing a shorter questionnaire (but again apparently including interviews as well), consisted of 552 responses, once more from members of A.A. Trice found that most "respondents reported a substantial decrease in work effectiveness during the middle stage of their alcoholism" (p. 500). This is not quite consistent with a premise on which occupational programs rest, that decreased efficiency is a sign of early-stage alcoholism. Also diverging from statements made in companies' program literature (but reinforcing Maxwell's conclusion) was his finding that alcoholics seemed no more likely than others to have accidents on the job. Trice did report that approximately 70 percent of his respondents indicated that increased absenteeism accompanied their developing alcoholism. However, he did not address the question of whether this poor attendance was an early-, middle-, or late-stage problem, nor did he make clear the extent of this increase in absenteeism. Trice wrote that "forty-three percent increased to one or more days per week or to the equivalent during concentrated drinking periods" (p. 501), but did not mention the frequency of such periods.

In his last reported research on the work-related symptoms of alcoholism, Trice (1964) endeavored to build on Maxwell's work, noting that all of the extant research literature on this issue was based on data provided by alcoholics themselves. Arguing that a broadening of this data base was called for, Trice gave Maxwell's list of 44 symptoms to "the immediate superiors of 72 employees who had been diagnosed as alcoholics" (the actual number of responding superiors was not reported and conceivably might have been very few). Except for the absence of some easily hidden symptoms, such as drinking before work, nervousness, and edginess, the supervisors' list of the most common symptoms closely matched the list Maxwell obtained from the recovered alcoholics. Additionally, Trice inquired into the timing and duration of these symptoms, that is, whether each had been seen early and frequently, late and only intermittently, and so on. He reported that the most common early and enduring work performance problems were absenteeism and lower quality of work. However, he provided no specific data to indicate that those problems occurred any more consistently among early-stage alcoholics than Maxwell had found to be the case.

Despite the high regard in which Trice is held among many in the occupational alcoholism field, his findings on this crucial question of diagnostic symptoms, as well as those of Maxwell, are disregarded. The available evidence strongly suggests that, although the behaviors that are stated in much company literature to be signs of early alcoholism accurately identify the experiences of some developing alcoholics, these symptoms appear among only a fraction of "early-stage alcoholics."

The inattention to systematic evidence on various issues related to drinking problems that run counter to assertions in companies' program literature might lead one to conclude that many corporations have been advancing a perspective on alcoholism that borders very closely on prevarication. The medical disease ideology of alcoholism seems to have facilitated the promotion of assertions concerning the seriousness of the problem that are substantially overstated, definitions of alcoholism that are palpably crude and seemingly self-interested, and diagnostic symptoms that are inaccurate or highly unreliable. These exaggerations, authoritatively expressed opinions, and pseudofacts may not be merely the result of corporate personnel functionaries failing to get the facts straight. Rather, they may serve the purpose of social control in the workplace, by legitimating management's search for, and sanctioning of, employees whose job performance is not up to management's standards. Not only can these components of the disease model serve to legitimate social control of poor performers by corporate management and those they employ specifically as agents of social control, but they may serve to motivate others to be participants (perhaps unwittingly so) in this process of identifying and disciplining those who deviate from managements' performance norms.

Motivating Referrals

By asserting that alcoholism is a serious, yet diagnosable and treatable problem, the disease model of alcoholism and its corollaries can attack what many program administrators consider to be the major impediment to identifying those whom they consider to be alcoholics. In discussions with this writer administrators often brought up the dilemma of supervisors covering up for their deviant subordinates. However, perhaps because programs do not wish to direct accusations at supervisory personnel, whose cooperation is crucial to a program's success, discussions of the supervisory cover-up generally do not appear in program literature. Nevertheless, this problem is often alluded to, as in a manufacturer's program pamphlet that warns, "You should make no attempt to conceal the impaired job performance or intentionally overlook evidence of a problem on the job," or a telephone company's advice, "Do not let friendship or sympathy mislead you into covering up for the employee with the idea that you are being helpful." The booklet describing a chemical firm's program devotes a full page to a listing of possible reasons for reluctance to identify alcoholic employees, including: "Reluctance to invade an employee's privacy," "The unpleasantness of facing up to the alcoholic," and "No one likes to stigmatize an employee—it's like calling him or her a communist."

Although a solid basis for the successful undermining of this supervisory cover-up is formed by the description of alcoholism as a disease that is progressive and fatal unless someone recognizes its symptoms and helps its victims receive treatment, many company promotional efforts make specific pleas for the supervisor's cooperation. One of the points frequently emphasized is that referring a subordinate to the alcoholism program is not an act of betrayal, but the most humanitarian possible response to the situation.

To advance this view, some companies unleash what is perhaps the most powerful semantic weapon in the war on organizational deviants— the promotion of a remarkable "symptom of the disease of alcoholism." As this writer was told by one of the country's most prestigious consultants on occupational alcoholism programming, "The number one symptom of alcoholism is denial." Thus, according to this Catch-22-type tenet, the best basis on which to positively identify someone as an alcoholic is for that person to deny having problems with alcohol.

In actuality, the only research bearing on this issue of denial directly contradicts this view. Trice (1964) asked his subjects, work supervisors of alcoholics, to describe a number of symptoms of their subordinates' alcoholism in addition to those on Maxwell's (1960) original list. According to Trice, the supervisors offered these new clues:

> First, they expressed the belief that the developing alcoholic is a chronic liar. Second, they noted his docility and willingness to admit his problem when directly approached about it. In the experience of these supervisors, alcoholic employees not only invented excuses for absences; they were also persistently untruthful about a host of work-related matters. At the same time, they readily and meekly admitted their problem, tending to throw themselves on the mercy of the boss if they were confronted with concrete evidence, outwardly, at least, accepting chastisement (1964, p. 23).

Notwithstanding the absence of evidence supporting the existence of this symptom (and, indeed, the presence of Trice's contrary evidence), many EAPs promote the view that "denial" is a symptom of alcoholism, as illustrated by the program guidelines distributed to supervisors in a chemical company: "Alcoholics are practiced at cover-ups to their colleagues, family and selves. There is a pattern of rationalization that allows the individual to deny completely that a problem exists. He may thus fool both supervisors and himself." Similarly, a metal company states: "It is important to keep in mind that a problem drinker is usually least able to recognize his problem. This is a characteristic of alcoholism—it is an illness of self-denial."

Understandably, those who write program policy statements may not be familiar with the findings of every research study conducted over the past quarter century. More surprisingly, the most vociferous champion of the importance of denial as a symptom of alcoholism has been Trice. Although he neither cited nor reported any research evidence that would dispute his earlier empirical findings, he has chastized "current articles and discussions of EAPs ... [because] there is little discussion about how to reduce the many facets of denial" (Trice and Sonnenstuhl 1985b, p. 12). Asserting that denial is not restricted to alcoholics, but that "the psycho-dynamics of denial are also present in other troubled employees" (p. 12), Trice explained that "the implications are clear": "those psychodynamics must be broken up," and constructive confrontation is the way to do so.

Without the contention that denial is a symptom of alcoholism and similar "diseases," the argument that it is necessary to threaten people with termination unless they are cooperative is much less compelling. Certainly, management still can attempt to motivate supervisors to refer poor performers to the program with the logic that the company has a right to expect good job performance. However, as suggested by the discussion of ideology and social control in Chapter 3, the supervisory cover-up seems likely to be dealt with more successfully to the extent that the managerial ideology does not appear as merely self-interested, but seems to reflect concern for employee health as well. The following excerpt from a chemical firm's program brochure, describing supervisory procedures, provides an example of the attempt to make the point that putting severe pressure on alcoholics is just what the doctor ordered:

> Since alcoholism is an illness of denial, persons may not be motivated to recovery until the circumstances of their continued drinking become more intolerable than the circumstances of abstinence. In other words, they must hit bottom before they are receptive to treatment.
>
> Experience has shown that a bottom can be artificially created before it normally would be reached if the illness was left to itself. This factor is one reason for our company program. When an employee's job performance is affected by the abuse of alcohol, he is surrounded by the facts of his condition. Thus, through a carefully planned effort, the employee is led to accept the facts of his illness and there is a good chance of persuading him to start a program of treatment.

The brochure provided to supervisors does not describe the details of the "carefully planned effort." In fact, the effort that this particular company carefully plans consists of the process of constructive confrontation, emphasizing "crisis precipitation" through the use of the "job threat." That is, by surrounding an employee with "the facts of his condition" (i.e., telling the employee that his job performance has been poor) he will "hit bottom" and can then be "led to accept the facts of his illness" (i.e., told that he will either shape up or be fired).

Other companies emphasize that referring one's subordinates to the program is both ethical and humanitarian by attempting to impress upon supervisors the dire consequences for an alcoholic subordinate of not receiving the program's aid. This interview with the administrator and the consultant for a utility company's program, published in the company's house organ, transmits this message with dramatic, even macho imagery.

> [The program administrator] tells it flat: "Alcohol, uncontrolled, is a killer, and the alcoholic who fails to arrest the disease is killing himself as surely as if he put a gun to his head. Those who can help him toward arresting the disease and don't are helping him toward an early death— and not a pleasant one." It is not pleasant news, for alcoholics, but there is no soft way to face the problem, in [the consultant's] view. "We call it 'tough love,'" says [the program administrator], "and I think it is often the only thing that can work."

The in-house newsletter of a major petroleum company also takes up this theme of referral as a humanitarian imperative. Although employing more gentle language, the following passage also implies that a supervisor who fails to refer an alcoholic subordinate is an accessory to suicide:

> Most problem workers won't act until a supervisor stands up to their performance and explains that it's time to seek some help. That, says [the program administrator], is the "key step" in starting an employee back in control of his life. The supervisor has to get the ball rolling. But often convincing the supervisor that he should do something is equally as difficult as convincing the person with a problem to do something.
>
> "Supervisors are like everyone else. They don't like to have these unpleasant talks. Their first reaction is to let things slide—to see what happens. But when something more serious occurs, they let it slide again."
>
> "By doing so," [the program administrator] says, "the supervisor provides the alcoholic time to get more involved with alcohol." By covering up this problem or procrastinating, they're contributing to a potentially fatal disease. This is the severity of alcoholism supervisors must realize. Once they do, they'll see that the only humanitarian solution is to immediately confront it."

Similarly, the house organ of a major banking institution, after explaining the nature of "constructive confrontation," concludes that "These are stern methods ... but the supervisor must understand if he is to help the staff member, their rigorous application is *the kindest thing he can do*—that anything less is a grave disservice to a seriously sick human being."

Once supervisors have been convinced that identifying a subordinate for referral to the alcoholism program is not an act of betrayal but one of helpfulness, they must then be convinced that they are competent to make such an identification. The approach to this issue in various companies' program literature appears to be fairly consistent. In response to the objections made by supervisors in early programs to being placed in the role of medical diagnosticians, companies now specifically aver that it is not their intention to do that. Rather, they maintain that the basic responsibility of supervisors under the program is to do precisely what they are expected to do as supervisors—monitor job performance. The following examples are illustrative:

> It is recognized that supervisors are not expected to distinguish what behavioral or medical problems an employee is having, just as they are not qualified to diagnose any other illness. Referrals for diagnosis and treatment will be based strictly on unsatisfactory job performance which results from an apparent behavioral-medical problem in a previously competent worker.
>
> —A farm equipment company

> Your Job as a Supervisor: THE TROUBLED EMPLOYEE WITH A DRINKING PROBLEM CAN BE IDENTIFIED ON THE BASIS OF POOR WORK PERFORMANCE. Poor work performance includes tardiness, absenteeism, poor performance on the job, on-duty accidents, unexplained absence from assignments, and difficulty with fellow employees and customers.
>
> Accompanying job-performance deterioration may be personality changes such as moodiness, irritability and chronic griping. There may be changes in physical conditions such as carelessness in dress and poor personal hygiene. You may hear rumors of financial problems and family difficulties. These symptoms may also be the result of health problems other than alcoholism. However, as a supervisor, you will remain on safe ground if you avoid the role of diagnostician and counselor and make your decision to confront the employee *only on the basis of work performance.*
>
> —A public utility firm

> It is not a function of managers and supervisors to diagnose alcoholism or drug abuse. Therefore, all referrals are based on job performance.
> I. Identification
> Supervisor:
> - monitors job performance and attendance;
> - documents any deterioration;
> - informally discusses with employee a need for improvement;
> - gives a time limit by which improvement must be demonstrated;
> - discusses case with department manager.
>
> —An insurance company

> Job performance is the focal point of this policy. It is the responsibility of officers and supervisors to refer to the medical department any employee whose unsatisfactory job performance does not respond to normal corrective action and results from apparent behavioral or medical problems, whatever their nature. It is not the officer's or supervisor's function to diagnose or make any judgment as to the nature of the problem.
>
> —A bank

The proscription against supervisors' involvement in diagnosis is sometimes presented as part of a list of "Supervisory Don'ts," such as a bank that advises:

1. The supervisor should not play the role of "amateur diagnostician." He is not qualified to judge whether or not a staff member is an "alcoholic" or a "drug dependent" person. The supervisor must stick to job performance.
2. The supervisor should not play the role of "lay counselor." He should not discuss whether or not the staff member has a drinking or drug "problem" or attempt to counsel him in this regard. This is a job for specialists.

Although such policies might seem to be reasonable responses to the complaints of supervisors about their role requirements in the earlier, medically-oriented programs, it does seem odd that, beyond the point of referral, supervisors have absolutely no role in the diagnostic process. Employees' immediate supervisors, after all, are presumably the individuals most cognizant of the symptoms being exhibited by program clients, a fact that should render them extremely helpful in breaking through the "denial pattern" of the alleged alcoholic.

Conversely, it could be argued that it is just this intimate knowledge of employees' behavior that makes some companies decidedly uninterested in supervisors' participation in the diagnostic process. That is, it seems likely that in many cases supervisors will have some idea of the reasons behind a subordinate's poor work performance. For example, an employee may frequently be late and absent and exhibit poor productivity because of frustration in performing at a task that has been designed to maximize the potential of capital rather than human resources, a situation that the employee's supervisor may be not only aware of, but sympathetic toward. However, to the extent that an employee's problem is something other than alcoholism, it may be in the alcoholism program's interest not to receive such information. This interest is likely to be shared by the company's management as well if, as is argued here, identification of employees as victims of the disease of alcoholism is believed to facilitate the sanctioning of deviance and maintenance of social control. Additionally, as Roman (1980) has implied, management would prefer to construe poor person-job fits as the result of individuals' deficiencies (even if pitiable ones), rather than systemic stressors (or, it might be added, failings on the part of management).

The typical program's policy, then, fits this strategy ideally; the supervisor is told to provide the program with *nothing more* than evidence of an employee's poor job performance. Furthermore, supervisors are told that they are extremely incompetent at diagnosis and that the company has specialized professionals for just that purpose. Odd as this approach may seem, it could be highly useful if these programs are falsely labeling individuals as alcoholics in order to facilitate controlling them. In particular, restricting immediate supervisors' contact with the program could be especially helpful for management in situations that have the potential to undermine the credibility of the program and the diagnoses it makes, such as one in which an employee was diagnosed as alcoholic even though the supervisor was quite certain that the problem was a conflict with a co-worker.

To further motivate supervisors to refer subordinates to the program, companies also appeal to supervisors' own self-interests. This tactic is illustrated by the following statement from a consumer products company:

> It is the supervisor who has to put up with the absenteeism, errors, personality problems, and deteriorating job performance of the developing alcoholic. It is the supervisor who ultimately may have to make the painful decision to recommend terminating a once valuable employee because drinking has destroyed the ability to function on the job. And it is the supervisor, second only to the alcoholic employee, who has the most to gain from a program which couples early identification of the problem with an understanding attitude and a prompt referral to a competent source of assistance.

Finally, and perhaps most importantly, program literature and training sessions emphasize that supervisors have, by far, the most central role in the identification process, and that their help is absolutely crucial. Statements such as the following are found in a number of company brochures:

> Often you are the only person who can motivate the employee to seek counseling. He probably has failed to heed friends and family urging him to "do something." Telling him to stop drinking is like telling a person with hay fever to stop sneezing. If he could control his drinking he would, and may have made repeated attempts to stop. The alcoholic has difficulty facing his problem. As the condition progresses, he becomes increasingly aware that his drinking is more and more uncontrollable. He only may be stimulated to action when confronted with the realization that his job may be at stake.
> AN EMPLOYEE WILL RARELY ACCEPT TREATMENT UNLESS THE CONSEQUENCES OF NOT ACCEPTING TREATMENT CREATES A SITUATION WHICH IS MORE INTOLERABLE THAN HIS FEAR OF THE RESULTS OF EXPOSURE.
> —A telephone company

> The most important aspect of a successful recovery from alcoholism or other drug dependence is the MOTIVATION TO ACCEPT treatment, rather than treatment itself. The supervisor has one of the most effective motivational tools known to date—that is, the desire of employees to hold their jobs. The role of the supervisor, then, is to identify the

alcoholics or other drug dependents through the company program, where they can get the specialized treatment essential to their recovery.

The key to the successful motivation of employees to seek help lies in the fair and constructive use of the *supervisor's authority*. Experience has shown a mere offer of treatment is as ineffectual as giving lectures or repeated "chances." The employees must be made to understand that unless the problem (whatever it is) is corrected and performance is brought up to standard, they will be subject to existing penalties for unsatisfactory job performance. They will also need assurance that acceptance of treatment will not jeopardize their job or opportunities for promotion.

Experience has shown that about half of those approached in this manner respond immediately. That is, they agree to accept help under a company program. About half of these need no further motivation by the supervisor. They cooperate with treatment from the beginning and solve their problem with a minimum of difficulty. For the others, who did not accept help or initially agreed to accept help and then faltered, the supervisor follows normal administrative procedures, which exist for unsatisfactory job performance situations, based on the facts of the poor job performance and tailored to fit the individual case. This process is known as "forceful coercion" or "crisis precipitation."

—A public utility firm

In their desire to convince supervisors that they should refer subordinates who perform poorly to the EAP, these excerpts, above, from companies' program materials go beyond the facts and, indeed, beyond internal consistency. The notion in the telephone company's brochure that one can exercise no more cognitive control over abusive drinking patterns than over hay fever is patently untrue, as is demonstrated by, for example, the many thousands of individuals who have stopped drinking through affiliation with Alcoholics Anonymous. Making the point that alcoholics' loss of control has rendered them unable to act on the basis of conscious, willful decision-making, the brochure first states that "telling [the alcoholic] to stop drinking" will not work. What it then claims *does* work, however, is telling the alcoholic to stop drinking or "his job may be at stake." The second paragraph of that brochure emphasizes that threatening an "alcoholic" employee is necessary because, otherwise, they "will rarely accept treatment." However, the results from a number of studies of the sources of referral in company alcoholism programs (reviewed in Chapter 5) suggest that roughly one-third of program clients are self-referrals.

The second brochure excerpted above notes that "motivation to accept treatment" is a far stronger predictor of successful rehabilitation than is "treatment itself." Much research evidence does, in fact, support the view that the threat of dire consequences for failure to recover is more significant than whatever "treatment" is, or is not, applied to the "alcoholic" employee (see Miller and Hester 1981). This utility company would seem anxious, however, not to lose whatever added motivation for referring deviant subordinates can be achieved by appealing to supervisors' humanitarian sensitivities. Despite their earlier downplaying of the role of "treatment itself," the brochure goes on to emphasize the importance of supervisors actually making the referrals, by pointing out that the company program is where employees "can get the specialized treatment" that is described as "essential to their recovery."

Justifying Sanctions

An attempt has been made here to demonstrate that the disease model of alcoholism facilitates the identification of deviant employees and their labeling as alcoholics. Perhaps as importantly, after clients have been identified, the disease model's explanation of the "progressive," "fatal" nature of this "illness of denial" serves to justify the coercive sanctions utilitized in the putative treatment of program clients. For example, program material from a manufacturing firm explains why severe sanctions are an integral part of their "enlightened" approach to helping victims of this disease:

> The present method of dealing with problem drinkers is with enlightened confrontation that helps motivate the drinker to change and with the offer of treatment where it is indicated or desired. These alternatives to punishment are definite procedures that should be carried out conscientiously and uniformly and with them we can solve most of these problems and restore troubled employees to health and productivity. Problem drinking employees usually are more powerfully motivated to overcome alcohol abuse when their job is at stake if they do not change their unacceptable patterns of behavior. It is well known in the alcoholism professions that the rehabilitation rates of industrial programs are amazingly high and it is agreed that it is principally due to the fact that constructive coercion is possible when the job is really in jeopardy.
>
> Even so, not all problem drinkers will cooperate in their rehabilitation so that termination of employment will be the only solution in some cases. When it is necessary to terminate it is done in the hope that this final step will provide the necessary shock to turn the employee to sobriety. It has long been known that a very high percentage of the most stable members of Alcoholics Anonymous report that it was the final loss of a valued job that finally brought them to this remarkably successful program.

Similarly, a metal company explains how firm punishment is the most efficacious technique for successfully dealing with this disease:

> Strong intervention is necessary to break through the denial often associated with the disease of alcoholism. Supervisors are in an excel-

lent position to make this intervention because they control employment. While it may seem harsh, the prospect of job loss frequently
motivates a problem drinker into treatment when nothing else will. The
employee needs the job not only for the income that it provides but also
for the "respectability" that it offers. The rationale is that having a job is
tangible evidence that drinking is still within acceptable limits. This is
not to say that employees with suspected drinking problems should be
treated differently from anyone else. When the supervisor encounters
performance deficiencies of any type, he or she should apply corrective
procedures firmly and consistently. With those people who do not
respond, progressively more severe steps are necessary up to and
including the possibility of termination. Frequently, conditions must
reach this rather drastic stage before the poor performer who has a
drinking problem will recognize that something must be done.

The material presented in this chapter has been emphasizing the
means by which the managers of capitalist enterprises have attempted to
control their workforces, and is thus consistent with a Marxian analysis of
the nature of the class structure and of class conflict. A Weberian
approach, however, would be interested, as well, in conflict occurring
among groups having the same relationship to the means of production,
and would argue that a source of power in such a conflict might be an
advantageous relationship to the means of administration. An example of
conflict between working class groups was illustrated earlier in this
chapter, in a discussion of a radical labor group's accusation that the
union representing the company's employees was colluding with the
company, through its access to advisory boards, in using the alcoholism
program to brainwash members of this dissident group.

Collusion, or less pejoratively, cooperation, among unions and
capitalist management has long been a feature of many occupational
alcoholism programs. Under the leadership of Leo Perlis the AFL-CIO's
Community Services Agency recommended that each company facility in
which a program was in operation have a committee to oversee the
program, composed of equal numbers of union and management representatives. Because of the "denial" supposedly characteristic of alcoholism's victims it was expected that some employees would appeal to this
committee that they were refusing to accept treatment because they were
not actually alcoholics. Perlis' concept, intended to motivate acceptance of
treatment, was that if all of the committee's members agreed that the
appealant was in fact an alcoholic (who might only be attempting to play
off the union and management against each other), the union would
refuse to defend that employee in any grievance procedure relating to the
problems that led to the referral into the program. In practice this meant
that the union would be party to decisions to fire union members. In an
interview, this writer asked Perlis his view of union participation in this
most extreme form of constructive coercion. Pacing back and forth across
his office floor, he acknowledged that, as a longtime union member he

had found it extremely difficult to accept the idea that it was the union's duty to help to fire an employee who did not seem to be cooperating with an occupational alcoholism program (as evidenced by a lack of remission of the "symptoms" of that disease). But, he said, he found it easier since having come up with a new name for this procedure. Pausing in the middle of his office and lifting his eyes skyward he said, "Now I call it Therapeutic Firing."

The view that would appear to serve as a philosophical underpinning for such harsh policies, whether propounded by trade unionists or corporate managers, was expressed by the administrator of an insurance company's alcoholism program. Interviewed in the company magazine he explained that, "I've now learned what love is. . . . I've come to believe it is really giving someone else the freedom to experience his own pain, and to take on the responsibility of his own actions." In addition to a copy of this interview with the program director, this company enclosed evaluation data from its program along with its response to the Conference Board survey. The data indicated that 43 percent of those diagnosed as alcoholic in this program leave employment with the company, a finding that suggests that the program administrator is indeed generous in expressing his love.

Many programs' supervisory procedure manuals specify the conditions under which employees will be given the opportunity to experience their own pain. As examples:

> If the individual refuses an appointment with the [alcoholism program's] coordinator, explain that his future with the bank will be seriously jeopardized if the problem continues.
>
> —A bank

> If the employee indicates an unwillingness to attempt rehabilitation or if at any time the Medical Director feels further treatment or efforts at rehabilitation should be discontinued, the employee should be dismissed as indicated in Policy A-41.
>
> —A dairy products company

> If an employee refuses or fails to respond to treatment, he or she will be subject to appropriate disciplinary action.
>
> —An aerospace manufacturer

> An employee's continued refusal to accept diagnosis and treatment, or continued failure to respond to treatment, will be handled in exactly the same way that similar refusals or treatment failures are handled for all other illnesses, when the results of such refusals or failures continue to affect job performance.
>
> —A farm equipment company

What is usually not stated among these written procedures is precisely what constitutes a "failure to respond to treatment." The job performance approach to alcoholism, however, provides an unambiguous answer to this question. Evidence of a program client's sincere cooperation with the treatment the company has offered (consisting, modally, of referral to a local A.A. group) would be demonstrated by remission of the symptoms of the disease. Because the symptoms of "early-stage alcoholism" are said to be absenteeism, lateness, and low productivity, the operational definition of "failure to respond to treatment" very clearly means "lack of improvement in attendance, punctuality, and productivity."

RESEARCH ON CLIENT OUTCOMES
UNDER COERCED TREATMENT

Simply to contend that the medical disease model of alcoholism is especially conducive to the adoption of practices that could be used for social control, rather than for their ostensible therapeutic purposes, certainly does not prove that such practices are occurring. Although the phrase "constructive coercion" has a rather authoritarian ring, this study has not yet demonstrated that coercion is not an efficacious means of dealing with alcoholics. Similarly, although the diagnostic symptoms of alcoholism proposed by the job performance perspective do seem to allow programs to cast a wide net, this study has not yet presented evidence that individuals who are not alcoholics are being unfairly labeled. This section will review reports of outcomes of programs using these procedures, with the intention of addressing these two questions. Unfortunately, the available literature will not permit an unequivocal resolution of these issues, and only inferential conclusions can be drawn.

A human resource specialist interviewed by Williams, DuBrin, and Sisk (1985) described the dynamics of the referral process in one company's program, stating that the employees "see the assistance program as a weapon used by their supervisors. They are told to sign up for the program or be fired. So a lot of them enter the EAP just to avoid getting canned" (p. 421). Attempting to explain the program's limited success this specialist stated that a result of this means of referral seemed to be that employees placed in the program "have no real desire for change."

The four published research reports that specifically are concerned with the efficacy of "constructive confrontation" have all shared this assumption, that in alcoholism treatment success depends upon "the person's entering with a desire to change" (Freedberg and Johnston 1980) or "self-generated motivation to improve" (Smart 1974). None of these articles either provided or cited support for this assumption; nevertheless, its assertion has served to focus these studies on the question of whether favorable outcomes can be obtained from patients who have been coerced into entering treatment for alcoholism.

Two of the articles were authored by researchers associated with the Addiction Research Foundation in Toronto and share some instrumentation. Smart (1974) described a Supervisor Rating Form (SRF), on which work supervisors of program clients provided ratings of these individuals on 16 work-related characteristics. Eleven of the characteristics are concerned with job performance (e.g., productivity and dependability), three with alcohol-related behavior (drinking on the job, working under the influence of alcohol, and effects of hangovers), one with absenteeism, and one with lateness. An Improvement Rating Scale (IRS) measured self-reported changes in drinking, work, family relations, and so on.

Comparing patients in an alcoholism treatment facility who had been admitted voluntarily to those whose attendance had been mandated by their employer, Smart reported that the two groups essentially had the same levels of improvement in both drinking behavior and overall behavior. However, the IRS appears to have been administered just once, and Smart did not report an initial baseline measure of patients' drinking or overall behavior, on which an assessment of actual improvement might be based. The lack of baseline data not only leaves open the question of whether these patients were helped by the treatment, it also leaves unanswered the question of whether they were all alcoholics to begin with. Supervisor ratings for the mandatory patients were said to have improved on a number of characteristics, including productivity, absenteeism, and lateness. Changes in SRF scores for voluntary patients were not reported.

In light of Smart's original concern that therapy would be unsuccessful if a patient lacked internal motivation, the finding of equal outcomes for both the internally and externally motivated groups suggests that in the absence of a self-generated desire to improve simple coercion will suffice. Reported but not explained was the finding that of the patients mandatorily referred from companies with alcoholism programs oriented toward job performance, 16 percent were terminated from their jobs, whereas none of the voluntary patients in the study lost their jobs. This seems inconsistent with the medical disease ideology of alcoholism, which would seem to predict that unless the mandatory and voluntary subsamples were at different stages of the disease they would both be exhibiting the same work performance problems, and their equal rehabilitation rates would lead to equal consequences for their employment status.

Freedberg and Johnston (1980) also administered the Addiction Research Foundation's Supervisor Rating Form to subsamples of mandatory and voluntary patients. Improving on Smart's Improvement Rating Scale, they used the Ontario Problem Assessment Battery (OPAB) (Freedberg and Scherer 1977) to measure problems in areas relevant to treatment goals, such as depression and marital sex. The OPAB, however, includes no questions related to actual alcohol use.

At the time of their admission to treatment, the voluntary patients in Freedberg and Johnston's study had far more problems than the mandatory patients, as measured by the OPAB. However, the SRF scores indicated that patients who had been mandatorily referred into the program were more likely to have been found drinking on the job and to have productivity problems. By the three-month follow-up, and sustaining through the six- and twelve-month follow-ups, both groups improved on both scales, and the differences between mandatory and voluntary patients (with the exception of the overassertion and marital sex scales on the OPAB) disappeared.

The findings, in Freedberg and Johnston's study, of equivalent therapeutic outcomes for coerced versus self-motivated patients replicate those of Smart. They also replicate Smart's in that, despite considerable and equal rehabilitation rates, 15 percent of the mandatory patients were fired from their jobs, versus only 7 percent of the voluntary patients. In fact, a number of studies of programs in which clients have been ordered to treatment by their employer (e.g., Clyne 1965; Thorpe and Perrett 1959) have found that approximately 15 percent lose their jobs.

Freedberg and Johnston did assess patients' drinking status, showing the extent of improvement at three-, six- and twelve-month follow-up intervals. They did not, however, report patients' drinking status on admission to treatment. Their finding that nearly two-thirds of the mandatory patients were abstinent three months after discharge from treatment indicates an impressive rate of recovery from alcoholism; unfortunately, the authors provided no data to show that these patients had ever been alcoholics to begin with. The only information presented concerning the mandatory patients' consumption of alcohol is that they were likely to have been found drinking on the job. Since, as discussed earlier, drinking on the job is by no means a reliable indicator of alcoholism (in fact, even the admitted alcoholics in this study were considerably less likely than the coerced patients to have this problem), the actual nature of the mandatory patients' problems (other than low productivity) is unclear.

Chopra, Preston, and Gerson (1979) were also concerned with the relative outcomes of coerced versus self-referred patients. Additionally they sought to answer the question, "Does a policy of constructive coercion allow earlier identification and treatment of workers with problem drinking?" Addressing this second issue, they wrote:

> While the time when alcohol-related problems began for any individual cannot be pinpointed, it seems reasonable to assume that the mean age of onset for drinking problems was the same for each group [i.e., the coerced and the self-referred patients]. Given this assumption, a finding that the coerced workers are younger than the volunteers would be proof that constructive coercion leads to early identification. Furthermore, a group identified earlier should have fewer problems associated with alcohol—they would have fewer years of risk.... Consistent with younger age, the existence of fewer social problems in the coerced group should serve as evidence of earlier identification (1979, p. 750).

None too surprisingly, Chopra, Preston, and Gerson indicated that their findings supported these hypotheses, concluding that:

> The evidence presented certainly supports the concepts underlying Employee Assistance Programs.
> 1. Patients referred under the policy of constructive coercion enter treatment at younger ages.
> 2. These patients have experienced fewer problems associated with alcohol.
> 3. A higher percentage report themselves abstinent during follow-up.
> 4. Compliance with follow-up is increased (1979, p. 751).

Regrettably, nowhere in this study was there any demonstration that the coerced patients were alcoholics. All that readers were told, in fact, was that the patients who were in treatment against their wishes were less likely to have had problems that are sometimes associated with alcoholism. Indeed, if these individuals were alcoholics, it was at an extremely early stage. Moreover, the abstinence rates reported by Chopra et al. were based entirely on patients' self-reports, and it is just possible that these individuals, who were threatened with the loss of their jobs, may have been particularly motivated to claim that they had achieved complete control of their drinking. The greater compliance with follow-up on the part of the coerced patients may also have been similarly motivated.

It is not possible to determine whether recovery rates in the Chopra et al. study were simply an artifact of verbal compliance on the part of clients who feared sanctions. However, the suggestion that this phenomenon might explain their findings is not merely surmise. DuBrin, for example, offered evidence that it does occur; he reported a conversation with a low-paid service employee who stated: "Supervisors here put a lot of pressure on the employee with a drinking problem to enroll in the assistance program. You are told that if you don't join up, you'll be canned. So you get a lot of workers claiming how great the program is and how it's cured their problem" (1985, p. 294).

The reasoning of Chopra, and his associates, followed to its questionably logical conclusion, would seem to imply that not only is mandatory therapy for alcoholism efficacious, but that it is most efficacious for children, who are even less likely to have had auto accidents, arrests for violent crime, and other problems associated with alcohol. Although labeling children as alcoholics is an irrelevancy for most work organizations,* the same logic does have the potential to enhance organizations'

---

*This is not to say that the principles of employee assistance programs are irrelevant to nonadults. An apparently emerging trend is the development of "student assistance programs" that according to the Director of the NIAAA, are "based on the highly successful employee assistance program model found in industry" (Niven 1985, p. vii).

abilities to label individuals as alcoholics. From this perspective a diagnosis of alcoholism applied to a poorly performing employee for whom no corroborative evidence of alcoholism (such as auto accidents) can be found would not indicate mislabeling, but rather the program's success in "early identification" of alcoholics, by which they were actually preventing the further development of the disease.

The notion that coercion is a prevention strategy might be highly appealing to those concerned about the credibility of programs whose justification for calling poor performers alcoholics and rehabilitating them with threats rests on claims that 60 to 80 percent of problem employees are alcoholics. Indeed, Trice, the originator of the constructive coercion/confrontation concept, expressing "a need to reaffirm the prevention potential that exists in job-based programs," explained that "drinking behaviors that precede chronic drinking problems tend to be manifest in impaired job performance relatively early in their development" (Trice and Roman 1978, p. xiv). That is, the combination of the job performance approach to diagnosis with the constructive confrontation approach to treatment is said to be effective not only for alcoholics, but for those who might become alcoholics in the future. Trice and Beyer (1982) are so convinced of the efficacy of constructive confrontation, in fact, that they suggest that managers apply it to not only alcoholic or prealcoholic employees, but also to those suffering from depression.

Unfortunately, Trice's own research (1962) indicated that individuals who developed chronic drinking problems did not manifest job performance difficulties early in the problem's progression. Even more problematic for his contention are the findings (Cahalan and Room 1974; Clark and Cahalan 1976; Roizen et al. 1978) that although it is males in their twenties whose job performance is most likely to be impaired by abuse of alcohol, this drinking pattern is not predictive of the development of long-term alcohol addiction.

Consistent with those findings, an examination of the Chopra et al. data indicates that it is precisely this group that is markedly overrepresented in their subsample of coerced clients. Thus a reasonable surmise is that many of the coerced patients in the Chopra study were young men whose referral to the program had been triggered by having exhibited some dysfunctional behavior on the job—perhaps associated with an episode of overconsumption of alcohol. To the extent that such behavior is construed as simply "young fellows kicking up their heels," however, the deficient work behavior might be overlooked by those in a position to refer employees into the program. In contrast, Trice and Roman's claim that such behaviors "precede chronic drinking problems" makes referral to the program a judicious preventive measure. Although their approach is essentially isomorphic to the NCA's construal of young adult overconsumption as "early stage alcoholism," Trice and Roman's version is perhaps more credible, and seems to provide an even more subtle basis for managerial control over deviant behavior.

Heyman (1976) interviewed "180 randomly sampled alcoholics from four industrial alcoholism programs." Although she provided no supportive data, she seems to have had no reticence about accepting the accuracy of the programs' diagnoses that all these persons actually were alcoholics. The same cannot be said for 10 percent of her sample, who were refusing to participate in the company programs. These refusers tended to be younger, tended to deny having a problem with alcohol, and were likely to have been referred by their supervisors. Cahalan and Room's findings, cited above, would seem to be applicable to interpreting this situation as well, and would tend to support the resistance to being labeled as alcoholics by the 10 percent who declined to cooperate with the program.

The focus of Heyman's analysis was on the incident that triggered the entry into treatment. She found that, of the 29 percent of the sample for whom impaired job performance was the trigger, 89 percent had an eventual outcome of improved job performance. Of the 17 percent whose treatment was triggered by family problems, only 44 percent improved on work performance; however, these subjects were less likely to have had job performance problems. Because of her assumption that job impairment is an early sign of alcoholism, Heyman concluded that the family-triggered patients must therefore be very early-stage alcoholics, as their work had not yet suffered. Concerning those patients triggered by impaired job performance, she wrote:

> The strong associations related to the impaired-work trigger support the purpose of the program and the use of coercion by the company as leverage. They also imply that the identification of these individuals as alcoholics was not made in the early course of their problem drinking, since their work performance had already noticeably deteriorated (1976, p. 906).

Although she thus concluded that patients triggered by job problems are relatively late-stage alcoholics, she noted that the supposedly early-stage, family-triggered patients were more than twice as likely as others to have been "detoxed." Detoxification is a hospital-based medical procedure employed in circumstances in which many years of extreme overconsumption of alcohol have resulted in an actual physical addiction. Confronted with this evidence, which clearly contradicted her analysis, Heyman admitted to mild confusion. Also confusing her was the finding that the specific problem that had triggered entry into the program was highly predictive of the eventual treatment outcome. Attempting to extricate herself from these inconvenient facts, she posited that there might be a variety of alcoholisms, such as "family problem-triggered alcoholism."

A far more parsimonious interpretation of her findings is simply that those clients whose treatment was triggered by job impairment were suffering primarily from job impairment—which may or may not have been related to some overt abuse of alcohol. If comparatively few of the patients triggered by family problems, 61 percent of whom needed detoxification, reported job performance problems, it was probably because, as indicated by the research reviewed here previously, job performance problems among alcoholics are far from universal.

Heyman is by no means alone in suffering from the puzzlement caused by the wide discrepancy between the explanations offered by the traditional medical disease model and the reality encountered in working with clients mandatorily referred to treatment in occupational programs. This was illustrated in a counseling session that the present author was invited to sit in on, in which an organization's EAP administrator talked with a young janitor who had been referred to the program as a result of an episode of drunkenness on the job, and whom the program administrator had subsequently diagnosed as an alcoholic. When asked whether he had had a drink since the last session, the janitor replied that while watching a ball game at the home of his wife's parents he had accepted one beer, but declined a second, telling his father-in-law that he was trying to cut down. This simple story, told by a young man whose drunkenness on the job had not recurred, presents a dilemma for the program administrator; either this diagnosis in particular, or the disease model in general, would seem to have been disconfirmed. According to the medical disease ideology, alcoholics are that small minority for whom alcohol is a poison, for whom even one drop of liquor triggers an uncontrollable craving for more alcohol. Yet, the client seems not to have exhibited that behavior, having stayed very much in control of his drinking since the one episode on the job. Like a great many who work in the EAP field, this program's administrator was a former alcoholic who had recovered through the help of A.A., in which the final, and ongoing, stage of the recovery program is to proselytize for new alcoholics. This "twelfth step work" mitigates against the administrator conceding that a client is not alcoholic, especially in this case, in which the diagnosis could be supported by direct evidence of disruptive alcohol consumption. Dealing with this conundrum much as Heyman had, the administrator maintained that this janitor was indeed a victim of the disease of alcoholism by inventing a new characteristic of this disease; leaning over his desk he told the employee "you know, alcoholism's a funny disease; one time you have a drink and nothing happens and, the next time maybe, you take a drink and the next thing you know you're in the gutter."

The first question posed in this section was whether "constructive coercion" is an efficacious means of dealing with alcoholics. Having reviewed the data, the answer that can now be given is that it appears that threats are a highly effective method (ethical issues aside) of getting people to change their behavior—at least as effective as getting them to develop some sort of internalized motivation to change. None of the studies were able to demonstrate at all convincingly that this is especially true of alcoholics, because none of them provided data to address the question of whether individuals being dealt with in these programs actually are alcoholics.

The research projects reviewed above, however, were designed specifically to investigate "constructive coercion"; the question of whether the clients of occupational alcoholism programs are actually alcoholics presumably would be addressed more directly in general assessments of program functioning. However, methodologically rigorous evaluative studies of individual company programs, examining the behavioral characteristics of clients both at entry into and completion of the program, simply do not exist. The available evaluative data on occupational programs, both published and unpublished, have been reviewed on three occasions (Edwards 1975; Kurtz, Googins, and Howard 1984; Weiss 1982a). It is clear from these assessments that the quality of the program evaluation literature is even poorer than that of the research on coercion.

Edwards' review, the most detailed of the three, was published in a book directed toward individuals working in the occupational programming field, and attempted to convey some of the rudiments of Campbell and Stanley's well-known discussion of quasi-experimental research designs (1966). He pointed out that, for those studies in which he was able to detect any type of research design at all, the majority were of what Campbell and Stanley diagrammed as the "X O" (experimental intervention followed by observation of subjects' behavior), or "one-shot case study," design—essentially a retrospective description of the phenomenon of interest. In no case did an evaluation include a control or comparison group. Edwards' summary of these studies indicated that the programs claimed rehabilitation rates ranging from 65 to 87 percent. These favorable conclusions, from studies that were all conducted by these programs' own staff members, were entirely predictable in light of Gordon and Morse's finding (1975) that evaluations by internal personnel are highly likely to indicate that the program being evaluated is successful. More importantly, Edwards pointed out that the research designs used in these studies did not control for various sources of bias that threaten the evaluations' validity, such as different definitions of alcoholism, case selection from special populations, rejection of applicants, refusal of referral, refusal to participate in follow-ups, the effects of testing, spontaneous recovery, deterioration effects, and regression effects. For the concerns of the present study, however, what is most remarkable about the research summarized by Edwards is that of the 16 evaluations only 2 included some measure of their patients' use of alcohol. Eleven evaluations used some criterion of job performance to measure program effectiveness, one stated an uninterpretable "rehabilitation rate," and two provided no measure of outcomes. Although not specifically discussed by Edwards, it is clear from his review of these studies (almost a third of which were unpublished) that in no case were the investigators able to determine whether incoming clients were in fact alcoholics.

Have program evaluations become more sophisticated in the decade since Edwards attempted to impart some of the most basic concepts of evaluation research? Neither Kurtz and associates' nor Weiss' reviews found substantially better evaluation studies than did Edwards'. Writing in *Personnel Administrator*, Starr and Byram (chairperson of the EAP subcommittee of the American Society of Personnel Administrators) identified what they considered to be state-of-the-art evaluation techniques in a discussion of "Cost benefit analysis for employee assistance programs" (1985). They noted that "Erfurt and Foote have developed a method of establishing return on investment for insurance utilization." This methodological development (Erfurt and Foote 1977) consists of subtracting medical costs incurred since the employee's entry into the program from those incurred before entering the program. A second technique described by Starr and Byram was designed to evaluate a program's return on investment for savings in costs of absenteeism. Specifically, Gaeta, Lynn and Grey (1982) used the difference between before and after treatment calculations of the number of days absent multiplied by the clients' daily wages. A third technique that Starr and Byram offered, to determine savings from reduced disability benefits, consisted of subtracting the costs of disability payments to an employee after the program from such payments to that individual before entering the program. For each of these three techniques, the subtraction's remainder constituted the program's economic "benefit."

As Edwards and Weiss both have noted, measures such as these tend to yield highly inflated estimates of program effectiveness. One reason for this is likely to be that individuals often enter a program when their problems are at the height of their severity; but large medical expenditures (for example) during one year do not necessarily mean that future years will see increasingly expensive medical bills. Rather, simply by statistical chance, extremely high medical expenses in one year will tend to be followed by less extreme expenses the next (see Campbell and Stanley 1966). Attributing the reduction in costs to any sort of program, rather than simply to "regression toward the mean," is unjustified. Indeed, Starr and Byram appear to pay no attention to any of the biases that, as Edwards explained, can threaten validity when simple pre- and post-treatment comparisons are made. The research design implicit in their recommended techniques is an improvement on the "X O," "one-shot case study" approach used by most alcoholism program evaluations, but not by very much. In Campbell and Stanley's classification, it is an "O X O" (observation - experimental intervention - observation) or "one-group pretest-posttest" design, a procedure for which they have so little regard that they note that its inclusion in their book is purely as a "bad example."

Although the methods suggested by Starr and Byram may not have been very good, two of the three factors they suggested measuring would seem to have potential to demonstrate that actual alcoholics were being treated. Information that an employee had been receiving health insurance benefits for the treatment of alcoholism prior to entering the program, or disability benefits because of incapacitation resulting from alcoholism, would provide more credible evidence of the individual's alcoholism than would the diagnosis made by an alcoholism program's administrator. Perhaps in the future such evidence will be reported.

Relatively few studies on clients' outcomes in a set of programs have been conducted by academically-oriented authors. Those that have, however, might be expected to exhibit greater sophistication than that of the various case studies of outcomes by staff members of individual programs. The previously discussed report by Roman and Thomas (1978) on their own and Opinion Research Corporation's data on large samples of programs had some information on program outcomes. In the study designed and conducted by Roman's research group, no data concerning any outcomes for clients have ever been reported. However, the ORC survey asked responding executives whether they had ever dealt with a problem drinking subordinate and whether the case had a successful outcome. Based on their analyses of the ORC data, Roman and Thomas reported that of cases of problem-drinking subordinates reported by executives in companies having programs, 62 percent were resolved successfully (measured as restoration to acceptable job performance). What Roman and Thomas did not report, although it can be determined from an examination of the ORC's report of their survey's frequency counts, is that 51 percent of cases of problem-drinking subordinates were reported to have been resolved successfully by executives in companies that did not have programs. Thus the ORC data indicated that having a program yielded only an 11 percentage point net increase in the rehabilitation rate. Of substantially greater magnitude was the programs' impact on the willingness of supervisors to report to management those subordinates who would not voluntarily seek help; 50 percent of respondents in companies with programs had referred subordinates to help for drinking problems, compared to only 32 percent in companies without programs. That is, the presence of a program is associated with a 22 percent greater likelihood of individuals identified as alcoholics improving their job performance, and a 56 percent greater likelihood that supervisors will coerce subordinates into a program. Whether employees who entered these programs were alcoholics or what changes occurred in their drinking behavior were not addressed in this study.

Hitchcock and Sanders' (1976) study of programs in the railroad industry employed a variety of outcome measures. In presenting their data on successes and failures, however, they duly reported that different programs in their study used different criteria of success and failure, including sobriety, abstinence, behavior change at work, and medical clearance. Of the 15 programs with usable data, the mean percentage of successful client interventions was 68.7, with a range of 50 to 84 percent. The mean failure rate was 24.2 percent, although this figure is highly influenced by an outlier that reported 50 percent failures (probably because they reported outcome data in only two categories, success or failure, leaving out the various intermediate categories—such as "in treatment"—used by most other programs). Although they at least attempted to provide some evidence on the drinking status of some programs' clients, as with other studies Hitchcock and Sanders were not able to report on the original problem status of the employees in these programs.

The Conference Board study (Weiss 1980) endeavored to avoid the problem of differing definitions of success encountered by Hitchcock and Sanders. Rather than inquire into "successes" and "failures," it asked for specific information concerning the current drinking behavior and current employment statuses of those employees who had been diagnosed as alcoholic. Weiss found that 63 percent of these individuals were reported as abstinent and that 14 percent were still drinking (others had "slipped" occasionally, or their drinking status was unknown). Sixty-two percent were still at the jobs they held prior to treatment and, corroborating the findings from studies of individual programs, 15 percent had been fired (others were in treatment, laid off, transferred, and so on). However, whether program clients were alcoholics was not assessed.

SUMMARY

Neither studies of constructive coercion, evaluations of individual programs, nor comparative analyses of program outcomes have been able to disconfirm the possibility, raised by critics of EAPs and implicit in program literature reviewed here, that, through the medical disease model and its corollary methods of diagnosis and treatment, EAPs may be mislabeling nonalcoholics as alcoholics and thereby exposing employees to disciplinary sanctions. Although it is undoubtedly true that a great many alcoholism programs act in good faith and do in fact deal with alcoholic employees, the troubling fact remains that in the entire literature on occupational alcoholism programming no evidence can be found to validate that these programs' patients are, in actuality, alcoholics. Based on the available data, what can be stated with reasonable assurance is that if 100 employed persons, most of whom have been performing poorly on the job, are labeled alcoholics and put into a "program" of "treatment," about a year later roughly two-thirds of them will have substantially improved their job performance and roughly one in seven will have been fired. Such a conclusion does little to reduce skepticism toward the putatively benevolent goals of these programs. What it does suggest is that the medical disease model of alcoholism may indeed serve as a managerial ideology that facilitates the implementation of programs in which employees are labeled alcoholics, subjected to severe sanctions (in the guise of therapy), and in many cases pronounced recovered from alcoholism, all without a single reference—at any point in the process—to their consumption of alcohol.

7

A National Survey of Alcoholism and Employee Assistance Programs

The Conference Board monograph *Dealing with Alcoholism in the Workplace* (Weiss 1980), written to provide empirically-based prescriptions for organizations operating or developing alcoholism and employee assistance programs, has already been discussed briefly in Chapters 5 and 6. This chapter describes the methodological details of the survey that formed the basis for the Conference Board report. In addition, it reviews the highly varied reactions to this report, primarily as an illustration of the ideological fervor associated with the medical model of alcoholism and its application to occupational programs.

This survey research project had not been designed solely to provide information for practitioners. A coequal purpose was to provide quantitative data to address the theoretical concerns of this book: Weber's and Bendix's hypotheses concerning the relationship of organizational structuring and managerial ideology to management's control of the workplace. For example, data on characteristics of organizational structure were collected both to address Weber's theorizing on bureaucracy and to determine if particular elements of alcoholism programs are differentially related to program effectiveness in differently structured organizations. Similarly, program administrators were asked their views of the etiology of alcohol problems, both to relate such perspectives to program success and to provide a quantitative assessment of what has been argued here is a managerial ideology.

The notion that elements of organizational structure can be identified, operationally defined, and assessed through survey procedures is a commonplace in the field of organizational sociology. After the analyses of Blau (1957) and Udy (1959), discussed in Chapter 2, this idea became what was perhaps the core methodological assumption underlying the mainstream of organizational research in the 1960s and 1970s. The assessment of ideology from survey responses, however, is a much less established procedure. In fact, in *Work and Authority in Industry* Bendix stated:

> By "ideologies" I do not refer to attitudes of the type that can be elicited in a questionnaire study, but to the "constant process of formulation and reformulation by which spokesmen identified with a social group seek to articulate what they sense to be its shared understandings" (1956, p. 443).

The qualitative analysis of managerial ideology presented in previous chapters has attempted to demonstrate the existence of various highly salient "shared understandings" among many individuals involved in operating EAPs. The strength of individuals' advocacy of the disease ideology, however, presumably varies. The quantitative assessments of individual expressions of ideologies were therefore intended to complement the qualitative analyses by capturing some of that variability and assessing its relationship to structures and processes of social control in organizations.*

RESEARCH DESIGN AND SAMPLING

As a visiting fellow conducting research in-house at the Conference Board, the methodological strategies employed by this author to conduct the survey were dictated primarily by the practices of that organization. Data for Conference Board studies generally have been gathered through surveys mailed to a few hundred companies whose names are drawn from the Conference Board's computerized data base of approximately 11,000 private sector firms in the United States. This data base is organized such that researchers may choose to stratify their sample by characteristics such as organizational size or total assets, or according to the range of Standard Industrial Classifications (SICs) to be included. A systematic sample is then drawn by choosing a skip rate that will yield the desired final sample size.

The present study's sample was drawn from this data base. However, because of concerns that relatively few of the sampled corporations might have alcoholism programs on which to report, the sample taken for this study was substantially larger than for other Conference Board projects. Because of the types of organizations to which the Conference Board's

---

*I have discussed this study's use of questionnaire data to assess managerial ideologies with Professor Bendix. He stated that he had always viewed his historical, qualitative work as essentially hypothesis-generating, and has often wondered why it has not been followed by research using other techniques. He raised no objection to the survey research approach taken in this study.

services traditionally have been directed, organizations falling in the health, legal, and educational services SICs were omitted (as well as those firms of undetermined SIC). Otherwise, all firms known to have more than 1,000 employees were drawn; this listing included 2,927 companies. Because all major domestic firms are included in the Conference Board data base, this listing comprised a census rather than a sample of firms with these specified characteristics (that is, every element of the population was included). Using the same SIC categories, firms having between 500 and 1,000 employees were studied as well. However, as a compromise to the costs of survey research, a systematic sample of half of these firms (a lower proportion of which were expected to have alcoholism programs) was drawn. In total, 3,586 questionnaires were mailed.

The mailing of these questionnaires was preceded by three distinct stages in the research process. First, the author conducted lengthy, in-person, open-ended interviews with a wide variety of individuals involved in occupational alcoholism and employee assistance programming. Among those interviewed were the executive director of ALMACA, the director of labor-management services of the NCA, the director of community services for the AFL-CIO, corporate-level personnel executives, international-level union community service executives, and administrators of occupational programs and of alcoholism treatment facilities.

On the basis of these interviews and a review of the extant literature on occupational programming, a draft questionnaire was developed for pretesting. This instrument was field tested in interviews with a dozen corporate personnel executives and program administrators in the metropolitan New York area. Averaging 90 minutes, the purpose of these interviews was to obtain responses to each of the survey questions, with interviewees explaining their reactions to items that they had found to be unclear, that asked for inappropriate information, or that missed important considerations. Finally, after incorporating suggestions made in these sessions, a pilot survey was mailed to 32 large corporations. Responses, often including extensive commentary in addition to answers to the specific questions asked, were received from 28 of the 32 firms, and led to further refinement of the questionnaire.

The survey that emerged from this process consisted of two instruments. They were enclosed in one mailing to the corporations' senior personnel executives, who were asked to personally check off responses to eight opinion-type items on the first questionnaire, whether or not the company had an occupational program. If the company did have a program, the executives were requested to fill out six additional, somewhat more specific items on that questionnaire, and to forward the second, highly detailed questionnaire to the individual who administered the program.

The choice of personnel functionaries as the initial respondents was based on previous research on occupational programming. As discussed in Chapter 5, the Opinion Research Corporation's reports of marginal frequencies from their Executive Caravan Survey (1972, 1974, 1976, 1979), indicate that personnel functionaries responded "don't know" to questions about their companies' alcoholism programs far less frequently than did survey respondents from other functional areas. Other research, reviewed along with ORC's in that chapter, noted that alcoholism and employee assistance programs were very likely either to be located in personnel departments, or to have a reporting relationship to personnel. Thus, on the basis of what they should know, given their frequent position of administrative responsibility for the alcoholism program, and on the basis of what they apparently do know, given the ORC findings, personnel executives were judged to be the most appropriate targets for a survey to examine these programs.

The Conference Board data base contained the names of key executives for many companies, so that specific respondents could be targeted. Because research has suggested that personalized queries will increase response rates (see Linsky 1975; Kanuk and Berenson 1975), personalized cover letters were used. After one follow-up to the original mailing, 1,347 companies had responded to the survey. Of the corporations responding, 346 stated that they did have at least one functioning occupational program and provided at least some of the requested information on its operation. This overall response rate of 38 percent was roughly 6 percentage points higher than the average for Conference Board surveys, which generally have been highly respected and influential. For example, the previous Conference Board study on alcoholism programs in industry (Habbe 1969), frequently cited approvingly by those in the occupational alcoholism field, received responses from 30 percent of the 520 companies to which surveys were mailed.

Nevertheless, those unfamiliar with survey research at the comparative organizational level of analysis may question the appropriateness of generalizing from findings based on a survey with a 38 percent response rate. Clearly, the representativeness of the 1,347 responding companies for the total population of large U.S. corporations is not determinable. Some SIC categories were more likely than others to respond, but the appropriate interpretation of that seeming bias cannot be determined. A basic dilemma in large sample, cross-sectional organizational research is that there is no widely accepted set of categories of organizations to guide sampling procedures (see McKelvey 1982). Similarly, in the absence of an accurate census of just how many corporations do have programs, the percentage of them that have been included in the study, and thus the representativeness of the 346 responding programs for the universe of occupational programs, is unknown.

However, correspondence and telephone conversations with executives at a number of the sampled companies strongly suggest a response bias of particular relevance to this study, specifically, that executives in many companies without programs chose not to complete the survey. That is, although the personnel executives were clearly asked to check off the first few questionnaire items (concerning their general views on alcohol problems, and taking about five minutes to complete) whether or not their companies had programs, many of those in companies with no program declined to answer any of the items. In a number of cases, personnel executives in companies with no program replied with fairly lengthy personal letters apologetically explaining that they could not respond to the survey because they had no program on which to report (a courtesy that must have taken more effort than filling in the requested checkmarks). Thus, although only 38 percent of the large domestic corporations sampled here responded, nonresponse appears to have been partly attributable to misreading the questionnaire's instructions rather than to indifference. Consequently, the 346 corporations that did describe their programs actually might represent substantially more than 38 percent of the true population of large corporations having occupational alcoholism and employee assistance programs.*

The uncertain representativeness of the responses analyzed here, as serious a problem as it may be, has been virtually the rule in comparative organizational research that has attempted to elicit participation from a large number of independent, private sector organizations. Perhaps because of this problem, much of the research that has compared sets of organizations has been conducted on samples of government agencies (e.g., Beyer and Trice 1979; Blau and Schoenherr 1971; Meyer 1972). In studying these organizations, access to research subjects and at least minimal cooperation from all operational facilities is virtually assured once approval is granted by the central headquarters. Not surprisingly, such research has been relatively successful at achieving high response rates.

In contrast, some of the difficulties involved in studying private sector organizations are illustrated in the presentation of the sampling procedures for the well-known study of organizational structure and operations technology conducted by Blau and his associates. They stated that

---

*Journalistic accounts of the growth of alcoholism and employee assistance programs frequently assert that the number of programs is in the thousands. The difference between those numerations and the present one is probably accounted for by two factors: their inclusion of public sector programs and their counting of programs rather than of corporations that have programs. That is, General Motors is counted once in the present analysis, but the programs at each of their many facilities may have been counted independently by others. Nevertheless, the assertions concerning the vast number of programs appear merely to be guesses.

they attempted to collect data from "a random sample of 331 New Jersey manufacturing establishments employing 200 or more persons," but that only "one-third of the plants in the original random sample agreed to participate in the study." They explained that "New Jersey was selected as the location of the study because its wide variety of manufacturing firms are representative of American industry as a whole. All the two-digit Standard Industrial Classification codes, for example, are found in this state" (Blau et al. 1976, pp. 21–22). Apparently, this major research study, conducted by a team led by the founder of the contemporary comparative organizational research paradigm, was based on responses from a sample of organizations in which two-thirds of the sampled firms refused co-operation. The authors' assertion that a sampling frame consisting of New Jersey manufacturing companies provides a basis for representativeness to all such establishments in the United States is also unsupported, other than by their observation that all two-digit SIC codes are found in the state (although not necessarily in their sample).

Clearly, studies that attempt to bridge various nominal categories of organizations (e.g., banks, department stores, manufacturing facilities) present greater sampling problems than do studies of a large multistore or multiplant company, or a multiinstallation government agency, for which access could be gained simply by approval from a headquarters or home office. However, data from what Kimberly (1976) has referred to as "intertypical" samples of organizations (that is, samples that include many types of organizations, as opposed to "intratypical" samples of one nominal category of organization) are necessary for the examination of variability attributable to differences among organizational forms.

Of course, the practical issues of effort and expense also serve as limiting conditions on the scientific precision of comparative organizational research. For example, the choice of Blau et al. of New Jersey as a site for their sample selection may be surmised to have been at least partly related to New Jersey's proximity to Columbia University, where Blau and his associates were located. Reviewing the methodologies of the research in this field, it is apparent that, as Beyer and Trice (1979) have observed, virtually all such organizational studies has been based on samples that have in common these substantial imperfections.

The sampling problems that have been described here are not, however, restricted to research at the comparative organizational level. Investigations of individual and group-level phenomena in organizations would seem to be less difficult to conduct rigorously. For example, eliciting responses to questionnaires from a fairly large sample of individuals might involve gaining access to only one or two organizations, necessitating far fewer resources. Nevertheless, some of the problems in the present sample are apparently the norm for microlevel organizational behavior research as well. Mitchell (1985) analyzed the sampling procedures of all correlational studies published in the three leading journals for organizational behavior research (*Journal of Applied Psychology, Organizational Behavior and Human Performance*, and *Academy of Management Journal*) for the period from 1979 through 1983. He found that, of these 126 studies, 105 employed convenience samples (as opposed to random, cluster, or stratified samples), only 11 of them compared respondents to nonrespondents, and 67 did not report a response rate. Mitchell noted that the failure to report a response rate occurs primarily when questionnaires are administered personally: "The researchers in most cases simply call their sample (those who show up) their population, and the concept of sampling loses its meaning altogether" (1985, p. 201).

Despite organizational researchers' difficulties in obtaining representative samples, there are reasons to conclude that not all social and behavioral science investigations of organizations are entirely invalid. One such reason is that sampling bias should do most harm in its effects on the accuracy of descriptive statistics. Clearly, analyses that have been reported in the organizational studies literature should not be used, for example, to determine the level of formalization in the general population of bureaucratic structures and, indeed, such conclusions are not drawn among the articles that comprise the mainstream of the comparative research literature. Relational statistics, however, are less obviously affected by nonrepresentative samples, with one of the most common problems being an underestimate of relationships due to restricted variability in the variables being correlated (Cohen and Cohen 1983). In research at the macroorganizational level, the fact that, across samples, consistent relationships among some elements of bureaucratic structure are obtained is an indication of external validity.

Although the sample of organizations to be reported on in the present study shares many of the problems of the mainstream of quantitative research on organizations, it has some advantages over other studies. One is that the survey's population constituted a census, rather than a sample, for the companies with more than 1,000 employees, allowing for the possible inclusion of all large U.S. corporations having programs. A related advantage is that the 346 responding corporations that have programs provide not only the broadest data set of any study of employee alcoholism and employee assistance programs, but the largest data set of any intertypical sample in the literature of comparative organizational theory.

Beyond any specific comparisons of this to other quantitative studies of organizational phenomena, it is clear that the methodological deficiencies adumbrated above, typical of such investigations, should not inspire unqualified confidence in the reliability or generalizability of findings based on statistically oriented research. Recognizing that quantitative methods, or any other modes of social scientific inquiry, are necessarily limited in the extent to which they can capture the essence of social phenomena, this study does not depend solely on the statistical relationships to be presented here. Rather, the quantitative data are intended to support, and are supported by, the theoretical analyses and qualitative descriptions of earlier chapters.

THE QUESTIONNAIRES

Personnel Executives' Opinions and Intentions

The first of the two survey instruments was to be answered by each corporation's senior personnel executive. These executives were first asked how serious a problem they believed alcoholism or problem drinking to be in their companies, on an eight-point scale ranging from 1 = "very serious problem" to 8 = "not a problem at all." Next, they were asked to indicate their beliefs regarding the percentage of their companies' employees whose work performance was frequently impaired as a result of alcohol abuse, on a scale with seven anchored categories ranging from 1 = "none at all" to 7 = "13% or more." Respondents were then asked to express their level of agreement with each of a list of eight possible reasons for the development of alcoholism or problem drinking, on six-point scales with 1 = "strongly disagree" and 6 = "strongly agree." Similarly, they were asked their opinion of the effectiveness of eight possible means of dealing with alcoholics or problem drinkers, on a six-point scale ranging from 1 = "highly counterproductive" to 6 = "very effective."

Following these general questions about alcohol problems, the personnel executives were asked if their company had an alcoholism or employee assistance program in operation. Those whose companies did not have a program were thanked for their cooperation and asked to return the questionnaire. The executives from companies with programs were asked to answer additional questions. The first of these listed seven possible reasons for their organization having started an alcoholism or employee assistance program; the reasons were derived from a literature review, the interviews that had been conducted, and responses to the pretest and pilot questionnaires. Respondents were asked to rate each of the reasons on a four-point scale scored 1 = "very unimportant" to 4 = "very important." As part of the previous chapter's discussion of research on expressed reasons for program implementation, Table 6.1 listed these responses' means and standard deviations, and Table 6.2 ranked the items checked as the two most and two least important of the seven. The correlations among the seven scaled items are shown in Table 7.1.

The executive respondents also were asked their subjective impressions of the programs' outcomes. Their overall evaluation of the program was assessed by an item that read, "In considering your company's overall goals in establishing an alcoholism program, how successful do you

TABLE 7.1. Correlations among Personnel Executives' Reasons for Program Implementation

	1	2	3	4	5	6	7
1. Recognition of alcoholism as a medical problem affecting employee well-being		.01 (158)	.18** (157)	-.09 (158)	.01 (156)	.08 (157)	.01 (154)
2. Concern over poor job performance			.05 (156)	.13* (158)	.22*** (155)	.17** (156)	.07 (153)
3. Assumption of an increased social responsibility				-.03 (157)	-.05 (155)	-.02 (156)	.01 (153)
4. Visible cases brought problem drinking to company's attention					.16** (156)	.22*** (157)	.10 (154)
5. Concern over high absenteeism						.25*** (155)	.32*** (154)
6. Efforts of an employee who had personal contact with the problem							.07 (153)
7. Concern over high turnover							

*$p \leq .10$
**$p \leq .05$
***$p \leq .01$
Note: Number of cases on which each calculation is based is shown in parentheses.

consider the effort to be?" Responses were scored from 1 = "extremely unsuccessful" to 8 = "extremely successful." Additionally, subjective evaluations were assessed for a variety of specific program outcomes, such as whether the program had resulted in lower employee absenteeism, improved employee productivity, or improved community relations. These were scored on 5-point scales with values ranging from 1 = "detracted greatly from a favorable evaluation" to 5 = "contributed greatly to a favorable evaluation of the program."

Response to the second questionnaire, designed to be sent to the administrator of the company's program, provided data on program structure, objective measures of program outcomes, the organizational structure of the responding company, and the "ideology of alcoholism" held by the administrator. The measurement of these variables is described below.

Program Structures and Outcomes

Information on program structure was obtained by having survey respondents check off from a list those features that were included in their program. A number of the characteristics on the list were especially pertinent to the dissemination of information about how the program operates. These included the existence of a written program policy statement, the existence of written procedures, and the distribution of each of these documents to only managers and supervisors, or to all employees. In addition, respondents checked off which groups of employees, such as the medical department staff, union stewards, top management, or all employees, received formal training in the operation of the program.

Information on objectively measured program outcomes was more difficult to obtain, as the review in Chapter 6, indicating a dearth of outcome data on these programs, suggests would have been the case. One reason for this difficulty is the inconsistency of recordkeeping from one program to another, as there are no widely agreed-upon sets of standards for what information should be kept. Another reason for the scarcity of outcome data, in any form, is that program administrators often resist this sort of accounting work, expressing concern that written records of program participation might risk client confidentiality. A number of administrators also have admitted that paperwork is neither their personal strength nor what they feel they were hired to do. It became apparent from interviews that this disinclination to keep records frequently is supported by the senior corporate personnel executives, a number of whom stated that if even one valuable manager's job performance had been saved by the program it was worthwhile and needed no further documentation to demonstrate its usefulness.

Nevertheless, the Conference Board survey requested various types of information (in aggregate form) about program clients, such as how many employees had been diagnosed as alcoholics and how many had been sent to residential treatment facilities, in the hope that respondents would be able to provide some, if not all, of these data. From this information, outcome measures have been constructed. For example, because abstinence is the most frequent therapeutic goal in treatment for alcoholism, the proportion of program clients diagnosed as alcoholic who are now abstinent would seem to be one appropriate operational measure of program effectiveness. Therefore, the survey reported here calculated an abstention rate by dividing the number of clients listed as currently abstinent by the total number of clients diagnosed as alcoholic. However, as discussed earlier, many alcoholism and employee assistance programs maintain the policy that an individual's drinking behavior is only the company's business to the extent that it affects the employee's job performance. It would be consistent with this policy to keep records not of drinking behavior, but of work performance. Moreover, because these job performance-oriented programs generally make clear that an individual's failure in the program—that is, his or her failure to improve deficient job performance—will result in job loss, an appropriate indication of a program's success, from this perspective, might be the proportion of program clients who have been fired from their jobs. In fact, as indicated in the previous chapter's review of evaluation studies, the proportion of program clients losing their jobs is one of the most frequently assessed measures in this literature. In the present study, respondents were asked how many program clients diagnosed as alcoholics had been terminated from their jobs; this number has been divided by the total number of program clients diagnosed as alcoholic to yield the termination rate.

Unfortunately, neither this termination rate nor the abstention rate has an unequivocal relationship to the concerns of the present study. Analyses using these rates as dependent measures in the Conference Board report allowed for conclusions of use to practitioners who might wish to know what particular program features are most likely to minimize termination rates and maximize abstention rates. However, these measures are less useful for addressing this study's concern with Weber's propositions concerning ideology, structure, and social control. A high termination rate, for example, may be indicative of managerial control being exercised through the removal of intransigent deviants and the consequent warning to others of the consequences of deviance. But a high termination rate might also be indicative of programs that fail to bring employees' deviant behavior back into line, so that program clients are fired essentially as a last resort. The problem in interpreting the abstention rate—given the lack of evidence that clients in these programs are in fact alcoholics—is that it may be measuring the control of drinking by at least some clients who had never lost control of it. Additionally, the data collected on abstention rates appear to be in part artifactual, tapping merely the existence of records on client alcohol consumption. That is, a low abstention rate may indicate only that the company's records of client outcomes were incomplete or nonexistent.

This study, consequently, will make use of a different outcome measure. As discussed in Chapter 5, Shain and Groeneveld (1980) assessed programs' success on the basis of their penetration rate, that is, the proportion of the organization's employees who enter the alcoholism program each year. Clearly, this usage disregards the question of whether program clients are "treated" successfully after being identified. Although clients referred into alcoholism treatment from occupational programs are alleged to have favorable treatment outcomes, even the NIAAA (1981), reporting to Congress on its activities, admitted that an average of 30 percent of program clients fail to rehabilitate.*

From the perspective of the company, rather than the employee, the penetration rate may well be an outcome of great interest. If it is true that these programs are sometimes used to enhance management's control of the workplace, then a key to company "success" may be the uncovering of a large number of deviants, who are put under surveillance and threatened with job loss. Therefore, one measure of program effectiveness analyzed in the present study will be the penetration rate, calculated as the number of employees entering the program with a diagnosis of alcoholism each year divided by the total number of employees.

Because of their use of the job performance approach to diagnosis, virtually all programs, whether they are "broad-brush" employee assistance programs or closely focused on alcoholism, find themselves with at least a few referrals who they acknowledge may be performing poorly for some reason other than alcoholism. As shown in Chapter 6, many organizations attempt to impute the same characteristics, and thus to justify the same "therapeutic" approach, to these other diagnoses. The consequence is that employees diagnosed as having "psychological problems" may be subjected to essentially the same surveillance and performance monitoring that accompanies being labeled an alcoholic. To examine the social control potential of diagnoses other than alcoholism, the present study will also report on the penetration rates for employees diagnosed with other "behavioral-medical" problems.

Two final objectively derived dependent measures will be employed in these analyses, self-referral and supervisory referral rates. The rates of these categories of referrals, which were found in a number of studies reviewed in Chapter 5 to be the two most frequent paths by which employees enter EAPs, are relevant to this study's focus on ideology and study follows these operational definitions.

---

*Oddly, however, they then stated that virtually nothing is known about the consequences of program participation for that sizeable group; from various studies reviewed in the previous chapter it is clear that what happens to about half of these unsuccessful patients is that they are fired.

control because of the necessity (as noted in the discussion of penetration rates) to first identify those employees whose behavior the organization wishes to control. A high rate of referrals from supervisors would suggest that they had concluded that making referrals to the program was in their interests. Similarly, high self-referrals would suggest that employees considered it in their interests to enter the program voluntarily. Of course, it is expected that the situations in which supervisors and employees regarded the programs as in their interests would often differ; in particular, a low self-referral rate would be expected when the programs were seen by the general employee population as oriented toward controlling deviant behavior rather than rehabilitating victims of an illness.

Organizational Structure

A number of items included in the Conference Board survey were adapted from studies designed to examine whether the elements of bureaucratic structure described by Weber covary and whether they lead to effectiveness. Although it has been argued here that such an emphasis misrepresents Weber's focus, this research tradition has succeeded in extracting and operationalizing variables from Weber's writings. Although the precise number of bureaucratic elements and their precise labels differ somewhat from author to author, most concur that bureaucratic organizations tend to be large, to be characterized by formal rules and procedural standards, to locate authority at or near the top of a hierarchy of command, and to have many departments, levels, and areas of specialization. A number of writers have labeled these concepts as size, formalization, centralization, and complexity, respectively.

Weber wrote that the conduct of bureaucratic administrative enterprises is associated with large size, and in the work of Blau and Schoenherr (1971), as well as Blau's student Meyer (1972), size emerged as the preeminent causal variable in the process of bureaucratization. The researchers known as the "Aston Group," centered around Aston University in Birmingham, England, also based their investigation of organization structure on Weber's writing (Pugh et al. 1963). They, too, concluded that size was a major causal variable in the analysis of organizational structure (Pugh et al. 1968). Although subsequent reanalysis of their data by Aldrich (1972) did call their causal logic into question, data to support the causal priority of size on structure do exist (see Meyer 1972).

In a review of 80 empirical studies concerned with organizational size, Kimberly (1976) found that in 65 of these size was operationalized as the number of an organization's employees. Although Hall (1982) argued that this head count technique correlates highly with other measures of size, such as net assets, Child (1973) pointed out that measures such as the latter create problems for drawing comparisons between, for example, manufacturing and service-oriented organizations. Two empirical studies (Agarwal 1979; Gupta 1980) also did not support Hall's view of the equivalence of size measures.

In the present study, although measures of financial scale were available, size was measured as the number of full-time equivalent employees (for example, two half-time employees equal one "full-time equivalent") on the payroll of the company or the particular company facility whose alcoholism or employee assistance program was being described. This operationalization was considered to be most appropriate for a number of reasons. First, the intertypical sample drawn here included manufacturing and service organizations, raising the interpretive difficulties with alternate measures that Child (1973) had pointed out. More importantly, in hypothesizing that increasing size leads to problems in controlling the behavior of members of the workforce, it is more likely that the problems are attributable to a greater number of employees than to higher net assets or sales volume.

Although the growth in an organization's employee population would be expected to heighten control problems, it should do so at a declining rate. That is, an increase of 100 employees at General Motors would be expected to have less of an impact on social control problems than would an equal increase at a local bank. Consequently, the measure of size was subjected to a logarithmic transformation, in order to provide a better fit for the prediction of a curvilinear relationship between size and control problems. Although the rationale for its use has not focused on its relationship to control problems, the log transformation of size has become virtually a standard procedure in organizational research (see Kimberly 1976).

The concept of complexity emerged from Weber's assessment that the work of his ideal-type bureaucracy is carried out by a variety of offices, each having a "clearly defined sphere of competence" (Weber 1968, p. 220) and staffed by individuals who have acquired specialized knowledge, either through training or experience. Complexity thus denotes a number of related ideas, all of which relate to differentiation.

One aspect of complexity in organizations is structural differentiation among organizational subunits such as divisions or departments. As the number of such units increases, so do problems of control and coordination among them, leading to increases in the number of levels in the administrative hierarchy (Beyer and Trice 1979). The latter of these two forms of complexity is referred to as vertical complexity or vertical differentiation, and has generally been operationalized as the number of levels of hierarchy from the lowest-level worker to the chief executive (Blau and Schoenherr 1971; Pugh et al. 1968). The former is referred to as horizontal complexity or horizontal differentiation, and typically has been operationalized as the number of heads of subunits reporting to the chief executive (Blau and Schoenherr 1971; Pugh et al. 1968). The present

Organizations may be complex not only in terms of differentiation among subunits, but in terms of differentiation among persons as well. Conceptually, person differentiation appears to include two distinct, virtually opposite types. Organizations may minutely subdivide tasks, lessening skill requirements; alternatively, organizations may create complex roles, requiring highly trained and skilled specialists. The first of these techniques has been referred to as division of labor and has been measured as the number of job titles used by the organization (Blau and Schoenherr 1971). The second has been referred to, by Blau and Schoenherr (1971), as personal specialization and has been operationalized as employees' salary and educational levels. Hage and his associates (Dewar and Hage 1978; Hage 1965; Hage and Aiken 1970) have referred to this latter concept simply as complexity and operationalized it as the number of different highly skilled occupational specialties.

Unfortunately, although these two aspects of person complexity may be conceptually distinct, they are not always measured readily. The studies cited above that did measure personal specialization employed intratypical samples. In Blau and Schoenherr's case, the research examined a national sample of units of the same government agency and, in the case of Hage's group, their analysis was of 16 social service agencies in Milwaukee. A measure of personal skill and training that would be comparable across a variety of nominal categories of organizations (e.g., banks, supermarkets, refineries) is not yet available. Consequently, the study reported here did not collect data on personal specialization but will report on organizations' division of labor, which was measured (following Blau et al. 1976) as the number of job titles in use at the responding organization. It should not be assumed, however, that this measure unequivocally permits expression to the level of work "rationalization" or fractionalization in an organization. Although, as Dewar and Hage (1978) pointed out, job titles most typically represent merely a variety of unskilled jobs, it would seem probable that at least some of an increase in the number of titles represents a proliferation of high-skill specialties.

One means by which organizations respond to the control and coordination problems attendant to increased complexity is through the use of written rules and procedures. This process is generally referred to as formalization (Hall 1982; Robbins 1983; Zey-Ferrell 1979) and research on this issue has taken two differing methodological approaches. "Subjective" opinion- or attitude-type measures of formalization (used by Hage and his associates) have attempted to assess the rule-boundedness of organizations by asking samples of employees about their level of agreement with statements such as "Most people here make their own rules on the job," and "People here feel they are constantly being watched to see that they obey all rules." "Objective" measures of formalization have been based on operationalizations such as the number of words in the organization's personnel procedures manual (Blau and Schoenherr 1971).

The objective approach would appear to provide data on the official status of rule formalization in an organization, whereas the subjective method, as illustrated by the two sample items above, appears to be assessing the extent to which rules are actually observed. Consequently, although it is disappointing, it is not entirely surprising that objective and subjective measures of this construct have been found to correlate only weakly (Pennings 1973; Azumi and McMillan 1974).

Because use of the subjective approach entails eliciting responses from a sample of members from each organization, it was not feasible for the present study, which gathered data from a very large sample of organizations. Instead, rule formalization was assessed "objectively," with measures that had been employed by the Aston Group and their replicators (Child 1972a; Hinings and Lee 1971; Inkson, Hickson, and Pugh 1970; and Pugh et al. 1968). Specifically, this study assessed formalization with an abbreviated version of Aston Scale 53.01 (Inkson, Hickson, and Pugh 1970), which asked respondents to indicate whether their organization had written policies, a manual of procedures, and written job descriptions for nonexempt workers, line supervisors, staff, and the head of the organization. In the present study these items were combined additively into a scale on which organizations could score from 0 to 6.

Weber's emphasis on the distribution of authority along hierarchical chains of command in bureaucratic organizations was the primary basis for a great deal of research on a fourth major characteristic of organizational structure, centralization. The dissensus concerning objective versus subjective approaches to measuring formalization extends, as well, to the assessment of this construct, which concerns the extent to which decisions are made at or near the top of an organization. Again, the present study used an objective approach, based on an abbreviated form of Aston Scale 54.10 (Inkson, Hickson, and Pugh 1970). Respondents were asked which of six managerial levels had the practical responsibility for making the following ten decisions: creating a new job, selecting and hiring temporary or part-time personnel, approving overtime, setting the price of the unit's output, approving a change in the physical layout of the work area, deciding what and how many employee services are to be provided, approving a change of day-to-day work procedures, deciding on a new product or service, approving annual vacations, and dismissing an employee. There were six response categories (that is, six managerial levels) for each item, and these were combined additively to form a centralization scale on which respondents' scores could range from 10 to 60.

Descriptive statistics and intercorrelations of the organizational structure variables are presented in Table 7.2, along with reliability scores (Cronbach's alpha) for the scaled items. Size was positively correlated with two measures of differentiation, horizontal complexity and division of labor, and with both formalization and centralization. Its relationship to vertical complexity, however, was not significant. With the exception of the positive correlation between size and centralization, these findings were consistent with those of Blau and Schoenherr (1971) and a number of Aston Group studies (Child 1973; Hinings and Lee 1971; Pugh et al. 1968).

Although the observed association between size and centralization was consistent with that of Hage and Aiken (1970), their result was based on subjective measures and would not have been predicted to be replicated here. The Blau and Aston studies, which had used objective measures, found negative size-centralization correlations—an inconsistency with the present study that may be attributable to two factors: the larger sizes of the organizations in the present sample, and the present sample's inclusion of both service and manufacturing operations. The mean number of employees in the best-known analyses of size and structure has not always specifically been included in the reports of these studies, but in many cases can be extrapolated from the published data: 1,538.7 in Child's national sample (1972a); 3,370 in the original Aston sample (Hickson, Pugh, and Pheysey 1969); and 1,194.7 in Blau and Schoenherr's sample (1971). In the Aston Group's Coventry study (Hinings and Lee 1971), size ranged from 114 to 2,454. For the sample reported on here, the mean number of full-time equivalent employees was 4,917.6. Analyzing only those organizations below this mean, the relationship between size and centralization appears comparable to these earlier studies, as it reverses and becomes negative ($r = -.25$). Additionally, results from data collected for this study appear to approximate earlier findings when the subsample of manufacturing organizations is examined separately. In the national study (Child 1972a), an analysis of size and centralization for the manufacturing subsample strengthened the negative association between these two variables, making it closer to that found by the original Aston researchers, whose sample had included only manufacturing firms. Similarly, an analysis of the manufacturing subsample from the present set of data produced a stronger negative correlation between size and centralization ($r = -.33$).

Other structural relationships shown in Table 7.2, such as the positive association between horizontal and vertical complexity and the negative relationship between formalization and centralization, were also consistent with previous research on organizational structure (see Jackson and Morgan 1982). These findings suggest that, although the organizational structure data analyzed here were collected through mailed questionnaires, they should not be dismissed as invalid. This method of data collection presumably introduced more error than would have resulted from on-site interviewing. However, although the relationships among these structural variables tended to be somewhat weaker than in

TABLE 7.2. Means, Standard Deviations, and Correlations among Organization Structure Variables

Organization Structure	1	2	3	4	5	6	7	Mean	Standard Deviation	n	Alpha
1. Size (log)†		.21*** (126)	.08 (197)	.43*** (159)	.15*** (252)	.08 (200)	.11* (164)	7.516	1.349	256	
2. Horizontal differentiation			.26*** (125)	.12 (93)	.00 (144)	.01 (126)	.18** (103)	11.933	8.540	150	
3. Vertical differentiation				.09 (148)	.07 (236)	-.10* (211)	-.06 (164)	6.890	4.378	236	
4. Division of labor					.17** (177)	-.05 (156)	.12* (126)	396.922	764.858	179	
5. Formalization						-.18*** (238)	-.19*** (194)	4.889	1.638	316	.81
6. Supervisor span							.04 (195)	13.849	10.171	238	
7. Centralization								34.240	9.072	196	.83

*p < .10
**p < .05
***p < .01

Note: Number of cases on which each calculation is based is shown in parentheses.

† Prior to log transform mean = 4,917.617, standard deviation = 10,016.238.

earlier research, they are of the same form as has been found in research using techniques that are considered to be less prone to error.

Ideologies of Alcoholism

This study has argued that ideologies arise under conditions in which the pertinent facts are not clearly understood or widely accepted, and debate is therefore possible. Orcutt and his associates (Orcutt 1976; Orcutt, Cairl, and Miller 1980) have investigated the patterning of espoused viewpoints on the development of alcohol problems, referring to them as "ideologies of alcoholism." It has been proposed here that these alcoholism ideologies (and especially the medical disease ideology) may function as managerial ideologies, that is, as sets of ideas used by managements to justify authority in the workplace. They have been operationalized in the present study as the alcoholism program administrators' ratings of the extent to which they believed that each of eight possible factors contribute to the development of alcoholism or problem drinking (this was the same list of items, with the same 6-point scales, as given to the corporate personnel executives).

The eight possible explanations of the etiology of alcohol problems were derived from responses of subjects in the preliminary stages of this research project and from the literature reviewed in Chapter 4. These eight viewpoints are a greater number than has been examined in other empirical analyses of alcoholism ideologies (Orcutt, Cairl, and Miller 1980; Tournier 1985); however, the present study is consistent with these others in assessing each ideology on the basis of one Likert-type item. The means, standard deviations, and intercorrelations of the eight items are shown in Table 7.3.

Two psychological models of alcoholism were represented by assessing agreement with the statements that alcoholism can result from "some problem of childhood development" or from "psychological problems." As shown in the table, the first of these two items, roughly approximating the psychoanalytic view of alcoholism, ranked fifth among the eight items. The second, more general, item was the highest ranking of all eight possible explanations of alcoholism's cause.

Ranked second was the view that alcoholism can result from "family-marital problems." Family therapy is a relatively new mental health semi-profession (see Guerin 1976) that explains alcoholism, predictably, as a "family problem." This possible explanation came up frequently among respondents to the pretest and pilot studies and is a response category that is at the interstice of the psychological and sociological models of alcoholism; it conceives of the problem as an interaction dysfunction in the microsocial environment and as one which is treated by essentially psychotherapeutic procedures.

Receiving a slightly less favorable reaction from the responding

TABLE 7.3. **Means, Standard Deviations, and Correlations among Program Administrators' Views on the Etiology of Alcoholism**

Alcoholism Can Result from:	1	2	3	4	5	6	7	8	Mean	Standard Deviation	n
1. Psychological problems		.48*** (333)	.29*** (334)	.01 (329)	.59*** (334)	.40*** (332)	.29*** (335)	.22*** (331)	4.801	1.067	336
2. Family-marital problems			.44*** (333)	−.17*** (328)	.25*** (331)	.75*** (332)	.44*** (334)	.40*** (330)	4.449	1.415	334
3. Associating with heavy drinkers				−.06 (329)	.15** (332)	.44*** (332)	.31*** (335)	.34*** (330)	4.310	1.418	335
4. Physiologically-based imbalance or dysfunction (or genetic inheritance)					.06 (328)	−.10** (327)	−.03 (330)	−.19*** (325)	4.269	1.482	331
5. Childhood psychological problem						.25*** (330)	.21*** (333)	.17*** (329)	4.105	1.291	334
6. Stressful job							.46*** (334)	.34*** (329)	4.096	1.478	334
7. Boring job								.27*** (331)	3.053	1.513	337
8. Weak character									2.474	1.569	331

*$p < .10$
**$p < .05$
***$p < .01$

Note: Number of cases on which each calculation is based is shown in parentheses.

program administrators was the third-ranked view, that alcoholism can result from "associating with people who drink heavily." This item was included to represent the differential association perspective in the sociology of deviance (Sutherland and Cressey 1960) and also was a factor mentioned by a number of those interviewed.

The medical disease model of alcoholism was represented by the response category stating that alcoholism can result from "a physio-logically-based imbalance or dysfunction (or genetic inheritance)." The appropriateness of this operationalization is suggested by Ward's char-acterization of the traditional disease ideology's definition of alcoholism as "a disease of the body" that is "either due to some inherited pre-disposition or to a changed physiological response" (1985, p. 4). Although this perspective received the fourth highest average rating, its mean score was not significantly different from that of the second-ranking ($t = 1.37$, $p = .172$) or the third-ranking ($t = .26$, $p = .795$) etiological explanations. It was, however, significantly less popular than the first-ranking view, that alcoholism results from "psychological problems."

The extent of agreement with two variants of the sociological model was examined by items that asked whether alcoholism can result from "a stressful job" or from "a boring job." These items ranked sixth and seventh, respectively. Program administrators, on average, responded that they "slightly agree" that job stress is an etiological factor and indicated that they "slightly disagree" that job boredom is a causative agent.

The lowest-ranked possible cause of alcoholism was "weak char-acter," a response category that was intended to assess agreement with the moral model of alcoholism. As discussed in the previous chapter, pro-motional literature for alcoholism and employee assistance programs frequently includes a specific disavowal of the idea that alcoholism is a characterological defect. Because the respondents to this item were the programs' administrators, who are often responsible for writing these brochures, their low ranking of this category was expected. Nevertheless, they did not, as a group, reject this view entirely; its average rating was between "slightly disagree" and "moderately disagree."

The views held by program administrators concerning possible causes of alcoholism appear similar to those indicated by research discussed in Chapter 4 to be held by the general population. Neither in the general population nor in the group of program administrators studied here was the medical model the most likely viewpoint to find acceptance. Rather, it fell into a category, along with family-marital problems and associating with heavy drinkers, that ranked below the most popular view, that alcohol abuse results from psychological problems. However, Tournier has noted "it is important to recognize that the medical model not only remains the standard against which other ideologies are inevi-tably measured, but is also the one most aggressively popularized both to professionals and to the general public" (1985, p. 41). The aggressive defense of the disease model and its corollaries is illustrated in the criticism that met the publication of the Conference Board report.

RESPONSES TO THE CONFERENCE BOARD REPORT

In light of the methodological procedures described here, even with their limitations, the Conference Board study would seem to have provided a source of information on program structures and outcomes that was far superior to the previously available literature. With its large sample and multivariate analyses of a variety of clearly-operationalized independent and dependent measures, this study presumably would have been considered an important source of information. Yet, in 1985, five years after the publication of the Conference Board study, the chairperson of the ALMACA research committee, and director of the Human Services in the Workplace Program at Boston University, stated:

> Despite the heralded acclaim which EAPs have received over the past several years, little substantive research has yet to be conducted to verify the effectiveness of these programs ... [and] a number of critically important research questions await study.
>
> - What types of changes do EAPs bring about?
> - Are EAPs responsible for increased productivity?
> - Why do some EAPs work better than others?
> - What are the most important elements of an EAP?
>
> [These questions] happen to be areas with little data outside of anecdotal reporting and brief reports of programs (Googins 1985, pp. 222–23).

Because the Conference Board data did address a number of these questions, with a statistical rather than an anecdotal approach, it seems odd that Googins appeared not to be aware of its existence. Did it simply get lost among the plethora of such studies issued annually, as is the fate of so much research?

This seems unlikely to have been the case, as evidenced, for example, by the interest shown in it by Googins' predecessor as chair of the ALMACA research committee. Walter Reichman devoted a talk at the National Council on Alcoholism's annual meetings and articles in the National Council's *Labor-Management Alcoholism Journal* (Reichman 1981a) and ALMACA's publication, *The ALMACAN* (Reichman 1981b), entirely to the Conference Board study. Additionally, a prominent member of the ALMACA research committee, writing in *Alcoholism: The National Magazine,* discussed "the recently published Weiss report, produced under the prestigious auspices of the Conference Board," and the "widespread publicity" it had been receiving (Roman 1981). In fact, there was a great deal of interest in this study even before it was released; prior to the report's publication its author delivered the keynote speech to ALMACA's national convention, discussing preliminary findings. The Mid-America ALMACA Chapter devoted two entire issues of its newsletter to a summary of the report, about which it said:

> This is the most extensive study of this type of programming that is currently available to people in this field to examine. The findings are important on several levels. They tell us some things that are quite different from what we have been taught were common practices. Naturally, they tell us some things we already know, which doesn't hurt anything. And finally, they shed some new light on the dynamics of setting up these programs (1980, p. 1).

> People in this field can learn a great deal from this extensive survey. Even if it is somewhat expensive, it will make a valuable addition to your library. (1980, p. 2).

Outside of the alcoholism community, the Conference Board report most certainly attracted far more than the usual share of attention paid to studies of personnel and human resource programs, including interviews with the author on network radio and television, and articles in periodicals as diverse as the *Chicago Tribune* (Kearns 1980), the *American Banker* (Smith 1980), and *Women's Wear Daily* (Feinberg 1983). However, the response to the Conference Board report was by no means uniformly favorable. In a letter to the Board's Canadian office, the national advisor to the Canadian government's EAP wrote, "I would urge you to consider suspending any further distribution of this material" (Corneil 1980). As extreme a response as book banning would presumably have an excellent justification; his was that the study contained

> a sampling bias which significantly distorts the findings. The data ... are drawn from a response of no greater than nine percent.... As a result of the sampling technique, some of the data are directly contradictory with a number of recent studies on EAP. These studies by Drs. Eurfort [sic], Foote, Manello, Roman and Trice are quite comprehensive and conform to normal research etiquettes. For example, the indepth study of Foote and Eurfort on referral sources does not correspond with the [Conference Board's] data (Corneil 1980).*

---

*Unfortunately, this was the only example of a "directly contradictory" finding that Corneil provided. He seems to have found this particular difference more dramatic than it has appeared to me. In Erfurt and Foote's study of 18 companies' programs in Detroit they found 41 percent of referrals coming from supervisors and 32 percent from self-referrals. With data on referrals from 192 companies' programs I found 65 percent supervisory referrals, and 30 percent self-referrals. My letter to Corneil requesting additional examples of directly contradictory findings has gone unanswered.

Corneil explained his reason for writing by implying expertise on matters of data analysis and sampling: "to me this represents an example of haphazard sampling which has questionable scientific merit. Unfortunately, I doubt that the majority of persons reading this report would be aware of this." The basis for his claims that the study had a response rate "of no greater than nine percent" will probably never be known. This writer's letter to Corneil, attempting to clarify what the study's sampling procedures actually had been, and asking for further explanation of his accusations, was not answered. A similar reaction to the Conference Board study came from Mannello, one of the researchers Corneil characterized as having done a "quite comprehensive" study (Mannello 1979). Mannello stated that he was "very disturbed" by the Conference Board report, citing poor sampling and use of inappropriate respondents for the information that the survey was designd to collect. In response to this criticism, Mannello was asked who, rather than personnel executives and program administrators, should be consulted about program structure, but there was no reply other than a lengthy silence over the telephone.

The work of Mannello and two of the other researchers held up as exemplars by Corneil has been discussed earlier in this book. Mannello was coauthor of an analysis of seven railroads' programs that strongly recommended a list of "ideal features," which apparently constituted a summary of the opinions expressed by an undefined sample of respondents. Roman coauthored a study based on a survey of organizations (probably about two dozen, perhaps fewer) conducted by a marketing research firm that specifically refused to disclose the sample's characteristics. Roman interpreted his analyses as supportive of the most frequently advised program features although he found that only three out of ten of these features were associated with even one of the predicted outcomes. Erfurt and Foote had authored a report of frequency listings of features in 18 company's programs and recommended, without any evidence, particular program components as causally related to effectiveness.

The research by Trice to which Corneil most probably was alluding has not been discussed here previously. This large project, generously funded by NIAAA, resulted in a book (Beyer and Trice 1978) that has made a substantial contribution to the literature on organizational change, and an article (Beyer and Trice 1979) that provided an important replication of Blau and Schoenherr's (1971) research on organizational structure, a purpose for which their study had been carefully planned. Its contribution to the understanding of alcoholism and employee assistance programs, however, is much less certain, primarily because the only outcome measured was whether supervisors had referred subordinates to the program (that is, irrespective of the results of that referral for either the employee or the organization).

The studies lauded by Corneil seem to have some common characteristics. In particular, they did not criticize current practices in the operation of alcoholism and employee assistance programs, nor, for that matter, did they collect data that would have allowed them to do so. His letter's complaint that "In the past, the Board has been most supportive of the developments in occupational alcoholism programs" suggests the possibility that the "normal research etiquettes" to which Corneil referred may have consisted of observing the courtesy of not questioning the efficacy of program practices.

Researchers in the alcoholism and employee assistance programming field also participated in the assault on the credibility of the Conference Board report. Reichman's comments on the report began by stating that it "is based on such poor quality research that the findings must be dismissed as invalid and ultimately meaningless" (Reichman 1981a, p. 76; 1981b, p. 5), and he protested that the Conference Board should not have released it "without review by recognized researchers in the field of occupational alcoholism" (Reichman 1981a, p. 76; 1981b, p. 5).* Claiming that he was only highlighting criticisms that, if fully presented, would be as extensive as the entire report, he made a number of accusations. These criticisms are so odd that an uncharitable reader might conclude that they were intended for no other purpose than to attempt to discredit the Conference Board study, which reported findings that were not uniformly supportive of practices in the EAP field.

For example, Reichman accused the study of being deceptive in its claim of analyzing a sample of over 1,000 respondents, noting that "some questions were answered by as few as 43 respondents" (Reichman 1981a, p. 76; 1981b, p. 5). As noted in this chapter, and on page iii of the Conference Board report, more than 1,300 companies reponded to the survey, over 300 of which stated that they had an alcoholism or employee assistance program. The only appearance of the number 43 in the study was as the number of cases in an analysis of one particularly unusual subsample, that of companies that *did* have programs, *did not* report union-management cooperation in their functioning, but *did* report that they engaged in cooperative activities with the union in other areas.

Reichman further accused the study of what he correctly pointed out is an incorrect practice, the reporting of "correlations as if they were indicative of causation." However, neither of the examples he gave from the Conference Board study, as follow, were guilty of that error: "programs with staff members who were chosen on the basis of being recovered alcoholics have higher penetration rates," and "executives who see employees as responsible for seeking help for their drinking problems have programs with lower retention rates."

---

*Reichman presumably was unaware that in the earlier stages of this research, the Conference Board solicited the advice of Paul Roman, Reichman's colleague on the ALMACA research committee. Roman stated that he would get in touch when his schedule permitted, but did not communicate with the Conference Board subsequent to that conversation.

In addition, Reichman accused the study of intentional misrepresentation in presenting a table in which executives' reasons for having started their programs were listed in rank order. He correctly noted that ranks can be a misleading guide to application of research findings because differences in rank order may not be statistically significant. Describing a rank order table in the Conference Board report, he stated that "The first ranked reason differs from the second ranked reason by .28 of a scale unit and from the third ranked reason by .83 of a scale unit. To draw any conclusions of differences in reasons for program establishment would be erroneous" (Reichman 1981a, p. 77-78; 1981b, p. 5). In fact, no such conclusions were drawn in the Conference Board report. Moreover, it is difficult to imagine why a table intended to misrepresent trivial differences as significant would have included those scale differences (indeed, it was precisely to avoid such misinterpretations that they were included).

Reichman also criticized the study for failing to caution readers that generalizing from the nonrepresentative sample of programs was inappropriate. The Conference Board report, however, had made no claims for the representativeness of its sample or the generalizability of the findings beyond the sample. In contrast, Reichman, in his own research, published the same year as his criticisms of the Conference Board report, argued for the representativeness of his sample consisting of just four organizations, because "we had organizations in the public and private sectors and a diversification of occupations" (Reichman et al. 1981, p. 209).

Roman (whose analysis of perhaps two dozen programs from an undisclosed sample was described earlier) characterized the Conference Board study as "fatally flawed" because "Readers are not provided with information as to the nature of the companies which were sampled, nor is information made available about the characteristics of the companies which completed the survey instrument" (Roman 1981, p. 37). That is, he condemned the study not because of specific defects of which he was aware, but rather because the report, written for a lay audience, did not indicate what its sampling methods were. At the same time that he criticized the Conference Board report because its sampling methods had not been reported, Roman also determined, somehow, that the Conference Board report's methods did not include the "adequate sampling from a known population [that is] vital ... in conducting a useful survey" (1981, p. 37). Roman told his readers that fortunately such high-quality data do exist—his own analyses of the Opinion Research Corporation Executive Caravan Surveys—which he claimed did not have the low response rates of the Conference Board study. However, as discussed in Chapter 5, not only would the ORC not disclose many details of its sampling, but what its representative did admit—that they request 15 interviews in each company, but may conduct as few as 7—is certainly not consistent with Roman's boast about the response rates in these data.

To respond to the legitimate curiosity of researchers concerning the methodological details of the Conference Board Report, the present author published a chapter, "The Conference Board Report: How and Why," in the *EAP Research Annual* (Weiss 1984). This chapter attempted to explain both how the study was conducted and the need for the study, in part by reviewing previous research on EAPs and describing the methodological deficiencies in that body of literature. The volume included a final chapter written by Trice (1984), commenting on each of the contributions.

Trice's critique of the chapter on the methods and rationale of the Conference Board report began with the complaint that it should have provided a detailed report of the study's findings because "Without the entire report in front of me at this time ... I can't be too certain of my facts" (p. 145). Instead, Trice argued, the chapter wasted too much time on "rather trivial controversies with other researchers" (p. 144). In particular, Trice was disturbed by the chapter's criticism of what he apparently considered one such trivial issue, that his expensive federally funded research (Beyer and Trice 1978) collected data on no outcome measure other than whether a manager had used the alcoholism policy. He responded that the Conference Board study's only outcome measure was precisely the outcome measure that his study had used. This comment seems difficult to understand in light of the fact that one table after another in the Conference Board report listed program components associated with such outcomes as "Proportion of clients still drinking," "Proportion of clients now abstaining from drinking," "Proportion of clients who return to their original job," and "Proportion of clients terminated from their job." Perhaps the explanation of Trice's misrepresentation lies in his comment that he didn't have the report in front of him as he wrote, and thus couldn't be too certain of his facts.

Trice expressed concern, as well, for the study's sampling procedure, finding it "difficult to believe that The Conference Board has a list of all U.S. corporations with at least one thousand employees" (1984, p. 144). Further, he wrote that "even if the U.S. Department of Commerce made such a claim there would be some reason to doubt it" (1984, p. 144), although he did not elaborate on what that reason might be. To impress upon his readers the perils of drawing any conclusions from a survey having the Conference Board study's 38 percent response rate from its census of large U.S. corporations, Trice explained how it "badly hampers the ability of researchers to represent with their limited responses ... companies in the population who did not fall into the sample. After all, there are almost six silent companies for every three and a half responsive ones" (1984, p. 144). With such an understanding of sampling, one can only imagine Trice's reaction to opinion polls, which typically use samples of about 1,500 individuals to represent the adult population of the United States—after all, there are over 10,000 silent individuals for every responsive one.

The fact that the Conference Board report drew the attention of Reichman, Roman, and Trice was itself noteworthy; these three scholars are the most esteemed researchers in the EAP field and their writing is frequently cited to confirm the perspectives of many practitioners. Just one indication of the regard in which they are held was the announcement, following Trice's summary chapter in the first annual volume of the *EAP Research Annual* (1984), of three awards: to Walter Reichman, for "outstanding leadership and dedication to research"; to Paul Roman, for "preeminent contributions to research"; and to Harrison Trice, for "pioneering accomplishments and encouragement to colleagues."

The Conference Board study, however, has not always been attacked when discussed by scholars in the field; on occasions it has simply been bent toward others' purposes. Trice and Beyer (1984) cited a paper using the Conference Board data as support for their contention that constructive confrontation/coercion is an effective technique for rehabilitating employed alcoholics. However, what the cited paper had said was: "It is, in a sense, an effective technique. Essentially, the findings demonstrate that if employees who have been frequently late or absent are labeled alcoholics and told they'll be fired if they don't shape up, their lateness and absenteeism improve dramatically" (Weiss 1982a, p. 130).

In a book on employee assistance programs, Professor Dale Masi of the University of Maryland, a leading proponent of these programs, offered the following as a direct quote from a corporate policy statement excerpted in the Conference Board report:

> The employees must be made to understand that unless the problem (whatever it is) is corrected and job performance is brought up to standard, they will be subject to existing procedures for unsatisfactory job performance. They will also need assurance that utilization of the program will not jeopardize their job and opportunities for promotion (1984, p. 42).

This policy would sound considerably more harsh and coercive if the word "penalties" was substituted for the word "procedures" in the above quote, and the phrase "utilization of the program" was replaced with "acceptance of treatment." Unfortunately, those changes would be necessary to make it an accurate quote from the Conference Board report. These and other subtle distortions of what are cited as direct quotes from the Conference Board report, along with some parallelisms between Masi's and the Conference Board report's text, cannot be attributed to carelessness. Masi made repeated written requests of this author for permission to use material from the Conference Board report, and on each occasion was told that the discrepancies and parallel language, identified for her, would have to be removed. Regrettably, the changes were not made, and the permission form was not signed.

In the time since the initial attacks on its validity the most common fate of the Conference Board study has not been outright distortion, but merely the fate that it shares with most research publications—it is ignored. Certainly, some writers have cited this study; for example, the figure on the growth of EAPs mentioned in the first paragraph of the "About This Report" section preceding the table of contents was cited in an article by Diane Walsh (1982), one of the authors of NIAAA's *Fifth Report to Congress on Alcohol and Health*. However, she went on to make unsupported assertions about the prevalence of various program features, all of which contradicted information presented in half-page bar graphs inside the Conference Board report itself. Similarly, Iutcovich's doctoral dissertation (1982) on EAPs cited the Conference Board study, but made an unsupported assertion about the impact of federal support for these programs that contradicted an entire chapter of the Conference Board report, which presented data addressing that question.

One possible motive for the largely successful discrediting of the Conference Board study is implied in Roman's comment that the attention paid to it was "especially problematic because of statements in the report ... that union-management cooperation ... has been quite limited ... and that publicly funded demonstration and consultation projects have been relatively ineffective" (1981, p. 38). Had the findings come out otherwise, it seems unlikely that those in the occupational programming field would have suddenly developed an interest in sampling methodology. An example of this interest in research methods was a magazine column by a union EAP director (Stanford 1981) devoted to a discussion of the "now discredited Conference Board Report." The columnist explained the nuances of sampling techniques, repeated Reichman's attacks, and asserted that the data (such as those addressing the association between the presence of a union and outcomes such as the number of clients sent to a particular type of treatment) should have been collected from union officials.

Of course, the Conference Board study was not the first research to find data that suggest conclusions contrary to popular practice in the alcoholism and employee assistance programming field. The efficacy of practices engaged in by programs that are based on the disease model of alcoholism, especially the job performance criteria for diagnosing the disease and the constructive coercion approach to rehabilitating its victims, simply have not been supported by data from systematic investigations. Although typically not mentioned by those who have found such evidence, disconfirming findings include not only some in the Conference Board study, but Trice's finding that denial is not characteristic of alcoholic employees, and Roman's that very few of the generally recommended program features predict effectiveness.

As this book has noted, a major factor in the success of an ideology is the continuing absence of clearly disconfirming evidence. It would appear that the medical disease model of alcoholism, an ideology that has come to support what Trice and Roman (1978) have referred to as the "alcoholism industry," along with its operational corollaries, is protected from attempts to examine questions whose answers have the potential to undermine these programs' legitimacy. Thus the Conference Board study, criticized by "experienced researchers in the field" (Roman 1980) "from many very respectable quarters" (Trice 1984), has been subjected to the zealous protestations characteristic of those defending a faith ... or, an ideology.

8

Ideology, Bureaucracy, and
Social Control

This chapter offers quantitative analyses intended to test Weber's and Bendix's hypotheses regarding the uses of both ideology and elements of bureaucracy for purposes of social control. More specifically, the analyses examine how the medical disease ideology of alcoholism as well as various components of organizational structure are used to facilitate managements' control of the workplace. Intended not to supersede, but to complement, the qualitative analyses presented in previous chapters, they provide what Denzin (1978) has called a "between class triangulation" on this study's central problem, the means by which control is exercised over those who might deviate from managements' norms.

The hypotheses to be tested here were derived from classical analyses of social domination, which, as discussed earlier, contend that the modern form of bureaucracy arose in response to the difficulties encountered by political states in controlling increasing populations engaged in increasingly differentiated activities. Although Hegel had hailed these new mechanisms as the means by which the will of the populace would be served, Marx argued that the bureaucracy was an instrument of class domination, and that Hegel's analysis was little more than propaganda for the state. Weber, although concurring with Marx that bureaucracy was a mechanism of social control, maintained that it could be used not only for the domination of one economic class over another, but for a wide variety of systems of domination. Most significantly, Weber combined Marx's analysis with a Hegelian idealist viewpoint, theorizing that in addition to an administrative structure such as bureaucracy, the other crucial element in the general process of domination is a legitimating ideology. Bendix contributed to the development of this line of theorizing by suggesting that some characteristics of bureaucracy, rather than facilitating domination, may cause control problems. Specifically, he wrote that in the modern industrial era the large size and complexity of

178

enterprises have created control problems that make managerial ideologies increasingly necessary.

The quantitative analyses presented here address these issues by examining whether size and differentiation cause problems for managerial control of the workforce, and whether such problems are managed by means of bureaucratic and ideological mechanisms. More particularly, if, as Bendix hypothesized, size and differentiation cause difficulties for managerial control, and if EAPs are being used to facilitate such control, executives in large and in highly differentiated firms would be expected to rate concern over poor job performance as having been a more important motive for starting their EAPs than would executives of smaller, less complex firms. If, as Weber suggested, bureaucratic structuring is a means by which organizations attempt to cope with this problem, expressions of concern about employee work performance should also be associated with the use of bureaucratic control mechanisms such as written rules and centralized authority.

These analyses will also address the question of whether the medical disease view of alcoholism constitutes a managerial ideology, arguing that if it does serve as a mechanism of social control, a wide range of statistical associations would be expected. First, companies whose senior personnel executives reported that their alcoholism programs were started because of concern over poor job performance should have program administrators who subscribe to the disease perspective. Further, the usefulness of the disease ideology for social control purposes would be indicated by correlations—in companies whose programs were started because of concern about poor job performance—between the administrator's advocacy of the medical disease model and program structures conducive to control, such as training sessions to indoctrinate managers with the disease ideology. Finally, in organizations concerned about poor performance, both having an administrator who believes in the disease model and program components associated with that model should be associated with more employees being remanded into the program, and with favorable perceptions of the program's success.

DATA ANALYSIS

A rigorous statistical analysis of the beliefs, structures and outcomes measured in this study must contend with a number of problems. Foremost among these is the large proportion of cases with missing data. As noted earlier, the decision to inquire into a wide variety of objective program outcomes, with the expectation that any one company would maintain records for only a subset of them, virtually guaranteed this problem. Nevertheless, because one of the survey's purposes was to provide descriptive statistics for practitioners, this decision was an unfortunate necessity. The consequence is that analyses using multiple regression-based techniques, which necessitate listwise deletion of missing cases, suffer dramatic losses of sample size.

A problem for data analysis that is of more relevance for the theoretical concerns of this study is the simple fact that the correlations among the variables are, for the most part, very low. Thus, even with a willingness to accept the lower stability of a relationship based on a greatly reduced number of cases, statistically significant associations would be relatively difficult to detect. Moreover, because of these low inter-item correlations and the large number of missing values, attempts to use clustering techniques to reduce the dimensionality of the data were unsuccessful. In particular, canonical correlation analyses, seemingly appropriate for examining the relationships, for example, of sets of ideology measures with sets of outcome measures, failed to produce statistically significant relationships between canonical variates.

On the basis of these problems it might be concluded that the data (or perhaps the hypotheses they address) simply are not very good. Nevertheless, some evidence for the validity of the survey data was provided by the findings, reported in Chapter 7, indicating that the correlations obtained among various elements of organizational structure replicated those found in other studies, especially when data for subsets of organizations similar to those previously studied were analyzed separately. Moreover, the weak correlations to be reported in this chapter's tests of hypotheses regarding the use of the disease model of alcoholism for social control are entirely consistent with expectations. That is, weak correlations would be expected, in part, because it would not be intuitively obvious to all corporate executives who want their employees to work harder that they can achieve that end by starting an alcoholism program based on the philosophy that alcoholics are blameless victims of a disease. It seems reasonable to hypothesize that this peculiarly complex and nonobvious perspective would have been diffused to (or independently intuited by) only enough corporate personnel executives for a modest, perhaps mildly significant, pattern of findings to be obtained.

A more general basis on which weak statistical associations might be expected is that many of the relationships of interest in this study are, in essence, between behaviors and attitude-type measures. The typical inability to detect substantial correspondences between measures of behavior and measures of beliefs, opinions, and attitudes has been a major preoccupation of social psychologists for more than four decades. Just as a variety of factors intervene to attenuate the association between expressed belief in a deity and actual attendance at a church service, intervening factors probably reduce the association between a certain view of the nature of alcohol problems and the institution of a particular training procedure in a particular company's program. In many cases, correspondences between behaviors and affective or cognitive responses can be strengthened by assessing more specific rather than general views (Davidson and Jaccard 1979). For example, the expressed belief that one will attend church services would predict attendance at church services more successfully than would a general question about spirituality. For the present study, however, it is not a specific belief or opinion but a general set of politically relevant beliefs—that is, an ideology—that is of concern. Consequently, weak correlations, although unfortunate, are at least consistent with other studies facing similar dilemmas.

The point of these prefatory comments is not to argue that the low magnitudes of the relationships to be presented are of little consequence, but rather, to direct attention to the types of findings that are expected to provide support for the arguments advanced in this book. The findings will be presented primarily in the form of bivariate correlation matrices, such as the correlations between companies' reasons for program implementation and administrators' beliefs about the etiology of alcoholism. Although these analyses are very simple, they do provide the opportunity to overcome what Mitchell (1985) has identified as two of the most significant methodological deficiencies in contemporary organizational research: the inattention to effects of common method variance and to the establishment of convergent and discriminant validity. For example, the correlations can show whether the program administrator's espousal of the disease model correlates with the personnel executive's indication that concern over poor productivity was the company's reason for starting the program. In addition, they allow the assessment of whether that reason for starting a program is correlated with any other beliefs about the etiology of alcoholism held by the program administrator, and whether the administrator's espousal of the medical disease etiological perspective is correlated with any other reason for program implementation.

SIZE, BUREAUCRACY, AND CONTROL PROBLEMS

The consistent associations between organizational size and various aspects of bureaucratic structure are widely acknowledged, even by those who have otherwise concluded that the empirical prediction of organizational design from objective factors is essentially futile (for example, Nystrom and Starbuck 1984). However, the preferred interpretation of these empirical correspondences is a matter of some dissensus, and the positions taken have closely resembled those of Hegel and Marx. The mainstream view is directly descended from that of Parsons' interpretation of Weber's writing on bureaucracy, an interpretation that has been argued in this book to have little to do with Weber's actual position, but to represent Hegel's perspective fairly well. From this viewpoint elements of bureaucratic structure are seen as functioning to maintain organizational efficiency by facilitating the increasing coordination necessitated by larger scale and increasing complexity. This focus on coordination requirements as the underlying dynamic of organizational structure is a central theme in the work of Merton's former student Blau (1970), and has found its way into other mainstream organization structure research as well. For example, Beyer and Trice, discussing their finding of a positive correlation between formalization and division of labor, stated "apparently, greater codification of rules facilitated task specialization, probably because the existence of rules ensured some coordination" (1979, p. 54).

Whereas the term coordination is congenial with a functionalist framework, which emphasizes the systemic interrelationships among societal elements, it directs attention away from the potential conflict between coordinators and coordinated that would be of particular interest to Marxian and other conflict theorists, who might reconceptualize the neutrally-toned "coordination" as "control" or "domination." This rephrasing suggests the alternative, Marxian interpretations of the associations among size and aspects of structure that have been offered by Goldman (a former student of Blau) and Van Houten (1977). Actually, they seem to have been unaware of Marx's analysis of bureaucracy, described in Chapter 2 of this book as having been written in response to Hegel's panegyric on the administrative apparatus of the Prussian state; however, their own analysis is a remarkable recapitulation of Marx's, written more than 140 years ago. Goldman and Van Houten argued that division of labor serves to weaken the power of workers both by reducing their knowledge of the work process and by making them readily replaceable. Similarly, they argued that proliferating levels of organizational hierarchy serve to reduce workers' overall comprehension of organizational processes and isolate them from one another by promoting an illusion of the possibility of individual rather than collective mobility. Further, they viewed rules and regulations as necessary for accomplishing organizations' goals only because of the recalcitrance of workers under capitalist social relations of production. The qualitative studies they offered in support of their position made their explanation of organizational structure as appealing, logically, as Blau's. Yet, the testable hypotheses that would seem deducible from Goldman and Van Houten's and Blau's perspectives, such as a prediction of a positive correlation between size and formalization, appear not to differ.

The interrelationships among organizational characteristics shown in Table 7.2 are no more able than those of previous studies to differentiate predictions from these two perspectives; further analysis presented in this chapter, however, examines relationships that allow a testing of the domination perspective on the role of organizational structure. Specifically, whereas a finding that formalization correlates with size can be interpreted as indicating a response to either control or coordination problems, a finding that it correlates with a perception that the company had been suffering from poor employee job performance is clearer in its support for the view that it is used to effect control. Similarly, a correlation between formalization and having an EAP administrator who advocates the medical disease model, a view that has been argued here to constitute a deceptive strategy for sanctioning deviant employees, is difficult to interpret as demonstrating that formalization functions to facilitate organizational coordination.

The analyses presented here will employ what Dalton et al. (1980) identified as the key variables of organizational structure in their review of the literature on the relationship between structure and effectiveness. These are size, supervisory span (at the lowest level), flat/tall hierarchy (the number of levels in the administrative hierarchy divided by the total number of employees), division of labor, centralization, and rule formalization. Following Campbell et al. (1974), Dalton et al. (1980) considered formalization, centralization, and division of labor to be "structuring" variables, which they defined as "policies and activities occurring within the organization that prescribe or restrict the behavior of organization members" (Dalton et al. 1980, p. 51). The other variables—size, span of control, and flat/tall hierarchy—were considered to be "structural" variables, that is, "dimensions that define the physical milieu in which behavior occurs" (p. 57).

This dichotomization of variables typically used in analyses of the structure of organizations may help to clarify the divergence between Weber's and Bendix's perspectives. That is, Weber's view that bureaucracy was a response to control problems appears consistent with the role of Dalton et al.'s "structuring" variables, whereas Bendix's view that certain organizational factors cause control problems appears to refer to Dalton et al.'s "structural" variables.

The correlations of the structural and structuring variables with the seven potential reasons for program implementation given by senior personnel executives are presented in Table 8.1. Organizational size had a significant positive correlation with the executive's level of agreement with the statement that the company's program had been implemented because of concerns about poor job performance. Additionally, size was correlated positively with two other performance-related reasons for starting a program—concerns about absenteeism and about high turnover. Size had a significant negative correlation with the program having been started because of highly visible cases of problem-drinking bringing the issue to the company's attention, and it had a marginally significant negative correlation with having started the program because of the efforts of an employee who had personal contact with alcoholism. Starting a program because of a recognition of alcoholism as a medical problem affecting the well-being of the company's employees or because of the assumption of an increased social responsibility was not related to organizational size. In summary, these correlations between size and reasons for program implementation suggest that larger organizations were more likely than smaller ones to have started programs because of concerns about controlling poor employee behavior, rather than because of sympathetic acceptance of alcoholism as a health problem.

The surveillance of employee behavior should be more problematic, not only for organizations with more employees, but in particular for organizations with more employees reporting to each supervisor. In support of this latter expectation, Table 8.1 indicates that personnel executives were more likely, in companies with larger first-level spans of control, to indicate that concerns about poor job performance and high absenteeism motivated the implementation of their alcoholism programs. No other motives for program implementation were associated with span. This finding is therefore again consistent with the expectation, based on Bendix's work, that structural elements of organizations cause control problems and that personnel executives may seek to solve those problems through the implementation of an alcoholism program.

Table 7.2 indicated that the number of levels in an organization's hierarchy was negatively correlated with supervisory spans of control. Therefore, flat hierarchies, because their spans of control would tend to be larger, would be expected to be associated with greater control problems. Goldman and Van Houten, however, argued that hierarchies also have a direct impact on organizations' abilities to exercise social control, in that they keep workers isolated and keep them motivated by a sense (an illusion, in Goldman and Van Houten's view) that their hard work will afford them opportunities for individual mobility up through the hierarchy. From this perspective as well, then, a tall organizational hierarchy would help to vitiate control problems. These contentions are supported by the analyses shown in Table 8.1, which indicate that hierarchy has significant negative correlations with concerns about poor job performance and absenteeism. Because taller organizations are those with smaller spans, these findings also serve to corroborate the findings, above, concerning the correlations between reasons for program implementation and first-level spans of control.

The aspects of organizational structure that have been discussed so far as potential causes of control problems for organizations could, alternatively, be effects of such problems, as management could reorganize to deal with problems of employee productivity. Clearly, employees may be added to or subtracted from the payroll, and the number of levels in the administrative hierarchy and the number of subordinates for each supervisor can be altered. Nevertheless, it does not seem likely that many firms would decide permanently to forego expansion simply because increases in size seem to create problems of employee absenteeism or work productivity. Similarly, it seems unlikely that organizations would drastically alter reporting relationships for such reasons; adding new layers to management or adding supervisors to reduce spans of control can increase the cost of administrative overhead excessively. For

TABLE 8.1. Correlations of Dimensions of Organizational Structure with Executives' Reasons for Program Implementation

	Reasons for Program Implementation						
Structural Dimensions	Recognition of Alcoholism as a Medical Problem Affecting Employee Well-being	Concern about Poor Job Performance	Assumption of an Increased Social Responsibility	Visible Cases Brought Problem Drinking to Company's Attention	Concern about High Absenteeism	Efforts of an Employee Who Had Personal Contact with the Problem	Concern about High Turnover
Size (log)	.09 (183)	.15** (184)	−.05 (181)	−.13** (184)	.21*** (181)	−.11* (185)	.12** (182)
Supervisory span	.05 (166)	.12* (168)	−.02 (166)	.00 (166)	.18** (164)	.01 (166)	.06 (165)
Tall/flat hierarchy	−.12* (137)	−.15** (139)	.01 (137)	.10 (138)	−.18** (137)	.11 (139)	−.03 (138)
Centralization	.06 (138)	.11* (138)	−.07 (139)	.01 (140)	.03 (139)	−.23*** (140)	.05 (139)
Rule formalization	.00 (228)	.10* (229)	.03 (226)	−.01 (228)	−.01 (225)	−.07 (227)	−.01 (225)
Division of labor	.10 (126)	−.02 (128)	.11 (127)	.12* (128)	.12* (126)	.17** (129)	.13* (127)

*$p \leq .10$
**$p \leq .05$
***$p \leq .01$
Note: n's are in parentheses.

example, in many situations spans are tied closely to job design and technology, a situation that obviates incremental changes in the amount of direct supervision and only permits options that are too extreme to be justifiable. Shrinking the supervisory span in a technical operation that is designed for six operatives and one supervisor/inspector, for instance, would require the expense of having two supervisors for these same six employees. Consequently, although changing the configuration and limiting the size of an organization most certainly are managerial strategies that have been used (see, for example, Worthy 1950), in general it would be expected that more readily manipulated elements of organizational structure serve to ameliorate control problems. In particular, rule formalization and decision centralization can afford management a closer control over employees' activities with a comparatively small investment of human and capital resources.

As shown in Table 8.1, formalization and centralization ("structuring" variables) were positively, although marginally, correlated with the extent to which concern about poor job performance was stated as having been an important reason for starting the company's alcoholism program. Not one of the other six reasons for program implementation had a significant positive correlation with either of these variables. These findings suggest that increasing the purview of written rules and moving the locus of decision making to a more centralized level of authority may be responses to perceptions of control problems.

The third structuring factor identified by Dalton et al., division of labor, was not correlated with concern about poor job performance. As discussed earlier, greater division of labor may reflect fractionalization of work into simple tasks that are more readily evaluated and controlled. Conversely, however, it may indicate the presence in the organization of a wider range of highly trained specialists, whose work performance is less readily assessed. Thus the failure to observe an association between division of labor and concern about poor job performance may reflect the confounding of two phenomena, one of which would be expected to result in a positive, and the other in a negative, correlation with performance concerns. Division of labor did have marginally significant positive correlations with two performance-related motives for program implementation, concerns about absenteeism and turnover. However, it was also correlated positively with two employee welfare-oriented motives, the efforts of a recovered alcoholic employee and (marginally) the observation of visible cases of problem drinking.

These findings, indicating a somewhat consistent, if modest, set of associations between elements of organizational structure and expressions by corporate executives of concerns about poor job performance, offer some support for the Marxian and Weberian views that those at the apex of administrative hierarchies manipulate structures to enhance compliance with their goals. However, especially in light of findings from previous comparative organizational research, an alternative interpretation that must be addressed is the possibility that the consistency among these relationships is simply an artifact of the correlations that both performance concerns and organizational structure have with size. Following the practice of other analyses of the interrelationships among structural characteristics of organizations (see Kimberly 1976), the relationships examined in Table 8.1 were reexamined, statistically controlling for the effects of size.

Partial correlations were performed, removing the effects of size from the relationships between performance concerns and structure for the four variables that were not already ratios of size. The partial correlation coefficient between division of labor and productivity as a motive for program implementation was .0474 units higher than the zero-order relationship. The partial correlation coefficients between productivity concerns and formalization, centralization, and span of control were lower than the zero-order correlations by .0181, .0197, and .0159 units, respectively. These modest changes from the coefficients of the zero-order correlations suggest that size was not responsible for the link between organizational structure and the perception of problems with employees' job performance. Because of the problem of missing data, discussed earlier, even these relatively simple first-order partial correlations suffered from losses of 13 to 23 percent of cases compared to the bivariate correlations; the similarities of the coefficients across the differing (although not independent) samples suggests some stability in the relationships reported here.

These findings, indicating that concern about job performance as a reason for program implementation responds to differences in organizational structure, suggest that this item taps the entire organization's control problems, rather than simply the organization's concern about controlling the job performance of the relatively small proportion of employees who may be alcoholics. In the analyses that follow control problems will be linked to ideologies of alcoholism and the correlates of these ideologies will be investigated.

ALCOHOLISM IDEOLOGIES AND REASONS FOR PROGRAM IMPLEMENTATION

Both mainstream and Marxian perspectives have focused on the role of bureaucratic structural mechanisms in achieving coordination and control in organizations. This study has argued that Weber contributed to the analysis of processes of social domination by positing that problems of domination are resolved not only through organizational mechanisms but also through the promotion of an ideology. To address the questions of whether certain ideas about the nature and origins of alcoholism tend to be advanced in companies that perceive social control problems, personnel executives' stated reasons for their companies' implementation of an EAP were correlated with program administrators' ratings of agreement with possible factors in alcoholism's etiology. The results of these analyses are shown in Table 8.2. For a number of organizations, responses to both the executive and administrator questionnaires had been provided by the same individual (as indicated by the names filled in on the completed questionnaires). So that the correlations in this table would represent correspondences between the responses of personnel executives and those of program administrators, rather than the same individuals' answers to a variety of items, cases in which the same individual responded to both questionnaires were omitted from the analyses reported in the table.*

Table 8.2 indicates that companies whose executives were more likely to agree that their firms' programs had been implemented because of concern about poor job performance were also more likely to have administrators who believed that alcoholism could result from a physiologically-based imbalance or inheritance (that is, who agreed with the traditional medical disease model). Although this correlation was only marginally significant, the disease model was the only one of the eight beliefs about the causes of alcoholism that was correlated with personnel executives' concern for poor productivity as a motive for program implementation. Only one other reason for starting a program, recognition of alcoholism as a medical problem affecting employee well-being, was correlated with the administrator's belief in the medical disease model.

These data suggest that companies hire supporters of the medical disease model of alcoholism under two circumstances: when there is a concern for employee well-being, and when there is a concern for control over employee work performance. It is certainly not surprising that companies whose personnel executives accept alcoholism as a medical problem would hire administrators who believe that it is a medical problem. However, other than from the perspective offered in this book, it would seem somewhat counterintuitive to find that companies wanting to deal with poor job performance are also inclined to hire someone who views alcoholism as a pitiable medical condition.

ALCOHOLISM IDEOLOGIES AND PROGRAM STRUCTURE

Program administrators' beliefs about the nature of alcohol problems presumably are reflected in the manner in which they operate their

---

*Although the questionnaire and cover letter clearly indicated that it was the executive's view that was of interest for the initial items, many letters from executives indicated that they felt that they were less informed on this topic than the program administrator, to whom they had forwarded the questionnaire.

programs. Although it is this book's thesis that adherence to the disease model strongly disposes administrators toward implementing programs in ways that may serve the interests of managers concerned with problems of social control, the intention has not been to suggest that proponents of the disease model are themselves primarily motivated by a desire to root out poor performers and, by labeling them alcoholics, to threaten them into submission to management's performance norms. On the contrary, many program administrators who promote the disease ideology were themselves active alcoholics who recovered through Alcoholics Anonymous, in which the disease model serves a focal role, and their motivation appears to be a sincere desire to help others having the same problems that they were able finally to overcome. Many other administrators holding to the disease perspective have never been alcoholics but have been influenced by literature and training programs advancing the disease model as the most enlightened and sympathetic approach to this very serious health problem. Although certain aspects of disease model-oriented programs might appear unusually harsh, and would therefore seem to belie such sympathy, principles such as constructive coercion emerged out of, and consequently are highly consistent with, A.A. beliefs such as the necessity for "tough love" and for allowing the alcoholic to "hit bottom."

Similarly, the organizations that hire administrators who believe in the disease model are not all necessarily concerned with social control. The finding in Table 8.2 that the presence of a disease model-oriented administrator was associated with two reasons for program implementation, concern over poor job performance and recognition that alcoholism was affecting employee well-being, suggests a need to differentiate the effects of social control motives for adopting the disease perspective from more benign and sympathetic motives. The analyses presented in all subsequent tables will therefore indicate findings separately for two subgroups: companies for which a concern about poor job performance was checked as one of the two most important reasons for starting their alcoholism program, and companies for which it was not one of the two most important reasons.

The program components implemented in the hope of encouraging employees to make use of the program are expected to vary with the ideology of alcoholism held by the administrator. Those whose views of alcoholism are consistent with the general public's probably have the greatest chances of having their explanations of alcohol problems accepted by both the company's supervisory and nonsupervisory personnel. Although, as shown in Chapter 4, the general notion that alcoholism is a disease is accepted by many individuals, survey research has never delved into respondents' approval of the unusual specifics of the operation of occupational programs based on the disease perspective, such as using job performance and denial as bases for diagnosis and providing treatment that consists of "constructive coercion" through use of the "job

TABLE 8.2. Correlations of Executives' Reasons for Program Implementation with Program Administrators' Views on the Etiology of Alcoholism

Reasons for Program Implementation	Psychological Problems	Family-Marital Problems	Associating with Heavy Drinkers	Physiologically-Based Imbalance or Dysfunction	Psychological Problem of Childhood Development	Stressful Job	Boring Job	Weak Character
			Program Administrators' Views—Alcoholism Can Result from:					
Recognition of alcoholism as a medical problem affecting employee well-being	.04 (156)	.08 (154)	.03 (154)	.20*** (153)	−.01 (155)	.11* (155)	.10 (155)	−.08 (154)
Concern about poor job performance	−.06 (155)	−.03 (153)	.03 (153)	.11* (153)	−.05 (154)	.01 (154)	−.01 (154)	−.05 (153)
Assumption of an increased social responsibility	.07 (154)	.05 (153)	.00 (153)	−.01 (152)	.07 (153)	.02 (154)	.10 (154)	−.12* (153)

Visible cases brought problem drinking to company's attention	.04 (155)	.11* (154)	.06 (154)	-.05 (154)	-.03 (154)	.06 (155)	.04 (155)	.11* (154)
Concern about high absenteeism	.01 (153)	-.05 (152)	-.04 (152)	-.03 (151)	.05 (152)	-.03 (153)	.05 (153)	.01 (152)
Efforts of an employee who had personal contact with the problem	-.12* (154)	-.15** (153)	-.05 (153)	.01 (153)	-.10 (153)	-.09 (154)	-.04 (154)	-.05 (153)
Concern about high turnover	.02 (151)	.01 (150)	.02 (150)	.03 (149)	.13* (150)	.06 (151)	.17** (151)	.11* (150)

$*p < .10$
$**p < .05$
$***p < .01$

Note: n's are in parentheses.

threat." For program administrators who espouse the disease model, winning over their organizations' members to their own perspective on alcoholism may be especially crucial to program success. Unless they can get the workforce to believe that alcoholics are reliably diagnosed by poor work performance and efficaciously rehabilitated by being threatened, it seems likely that relatively few supervisors will be motivated to refer their subordinates. Consequently, those who operate under the set of assumptions comprising the medical disease model are expected to make extensive efforts to convince their companies' employees of the veracity of their message.

The analyses shown in Table 8.3 indicate that the associations between alcoholism ideologies and program structure were, as expected, moderated by the company's concern about poor employee performance. Moreover, the pattern of findings for the subsample of companies for which job performance had been a prime motive for starting the program contrasted with the pattern for companies for which performance had not been a prime concern in a manner consistent with the hypothesized role of the medical disease ideology in the social control process. One such difference between these two subgroups was in the correlation between the administrator's belief in the disease model and the existence of a written policy on alcoholism, a feature that frequently is said to be crucial for a program's success. As illustrated by the examples of such policies provided in Chapter 6, they often embody some version of the disease model, stating that the company now accepts alcoholism—and other "behavioral-medical" problems, in the case of the broader employee assistance programs—as an illness or disease that should be treated as any other. It would therefore be expected that medical model proponents, who believe themselves to be the bearers of the "true understanding of the disease of alcoholism," would be especially determined to promote the development and acceptance of a written policy. Table 8.3 provides some support for this prediction, indicating that the medical disease ideology was the only ideology of alcoholism that had a positive correlation with the existence of such a document. However, the table shows that a program administrator's advocacy of the disease approach was correlated with the existence of a written policy only in those organizations that started the program because of concerns over poor job performance; when the personnel executive indicated that productivity was not a reason for program implementation there was no association between the program administrator's belief in the disease model and the existence of a policy statement.

As noted in Chapters 5 and 6, policy statements typically do not detail the specifics of the program, such as the possibility that the sympathetic help offered to treat this illness might feature "constructive coercion" through the use of "crisis precipitation" and the "job threat." Rather, it is in the detailed written procedures that some of the less intuitive aspects of the program are more likely to be explained, including the coercive thrust of therapy and the identification of employees as appropriate program clients on the basis of poor work performance rather than on the basis of evidence of drinking behavior. Table 8.3 indicates that the existence of a written procedure for the identification of problem employees was positively correlated with the presence of an administrator who believed in the disease model, but with no other views of alcoholism. Once again, however, it was only when the personnel executive rated job performance concerns as a major reason for starting the program that the administrator's belief in the disease perspective was associated significantly with this program feature. In fact, in this situation all other alcoholism ideologies were negatively correlated with the existence of written procedures, significantly in four of seven cases.

Companies not only vary in terms of whether written policies and procedures relating to their alcoholism or employee assistance programs exist, they also vary in the breadth of distribution of these documents. The extent to which a company distributes explanations of its program's procedures may be an indication of the program's motives. When the interest is in controlling deviants by getting supervisors to label poor performers as candidates for the alcoholism program, the brief, upbeat policy statement might be expected to be distributed to everyone, but the specific details of diagnosis and its consequences might be given only to supervisory personnel. Conversely, a program that was intended as a health benefit for its employees might be predicted to distribute both the policy and the detailed procedures widely.

The data in Table 8.3 are substantially consistent with these expectations. Whereas the seven other etiological perspectives were either uncorrelated or negatively correlated with policy distribution, the disease model correlated positively with distributing the policy statement both to supervisory personnel and to all employees. Moreover, both of these relationships (although the latter was only marginally significant) existed only when the program was started because of a concern about job productivity. Belief in the disease model was also the only etiological perspective positively correlated with the distribution of program procedures to supervisory personnel. In this case, the relationship existed both when productivity was and when it was not the basis for program implementation. As predicted, however, belief in the disease model was only associated with distributing procedures to all employees when job performance concerns had not been paramount in motivating program implementation. In companies where performance had been an important reason for adopting the program, the correlation of the disease model with the distribution of procedures to all employees turned negative (although not significantly so). In contrast, the correlations between the

TABLE 8.3. Correlations of Program Administrators' Views on the Etiology of Alcoholism with Elements of Program Structure

Program Administrators' Views—Alcoholism Can Result from:	Program Structures									
	Written Policy on Alcoholism		Written Procedure for Identification of Problem Employees		Distribution of Policy Statement to Managers and Supervisors		Distribution of Policy Statement to All Employees		Distribution of Program Procedures to Managers and Supervisors	
	Unimp.[a]	Imp.[b]	Unimp.	Imp.	Unimp.	Imp.	Unimp.	Imp.	Unimp.	Imp.
Psychological problems	-.06 (200)	-.02 (117)	-.04 (200)	-.06 (117)	-.09 (187)	-.11 (114)	-.14** (187)	-.05 (114)	-.23*** (187)	-.13* (114)
Family-marital problems	-.09 (200)	-.13* (115)	-.08 (200)	-.15* (115)	-.09 (187)	-.16** (112)	-.17** (187)	-.09 (112)	-.19*** (187)	-.13* (112)
Associating with heavy drinkers	-.04 (200)	-.04 (116)	.01 (200)	-.05 (116)	-.09 (187)	-.02 (113)	-.10* (187)	-.03 (113)	-.08 (187)	-.01 (113)

Physiologically-based imbalance or dysfunction (or genetic inheritance)									
−.01	.32***	.08	.27***	.03	.27***	.08	.12*	.11*	.18**
(195)	(117)	(195)	(117)	(184)	(114)	(184)	(114)	(184)	(114)
Childhood psychological problems									
−.11*	−.03	−.12**	−.02	−.10*	−.05	−.14**	−.03	−.29***	−.15*
(198)	(117)	(198)	(117)	(185)	(114)	(185)	(114)	(185)	(114)
Stressful job									
−.07	−.23***	−.04	−.14*	−.03	−.13*	−.09	−.10	−.01	−.18**
(201)	(115)	(201)	(115)	(186)	(112)	(186)	(112)	(186)	(112)
Boring job									
.02	−.08	−.10*	−.15*	−.04	−.06	−.09	−.02	−.09	−.18**
(202)	(116)	(202)	(116)	(188)	(112)	(188)	(112)	(188)	(112)
Weak character									
−.23***	−.06	−.25***	−.16**	−.20***	−.03	−.08	.02	−.21***	−.09
(197)	(115)	(197)	(115)	(184)	(112)	(184)	(112)	(184)	(112)

[a]Concern about poor job performance was unimportant as a reason for program implementation.
[b]Concern about poor job performance was important as a reason for program implementation.

*$p < .10$
**$p < .05$
***$p < .01$

Note: n's are in parentheses.

(continued)

TABLE 8.3 (continued).

Program Administrators' Views—Alcoholism Can Result from:	Distribution of Program Procedures to All Employees		Program Structures Training of Top Management		Training of Middle Management		Training of Union Leadership		Training of First-level Supervisors	
	Unimp.[a]	Imp.[b]	Unimp.	Imp.	Unimp.	Imp.	Unimp.	Imp.	Unimp.	Imp.
Psychological problems	-.19*** (187)	.02 (114)	-.22*** (171)	-.24*** (101)	-.15** (171)	-.17** (101)	.01 (86)	-.28** (45)	-.16** (171)	-.10 (101)
Family-marital problems	-.11* (187)	.05 (112)	-.13** (171)	-.14* (100)	-.17** (171)	-.16* (100)	.07 (85)	-.26** (45)	-.21*** (171)	-.13 (100)
Associating with heavy drinkers	-.07 (187)	.05 (113)	-.03 (171)	-.04 (100)	-.04 (171)	-.08 (100)	.01 (86)	-.08 (45)	-.13** (171)	-.08 (100)
Physiologically based imbalance or dysfunction (or genetic inheritance)	.14** (184)	-.06 (114)	.10 (168)	.19** (101)	.20*** (168)	.24*** (101)	.12 (84)	.17 (45)	.17** (168)	.26*** (101)
Childhood psychological problems	-.07 (185)	.04 (114)	-.16** (169)	-.33*** (101)	-.18*** (169)	-.25*** (101)	-.14 (86)	-.25** (45)	-.13** (169)	-.14* (101)
Stressful job	-.06 (186)	.02 (112)	-.05 (170)	-.13 (99)	-.03 (170)	-.08 (99)	.12 (85)	-.06 (44)	-.14** (170)	-.03 (99)
Boring job	.04 (188)	-.03 (113)	.01 (172)	-.26*** (100)	-.08 (172)	-.07 (100)	.22** (86)	-.20* (45)	-.09 (172)	-.09 (100)
Weak character	-.13** (184)	.19** (112)	-.14** (169)	-.17** (100)	-.18*** (169)	-.16* (100)	-.09 (84)	-.19 (45)	-.28*** (169)	-.07 (100)

| | Program Structures | | | | | | | |
| | Training of Union Stewards | | Training of Medical Department Staff | | Training of Personnel and Industrial Relations Staff | | Training of All Employees | |
Program Administrators' Views—Alcoholism Can Result from:	Unimp.[a]	Imp.[b]	Unimp.	Imp.	Unimp.	Imp.	Unimp.	Imp.
Psychological problems	-.04 (86)	-.34** (45)	-.08 (171)	-.22** (101)	-.12* (171)	-.19** (101)	-.18*** (171)	.05 (101)
Family-marital problems	.09 (85)	-.28** (45)	-.13** (171)	-.23** (100)	-.19*** (171)	-.26*** (100)	-.09 (171)	.00 (100)
Associating with heavy drinkers	.01 (86)	-.12 (45)	-.07 (171)	-.09 (100)	-.08 (171)	-.17** (100)	.00 (171)	-.14* (100)
Physiologically-based imbalance or dysfunction (or genetic inheritance)	.01 (84)	.15 (45)	.21*** (168)	.24*** (101)	.20*** (168)	.26*** (101)	.00 (168)	.01 (101)
Childhood psychological problems	-.04 (86)	-.14 (45)	-.12* (169)	-.26*** (101)	-.13* (169)	-.31*** (101)	-.16** (169)	.09 (101)
Stressful job	.04 (85)	-.20* (44)	-.08 (170)	-.22** (99)	-.09 (170)	-.22** (99)	-.03 (170)	.05 (99)
Boring job	.23** (86)	-.18 (45)	-.08 (172)	-.06 (100)	-.03 (172)	-.04 (100)	-.06 (172)	.01 (100)
Weak character	-.02 (84)	-.21* (45)	-.06 (169)	-.20** (100)	-.19*** (169)	-.29*** (100)	-.03 (169)	-.09 (100)

Note: See p. 195 for table notes.

broad distribution of procedures and six of the other seven etiological perspectives reversed signs from negative to positive when job performance concerns had been important to the company.

In addition to the distribution of written procedures, occupational programs communicate their methods of operation through training sessions, examples of which were provided in Chapter 5. Organizations consider training to be an expensive endeavor, particularly in contrast to distributing policies and procedures, both because of direct costs and because of lost time on the job. Consequently, the range of staff members to whom training is given is often considered an indication of the strength of a company's commitment to the implementation of an alcoholism or employee assistance program. On the basis of Chapter 5's examples of supervisors' and union officials' resistance to the disease model's corollaries of diagnosis based on job performance and rehabilitation through job termination, it might be expected that adherents of the disease perspective would wish as many opportunities as possible to proselytize for their nonobvious viewpoint that alcoholics can be identified on the basis of poor performance and denial, and "treated" with discipline. However, this message is really only relevant for organizational personnel who either are line supervisors or otherwise have the authority (perhaps as medical personnel) to refer other employees into the program. Consequently, administrators advocating the disease model and its accompanying job performance diagnostic criteria might consider training those with no such responsibility to be of less urgency.

Consistent with this social control perspective, Table 8.3 indicates that the training of personnel at a variety of organizational levels and engaged in a variety of functions was associated with greater advocacy of the disease model by program administrators. Although the relationship between the disease ideology and training was in each case stronger when the program's origin had been an interest in controlling work performance, it also appeared when that was not the company's motive. The cases where the disease perspective was not associated with training sessions are also consistent with this interpretation. The correlations between belief in this model and the training of union leaders and union shop stewards, who are not generally regarded as among managements' social control agents (although the radical labor caucus mentioned in Chapter 6 argued that unions share managements' interest in deviance control), were positive but nonsignificant. Of most direct relevance to the predictions made here, administrators who agreed with the disease ideology did not demonstrate a tendency to provide training for all of the company's employees.

Views of alcoholism other than the medical disease model had a pattern of relationships with the provision of training sessions that was somewhat similar to their associations with the distribution of detailed program procedures. That is, the signs of the correlations between these other beliefs about the etiology of alcoholism and the provision of training sessions for line and staff supervisory functionaries were consistently negative. Training for all employees was correlated negatively with these perspectives—when job performance was not a major reason for starting the program. However, for five of these seven viewpoints the signs of their correlations with this program feature reversed to positive when performance was an important motive.

The various measures of program structure have demonstrated a consistent pattern of relationships with the eight perspectives on the etiology of alcoholism. Table 8.3 indicated that program administrators' agreement with the view that alcoholism is a "physiologically-based imbalance or dysfunction (or genetic inheritance)" was associated with different program structures than were associated with agreement with the other seven perspectives on the etiology of alcoholism. Specifically, when job performance was one of the two most important reasons for implementing the program, the physiological disease model was unique in its positive correlation with a variety of efforts to inform potential social control agents of the workings of the program. Particularly when job productivity was the reason for starting the program, advocates of the disease model appeared no more likely than proponents of other views of alcoholism, or perhaps even less likely, to extend such informational efforts to the entire employee population.

Given the number of program features predicted by the disease explanation of alcoholism, one interpretation of these findings is that administrators who advocate it are simply more activist in their orientation to program development than are administrators who see alcoholism as related to stress, boredom, psychological problems, weak character, or "hanging out with the wrong crowd." However, the data seemed to indicate that this activist orientation blossomed primarily when the company intended the program to serve the interests of job performance control, rather than of health or welfare concerns. Additionally, this activism did not appear to extend to all aspects of program development; especially when job performance had been a major reason for starting the program, disease model proponents were unlikely to explain the program and its philosophy to the broad employee population, either in writing or in training sessions.

PROGRAM STRUCTURE AND OUTCOMES

The results in Table 8.3 have shown that the disease ideology is associated with a number of program components in a manner that could potentially facilitate social control. To examine whether these particular features actually do lead to control, the correlations of program features with the objective and subjective outcomes discussed in Chapter 7 are presented in Table 8.4. Consideration of the findi   n examination of the associations between program structural elements and the routes by which employees enter the program. These are not ultimate outcomes of the program, but are among the results of the program's design and are relevant, as well, to the issue of social control.

As discussed in previous chapters, the two main paths by which individuals enter occupational programs are self-referral and referral from a supervisor. Many program administrators strive for self-referrals, aware that, ceteris paribus, a high level of self-referrals probably indicates the employees' trust in the good intentions and effectiveness of the program. Other administrators employ the disease ideology to motivate supervisors to expose their poorly performing subordinates to the sanctions that management can exercise through the EAP, arguing that self-referrals reach individuals who are in too advanced a stage of the disease for the prognosis to be favorable. They aver that supervisory referrals are necessary to break through the denial that they claim is a symptom exhibited by the disease's victims.

The frequent exhortation to supervisors, in program literature, that they must mandate subordinates' participation in the program—for their subordinates' own good, of course—suggests that enhancing the rate of supervisory referrals may be used as a managerial control strategy. If this is indeed a strategy employed in these programs, program features oriented toward control of the general employee population would be predicted to be associated with high supervisory referral rates and low self-referral rates.

Table 8.4 indicates that when job performance concerns were important in the founding of the program, various efforts to communicate information about its operation were associated with lower proportions of clients referring themselves into the program. Specifically, the existence of a policy and written procedures and their distribution to supervisors, as well as the training of supervisors and personnel department functionaries, were correlated negatively with the self-referral rate. When productivity had not been a major factor in program implementation, however, the associations between oral or written dissemination of program information and lower self-referrals largely disappeared. Programs that explained the details of their functioning not only to the organizations' social control agents, but to all employees (a feature that was not associated with the medical model), did not experience lower self-referrals, even when job performance had been an important motive for implementation.

The rates of referrals from supervisors do not necessarily have correlations with program components that are the inverse of those with self-referral rates; in addition to these two paths into the program, referrals might come from unions, families, or company medical departments. However, it has been suggested here that the correlations of supervisory referrals and self-referrals with elements of program structure would have opposite signs if the programs were being used to extend managements' control over employee behavior. The data in Table 8.4 provide some support for this view, indicating opposite signs for these relationships in twelve of fourteen cases for the subsample of companies for which a concern over poor job performance had been one of the major reasons for starting the program. For example, in that group of respondents, the existence of a written policy and written procedures, which were associated with lower proportions of self-referrals, were related to higher proportions of supervisory referrals.

For companies in which concerns about employee performance had not been the motive behind program implementation, the correlations of supervisory referral and self-referral rates with structural features had opposite signs in eleven of the fourteen cases. For this group, however, the signs of the relationships were reversed from what they had been for those firms in which performance *had* been a major program motive. That is, when job performance had not been an important reason for starting the program, various methods of informing the organization's members about the program appeared to result in employees entering without having been forced to do so by their supervisors (that is, through a combination of referrals from their union, the medical department, family members, and self-referrals).

Program components that did not follow this general pattern of positive correlations with supervisory referrals when job productivity had been a program motive, and negative correlations when it had not, tended also to be those that were less likely to be found in programs whose administrators subscribed to the view that alcoholism is a physiologically-based disease. For example, two such variables, training union leaders and stewards, had relationships with supervisory referrals that were the opposite of those between supervisory referrals and training of management groups; these two variables correlated negatively with supervisory referrals when job performance was a motive for program implementation and reversed to positive when productivity was not one of management's two most important motives. Because it is the medical disease model that legitimates constructive coercion, information about programs based on other views of alcohol problems—although they may have been intended to enhance productivity—seem likely to render union functionaries less circumspect about the potential consequences of recommending cooperation with the program to their members.

The findings on the sources of referral into EAPs appear to be consistent with the interpretation that efforts to disseminate information about these programs may communicate very different content and thus obtain different results, depending upon the company's motive in implementing the program. Specifically, when improving control over employee work performance had been a major impetus for starting a

TABLE 8.4. Correlations of Elements of Program Structure with Program Outcomes

	Program Outcomes											
	Percent Self-Referrals		Percent Supervisory Referrals		Alcoholism Penetration Rate		Nonalcoholism Penetration Rate		Overall Evaluation of Success		Improved Productivity	
Program Structures	Unimp.[a]	Imp.[a]	Unimp.	Imp.	Unimp.	Imp.	Unimp	Imp.	Unimp.	Imp.	Unimp.	Imp.
Written policy on alcoholism	-.05 (98)	-.22** (58)	-.14* (101)	.17* (62)	.06 (89)	.05 (58)	.08 (125)	-.23** (89)	.09 (81)	.06 (84)	.10 (80)	.00 (81)
Written procedures for identification of alcoholic employees	-.06 (98)	-.24** (58)	-.08 (101)	.21* (62)	-.15* (89)	.17 (58)	-.14* (125)	-.18* (89)	-.05 (81)	.05 (84)	.14 (80)	.05 (81)
Distribution of policy statement to managers and supervisors	-.11 (96)	-.13 (58)	-.14* (98)	.19* (62)	.04 (88)	.17 (56)	-.05 (122)	-.24** (86)	.03 (76)	.06 (82)	.05 (76)	-.11 (79)
Distribution of policy statement to all employees	.06 (96)	.05 (58)	-.21** (98)	-.09 (62)	.09 (88)	-.04 (56)	-.10 (122)	-.16* (86)	-.16* (76)	.16* (82)	.02 (76)	-.08 (79)
Distribution of program procedures to managers and supervisors	.05 (96)	-.23** (58)	-.18** (98)	.10 (62)	.13 (88)	.13 (56)	-.05 (122)	-.19** (86)	.08 (76)	.12 (82)	.08 (76)	-.10 (79)
Distribution of program procedures to all employees	.11 (96)	.03 (58)	-.34*** (98)	.10 (62)	.22** (88)	-.05 (56)	.01 (122)	.14* (86)	.06 (76)	.11 (82)	.03 (76)	-.04 (79)

Training of top management	.00 (89)	−.03 (51)	−.26** (91)	.08 (54)	.16* (84)	.00 (50)	−.01 (113)	−.08 (76)	.29*** (71)	.32*** (76)	.36*** (71)	−.01 (73)
Training of middle management	.03 (89)	−.12 (51)	−.21** (91)	.14 (54)	.16* (84)	.15 (50)	.08 (113)	−.22** (76)	.04 (71)	.19* (76)	.22** (71)	.02 (73)
Training of union leadership	−.10 (51)	.04 (22)	.20* (57)	−.21 (24)	−.16 (49)	−.16 (24)	.18* (58)	.00 (37)	−.02 (62)	.39*** (44)	.20* (59)	.10 (44)
Training of first-level supervisors	.01 (89)	−.23* (51)	−.16* (91)	.06 (54)	.08 (84)	.11 (50)	−.01 (113)	−.16* (76)	−.04 (71)	.31*** (76)	.13 (71)	−.02 (73)
Training of union stewards	−.20* (51)	.09 (22)	.10 (57)	−.06 (24)	−.24* (49)	−.21 (24)	.14 (58)	.05 (37)	.25** (62)	.34** (44)	.13 (59)	.19 (44)
Training of medical department staff	−.17* (89)	−.12 (51)	.07 (91)	−.05 (54)	.11 (84)	.12 (50)	−.01 (113)	.01 (76)	.16* (71)	.16* (76)	.39*** (71)	−.02 (73)
Training of personnel and industrial relations staff	.06 (89)	−.23** (51)	−.14* (91)	.17 (54)	.14* (84)	.19* (50)	.10 (113)	−.15* (76)	.10 (71)	.16* (76)	.29*** (71)	.04 (73)
Training of all employees	.11 (89)	.13 (51)	−.28*** (91)	−.05 (54)	.30*** (84)	.01 (50)	.08 (113)	.33*** (76)	.03 (71)	.23** (73)	.14 (71)	.25** (69)

[a] Concern about poor job performance was unimportant as a reason for program implementation.
[b] Concern about poor job performance was important as a reason for program implementation.

*p < .10
**p < .05
***p < .01

Note: n's are in parentheses.

program, information regarding its operations left employees less inclined, and supervisors more inclined, to use them. This suggests that pointing out the connection between the program and organizational control processes, rather than just the program's link to employee health and welfare, was an important aspect of the content of program literature and training sessions for firms that had adopted programs with the intended purpose of enhancing control. Thus, these data support the characterization of many training sessions and program materials as being designed to convince supervisors that to do anything less than order their employees who perform poorly into the program is a disservice to themselves and to their unfortunate subordinates, whose poor productivity is pointed to as proof that they are suffering from a progressive and fatal disease.

The data on referral sources address only the question of *how* clients enter the program, not *how many* enter. Because of their view that alcoholics cannot be saved unless they are uncovered, a central concern for most program administrators is the proportion of the entire organization's workforce that are defined as "troubled employees" and made into program clients. Table 8.4 presents correlations of program structure with two measures of success in bringing employees into the program, the alcoholism and nonalcoholism penetration rates. As discussed in Chapter 7, the alcoholism penetration rate is the proportion of an organization's employee population that is diagnosed as alcoholic and enters the program each year (from any of a variety of referral sources) and the nonalcoholism penetration rate is the proportion entering with some other diagnosis. It is predicted that program elements more likely to be found when medical disease model proponents are administrators will be associated with higher proportions of the workforce being identified as alcoholics. The logic of the medical model, however, is probably more convincing when applied to alcohol abuse than when, for example, drug abuse is described as an inherited, progressive disease. Consequently, the presence of the supervisory training and information dissemination efforts that are associated with programs administered by advocates of the disease ideology is not expected to increase the nonalcoholism penetration rate.

The relationships between alcoholism penetration rates and a number of program features relevant to social control, shown in Table 8.4, were at best only marginally significant. Higher alcoholism penetration was weakly associated with training middle management and personnel functionaries, and lower alcoholism penetration with training union leaders and stewards; moreover, these effects were not moderated by company concern for productivity. The nonalcoholism penetration rate was associated with a majority of program components, but only when job performance had been a prime motive for program implementation. In that circumstance the proportion of an organization's workforce entering the program each year with a diagnosis other than alcoholism tended to be lower when policies and procedures on alcoholism existed and were distributed to supervisory personnel (but not to all employees), and when the personnel staff and first-level and middle managers were trained.

Two program features that are not correlated with administrators' agreement with the medical model, the provision of training and distribution of procedures to all employees, were associated with higher penetration rates. However, whether it was the alcoholism or the nonalcoholism penetration rate that was elevated by the existence of these program components depended upon the reason underlying the program's initiation. When concern about poor job performance had not been an especially salient motive, broad oral and written communications about the program correlated positively with the alcoholism penetration rate. However, in cases where performance concerns had been salient, these features were uncorrelated with the alcoholism penetration rate and instead were correlated positively with nonalcoholism penetration. These findings suggest the possibility that programs that wish to have an impact on job performance but are not based on the disease model (in which case they are slightly more likely to include training and distribution of procedures to all employees) are able to lure employees into the program. However, under these circumstances, employees seem to enter the programs diagnosed as having some "behavioral-medical" problem other than alcoholism.

The subjective measures of program outcomes were obtained from the corporate senior personnel executives, who were asked to provide ratings of both their program's overall success and its specific success in leading to improved productivity. In light of the ambiguities that arise in interpreting the social control implications of each of the available objective dependent measures, as discussed in Chapter 7, these subjective measures were employed not only to corroborate the findings associated with the objective measures, but also to allow for additional insights into the control functions of these programs. In particular, although identifying deviants is crucial to exercising control over their behavior, the punishment of counternormative behavior in a social system often enhances social control in more ways than merely by altering the behavior of those individuals who have been caught in the act of deviance. As Toby (1964) has noted, the punishment of deviants may also warn others of the consequences of such behavior and thus deter them from engaging in deviance. If alcoholism and employee assistance programs are indeed effecting such deterrence, individuals wishing to avoid being labeled as alcoholic would be careful not to engage in behaviors that would permit them to be labeled. Because those behaviors are absenteeism, lateness, and poor productivity, their avoidance by the employee population would be expected to lead to personnel executives' perceptions of the program as having resulted in improved employee productivity.

Table 8.4 indicates that perceptions that the program was a success were broadly associated with program structure; when productivity was an important concern, all fourteen program features had positive correlations with perceived success (significant in nine cases). When productivity was not a major impetus for program implementation, the relationships attenuated and in some cases disappeared.

The findings concerning executives' evaluations of their programs' specific effectiveness in improving productivity indicate that in companies in which improved job productivity was not one of their original intentions for starting the program, conducting training for a wide variety of the company's personnel was associated with the perception that improved productivity had been one of the program's results. Because the survey's respondents and the other executives with whom they interact are among those who are more likely to have contact with the program when training is offered broadly, this perception may be an artifact of a favorable reaction to training, rather than indicative of specific knowledge of the programs' actual results.

The correlations between subjective perceptions of improved performance and program structure that are of greatest interest are those for the subsample of respondents for which the improvement of employee work productivity had been a major reason for program implementation. This set of associations examines the conditions under which organizations desiring improved productivity were able to achieve that end through their EAP. It would seem more likely that in these firms personnel executives would be monitoring the programs' specific outcomes. The relevant findings, shown as the last column in Table 8.4, indicate that only one program feature—training of all employees—was significantly correlated with the perception that improved performance had been a result of the program.

The fact that none of the features that are somewhat more apt to be adopted by advocates of the disease model were correlated with the perception of improved performance would seem highly problematic for this book's thesis. Rather than disconfirmation of the thesis, however, these analyses appear to indicate a point of divergence between the interests of management and of alcoholism program administrators. If administrators who are adherents of the disease model of alcoholism are often anxious to label individuals as alcoholics, it is no doubt in considerable part because of a sincere concern about helping those who may be suffering from this recalcitrant problem; the less altruistic aspect of administrators' zeal in many cases is their assumption that it is by maintaining a high patient load that they justify their jobs to their superiors. Each client whose job performance becomes satisfactory again during the time he or she is in the program is another employee whom the administrator claims to have restored to full productivity. In this author's discussions with corporate personnel executives, however, many of them made it clear that they give little credence to the dollar figures (usually based on the assertion that alcoholism causes productivity to be reduced by at least 25 percent) that administrators purport to be the savings resulting from their programs. Therefore, a possibility that these data suggest is that the executive's rating that the program had resulted in improved employee productivity is not based only (or even primarily) on improved performance from former alcoholics. Instead, the finding that this perception is predicted statistically by the training of all employees fits the interpretation, suggested above, that dissemination of information about how these programs operate may well motivate employees to not exhibit the behaviors that would allow them to be diagnosed as in need of "assistance."

ADMINISTRATOR IDEOLOGY AND OUTCOMES

The influence of program administrators should extend beyond their choice of the components of program structure measured here. The views they hold about the problems with which they are charged to deal would be expected to have broad effects on their interactions with clients, supervisors, and staff personnel. For example, not only are administrators' differing beliefs about the nature of alcohol problems somewhat pre-dictive of whether training and information sessions will be conducted, but these beliefs are likely to be associated with differing content and emphases in these sessions, and thus to hold differing appeal to occupants of various organizational roles.

This study has contended that the perspective that views alcoholism as a physiological or, in some similar sense, medical disorder is unique in its ability to facilitate managerial control over employee work perfor-mance. However, the quantitative analyses offered so far have addressed this proposition only indirectly, through examination of the social control implications of program components that tend to be found when pro-grams are administered by proponents of the disease model. The findings in Table 8.5 allow for a more direct assessment of this hypothesis, presenting the relationships among program outcomes and program administrators' ideologies of alcoholism.

The table indicates that in programs that were not initiated because of productivity concerns, supervisory referral rates were higher and self-referral rates were lower to the extent that the administrators expressed agreement with the views that alcoholism may result from childhood or other psychological problems, or from associating with heavy drinkers. However, when productivity had been an impetus for program imple-mentation, those relationships disappeared. Confirming this study's expectation, in that circumstance the only ideology of alcoholism that

TABLE 8.5. Correlations of Program Administrators' Views on the Etiology of Alcoholism with Program Outcomes

Program Administrators' Views—Alcoholism Can Result from:	Program Outcomes											
	Percent Self-Referrals		Percent Supervisory Referrals		Alcoholism Penetration Rate		Nonalcoholism Penetration Rate		Overall Evaluation of Success		Improved Productivity	
	Unimp.[a]	Imp.[b]	Unimp.	Imp.	Unimp.	Imp.	Unimp.	Imp.	Unimp.	Imp.	Unimp.	Imp.
Psychological problems	-.15* (98)	-.09 (57)	.27*** (101)	-.03 (61)	-.33*** (89)	-.01 (57)	-.03 (123)	.15* (87)	-.29*** (80)	-.24** (81)	-.21** (79)	.05 (78)
Family-marital problems	.01 (98)	.06 (56)	.10 (101)	.04 (60)	-.20** (89)	-.08 (57)	-.08 (123)	.02 (86)	-.24** (80)	-.27*** (80)	-.12 (79)	-.04 (76)
Associating with heavy drinkers	-.15* (97)	-.07 (57)	.19** (100)	.20* (61)	-.19** (88)	-.05 (57)	-.09 (122)	-.04 (86)	-.03 (79)	-.13 (81)	-.13 (78)	.17* (77)

Physiologically-based
imbalance or

dysfunction (or genetic inheritance)	.06 (95)	-.29** (57)	.01 (97)	.38*** (61)	.12 (88)	.12 (57)	.08 (121)	-.27*** (86)	-.01 (78)	.14 (82)	.13 (77)	.18* (78)
Childhood psychological problems	-.15* (97)	.12 (57)	.17** (99)	-.14 (61)	-.27*** (88)	.23** (57)	-.06 (122)	.22** (87)	-.16* (79)	-.05 (81)	-.13 (78)	-.08 (78)
Stressful job	-.07 (98)	-.06 (57)	-.03 (101)	.00 (61)	-.19** (89)	-.10 (57)	-.06 (124)	.01 (85)	-.24** (80)	-.30*** (80)	-.04 (79)	-.08 (76)
Boring job	-.08 (98)	.01 (57)	.09 (101)	.01 (61)	-.15* (89)	-.14 (57)	-.03 (124)	-.11 (86)	-.11 (80)	-.16* (81)	.05 (79)	-.03 (77)
Weak character	-.04 (97)	-.21* (57)	.10 (100)	.04 (61)	-.05 (87)	-.13 (57)	.02 (121)	-.08 (85)	.02 (79)	-.24** (81)	.04 (78)	.01 (77)

[a]Concern about poor job performance was unimportant as a reason for program implementation.
[b]Concern about poor job performance was important as a reason for program implementation.

*p < .10
**p < .05
***p < .01
Note: n's are in parentheses.

predicted higher rates of supervisory referrals and lower self-referral rates was the medical disease model.

The alcoholism penetration rate had negative correlations with seven of eight perspectives on the etiology of alcoholism, in six cases reaching at least marginal statistical significance, when concern about job performance was not a highly salient program motive. The only belief associated with higher alcoholism penetration rates was the medical disease model, although the relationship was nonsignificant. When job performance was important, the level of statistical association between alcoholism penetration and belief in the disease model remained the same, and most of the other views on alcoholism became less negatively related to this rate. In the previous table, when productivity concerns had been a motive for starting the program, the nonalcoholism penetration rate had negative correlations with most of the program structural features that were associated with the disease model. Corroboratively, Table 8.5 indicates that when productivity had been a key motive, espousal of the disease ideology was itself inversely correlated with this rate.

The personnel executive's subjective assessment of the overall success of the program had significant negative correlations with a number of program administrator beliefs when poor job performance was not a major concern in starting the program. For this subsample, none of the eight alcoholism ideologies were positive correlates of this outcome measure, including belief in the medical disease model, which was uncorrelated with the executive's perception of success. However, when job performance was a major concern, a clearer pattern of associations emerged. Seven of the eight beliefs had negative correlations with program success, five of which were at least marginally significant. The one administrator viewpoint that correlated positively (although not quite significantly) with the perception of overall success was the medical disease ideology.

Similarly, when productivity was an important concern, a positive correlation emerged between the administrator's belief in the disease ideology and the executive's perception that improved productivity had resulted from the implementation of the alcoholism or employee assistance program. Other than espousal of the notion that associating with heavy drinkers can cause alcoholism, which also had a marginally significant correlation with perceptions of productivity improvements, no other administrator ideology was associated with the perception that this had been a result of the program. With that exception, the findings relating administrators' ideologies to the two subjective outcomes suggests that programs that executives tended to perceive as having led to outcomes that were in management's interests were those run by administrators who expressed greater agreement with the disease explanation of alcoholism's etiology.

SUMMARY

At the outset of this chapter, a set of general hypotheses was stated. It was predicted that aspects of organizational structure would be correlated with the level of concern about control of poor employee performance and that this concern would be associated with having a program administrator who espoused the ideology that alcoholism is a physiologically-based medical disease. Administrators subscribing to that viewpoint were predicted to operate programs in a manner conducive to the exercise of managerial control. Examined in isolation, the variables of interest did not appear to demonstrate strong interrelationships. However, by placing them in the context of other variables that were measured on the same scales, given to the same individuals, and which assessed the same issues, the concepts did appear to show patterns of correlations that were different from those of other similarly measured factors and consistent with the expectations derived from theory. The prediction that organizational structures would be associated with perceived employee performance problems was intended to address Weber's hypothesis that bureaucratic structure was one means by which problems of domination are managed, as well as Bendix's elaboration on Weber in which he contended that size and differentiation might be causes of, rather than solutions for, problems of control. Correlations between measures of organizational structure and companies' expressions of concern over poor work performance as a prime motive for starting their programs had not been expected to be strong. In themselves, the findings that this concern had positive, significant (or marginally significant), correlations of .15, .12, .15, .11, and .10 with size, span of control, tall/flat hierarchy, centralization, and formalization, respectively, are not especially impressive. Yet, of the seven reasons for program implementation to which personnel executives were asked to express their level of agreement, it was only job performance concerns that demonstrated this consistent link with structure.

The other analyses presented in this chapter, investigating the role of ideology, were directed to the examination of the second component of the Weberian perspective on processes of domination. The correlation between companies' concerns about job performance as a motive for program implementation and the choice of a program administrator who espoused the medical disease ideology was, in isolation, modest. However, of the eight alcoholism ideologies with which program administrators were asked to express their agreement, the medical disease model was the only one that was correlated with the personnel executive's response that concern for performance had been a major reason for starting the program. And this finding was not the result merely of the disease model being correlated with most reasons for starting a program; of the seven potential motives, the medical ideology was associated only with concern about poor job performance and, for obvious reasons, the recognition of alcoholism as a medical problem.

The findings presented here also exhibited patterns that seemed to be supportive of the remaining hypotheses, concerning the procedures and outcomes associated with programs administered by individuals who are committed to the disease ideology of alcoholism. Administrators who advocated the disease model engaged in a wider variety of activities relevant to exercising control over employees than did supporters of other explanations of alcoholism. The disease model proponents were not, however, simply more actively committed to fuller program development; features that are less clearly conducive to social control were not associated with disease model proponents, but instead tended to be associated with programs run by individuals with some other understanding of alcoholism. Moreover, the association between advocacy of the disease model and the implementation of many program components was found only among programs that had been started by management in order to deal with poor employee performance. Among programs in that subsample, administrators favoring the disease ideology had a variety of "successful" program outcomes; compared to proponents of other beliefs about the nature of alcoholism, their programs tended to have higher penetration rates and to be viewed more favorably by the personnel executive.

Preceding chapters attempted to illustrate the specific mechanisms by which alcoholism programs based on the medical disease ideology could be used for purposes of social control. This book's initial chapters had attempted to specify, based on classical statements in sociological theory, the conditions under which an ideological control mechanism would be needed. The quantitative data that have been presented here do provide some support for what has been argued to be the Weberian position, that control is accomplished through the combination of bureaucratic mechanisms and a legitimating ideology. In doing so, these data have also helped to illuminate the particular conditions under which a view of alcohol problems that appears to offer sympathy, support, and forgiveness to its victims is used for ends that would seem to invert the purposes of those who battled for the acceptance of "alcoholism as a disease."

9

Conclusion

Analyzing the functions of theory in sociology, Denzin (1978) stated that not only must it "provide explanations of the phenomenon under analysis," but that "it must also generate new images of reality, new hypotheses, and new propositions; it must move sociologists toward the goals of explanation and prediction" (1978, p. 56). Similarly, Wallace (1969) contended that not only must theoretical propositions be induced from empirical generalizations, but new testable hypotheses must be deducible from theory. Although the training of sociologists most typically puts substantial emphasis on what Mills (1960) called the classic tradition in sociological theory, in which the work of Marx and Weber is prominent, it would appear that a rather small proportion of empirical social research is concerned with directly addressing the hypotheses these theorists proposed (see Stinchcombe 1982).

In the sociology of organizations, quantitative empirical research has been concerned with issues of theory to a particularly limited extent, rarely going beyond the obligatory reference to Weber—that is, to the incorrect Parsonian version of his work. That view of Weber, in which, it has been argued here, the most central theoretical concern of his analysis of bureaucracy has been whether size, complexity, formalization, and centralization lead to efficiency, has isolated organizational research from the questions around which sociological theory has developed. But it has not only been the development of theory in this field that has failed to advance substantially; empirical research on the sociology of organizations has been perceived, with some justification, as having been very unsuccessful in uncovering significant and consistent relationships. Although the correlations among many of the most basic variables in organizational analysis, such as size, structural complexity, centralization, and formalization, have been replicated in numerous studies (see Jackson and Morgan 1982), a great number of remaining inconsistencies have caused many scholars to conclude that this research paradigm will never yield either important theoretical insights or practical knowledge.

This concluding chapter argues that the present study should help to restore Weber's analysis of bureaucracy to its appropriate status as a major contribution to sociological theory rather than as a mere point of departure for management research. The usefulness of Weberian theory for the analysis of organizations is compared here to the Marxian perspective, as well as to that of current fashions in organization theory, including the ecological perspective, organizational culture, and recent analyses of ideology. It is argued that these latter approaches are closely descended from theories that are not especially newer than Weber's. Rather, their apparent novelty derives from their parent theory having been discovered, tried out, and then disregarded so completely that few contemporary organization theorists seem aware that they ever existed.

RESISTANCE TO THEORY DEVELOPMENT AND TESTING IN THE CONTEMPORARY SOCIAL SCIENCE OF ORGANIZATIONS

The present study is not the only evidence of a desire to move the sociology of organizations beyond sterile "Weberian" analyses of structure and efficient coordination to issues of greater sociological concern and intellectual content. Yet, Weber is by no means ignored in the current organization theory literature; he is still the target of those who wish to demonstrate the profundity of their favorite perspective by touting its advantages over Weber's. Just as textbook authors have, for decades, claimed that Weber did not account for human relations or for environmental turbulence, Weber has recently been compared, invidiously, to current versions of social Darwinism, which lately have gone by names such as "population ecology" (Hannan and Freeman 1977) and "organizational systematics" (McKelvey 1982).

For example, Langton (1984), writing in what is perhaps the most scrupulously peer-reviewed journal in organization theory, offered such an attack on Weber, demonstrating an understanding of his work that is remarkably different from that which has been presented here. Langton alleged that Weber's analysis of bureaucracy "glosses over certain fundamental questions": how and why bureaucratic rationalization occurs and "how individuals are induced to accept the constraints of work in a bureaucratic environment" (1984, pp. 334–35). The present study, however, has suggested that Weber did indeed address directly the questions that Langton felt were glossed over. How did bureaucratic rationalization occur? According to Weber, through the differentiation of organizational roles and structural units, and their direction and coordination through a hierarchy of authority to monitor compliance with codified rules. Why did it occur? To enhance the domination of those at the top of the organization over those subordinated. How were individuals induced to accept these constraints? Through the use of a set of ideas—a managerial ideology—to make individuals believe that the circumstances in which they find themselves are legitimate and acceptable.

Langton, attempting to demonstrate how the "ecological theory of bureaucracy" provides a more fruitful analysis than Weber's, offered an historical description of Wedgewood's bureaucratized pottery factory. He described the factory's adoption of some bureaucratic techniques, noted the operation's subsequent profitability, and observed that "it seems clear that the bureaucratization of Wedgewood's firm had a series of functional consequences" (p. 347). On the basis of "ecological" theory, which emphasizes how organizational forms evolve through the processes of variation, selection, and retention, Langton concluded that "bureaucratic structures were selected for retention because they increased profitability" (p. 347). Additionally, he noted that the bureaucratization of the pottery industry was a case of the "diffusion of innovation," in which an innovation "either stabilizes or declines depending upon its functional value" (p. 350).

Half a century ago, however, the assessment that social structures survive because they serve a function, such as enhancing a firm's profitability, was neither a noteworthy research finding nor an interesting empirical question. Rather, it served as a starting assumption for Parsons, Warner, and the other structural functionalists who were prominent in the founding of the sociology of organizations. By the end of the 1940s, Merton had published a widely read essay (1949) in which he pointed out the inadequacy for sociological theory development of noting the historical existence of a social structural phenomenon and, on the basis of its continued survival, assuming that it must be a source of improved functioning and survival capacity. Although seemingly not aware of this critique, at one point in his article Langton did indicate an awareness of the shortcomings of his perspective for purposes of framing and testing hypotheses. With remarkable candor, he admitted that the ecological theory is impossible to falsify and does not "permit precase predictions" (although he claimed, later in his paper, that the theory could be useful in generating testable hypotheses).

The frustration with the mainstream, intendedly Weberian, approach to organizational analysis seems also to have motivated a number of scholars in this field who represent the Marxian tradition. These individuals, however, have tended to view themselves as politically radical theorists, rather than as researchers. This orientation away from research may have been due to the difficulty of translating Marxian theory into distinctive, testable hypotheses; as discussed in Chapter 8, the Marxian contribution has been primarily in offering new interpretations of observed relationships.

More than simply being disinclined to operationalize concepts and measure data, however, many Marxian theorists have expressed a strong antipathy toward quantification. Burrell and Morgan (1979), in presenting the "radical structuralist" attack on organization theory, encouraged scholars not to feel constrained by the facts, stating that "Radical organization theory should seek to assert the primacy of a coherent theoretical perspective which is not necessarily subject to the tyranny of data" (p. 367).

Goldman and Van Houten (1977), attempting to explain the failure of two quantitative studies that tested, but did not support, Marxian hypotheses, offered only the cryptic footnote that "Blauner's (1964) and Zwerman's (1970) attempts to test derived hypotheses falter because they have not related their research to the larger context of the theory" (p. 109). Offering their own analysis of organization structure, they distanced themselves from the actual testing of theory, noting that the Marxian concepts that they were about to detail "represent less a source of derivable propositions to be tested than a set of guidelines to be followed in analyzing bureaucratic behavior" (1977, p. 109).

To a skeptical reader of Goldman and Van Houten's work it might appear that they are unwilling to expose Marxian propositions to empirical examination, and in cases where this was done and the Marxian view was not supported, they have simply asserted that the theory must not have been tested correctly. More charitably, it may be suggested that Marxian scholars essentially are pessimistic about the possibility of gathering accurate data. According to Goldman and Van Houten, "The precise impact of managerial motivations on policies affecting the lives of workers is of course difficult to specify with any precision since unobtrusive access to the executive suite is almost impossible for Marxist scholars" (1977, p. 114). The problem this creates for researchers, in their view, is that "it is unclear whether organizational practices result from real *intentionality* on the part of management" (1977, p. 114). Writing six years later, Goldman (1983) again noted that this refractory problem of determining managers' intentions was a dilemma that the analysis of organizations had yet to overcome.

The apparent aversion to collecting data that might permit the testing of hypotheses is certainly not limited to those of one particular political orientation. It is found, as well, among academics in the contemporary mainstream of organization theory, as taught in the conservatizing environment of schools of business administration. As organizational sociologists have responded to shifts in the labor market for Ph.D.s and migrated to business schools, reemerging as organization theorists, their political values and research concerns, when looked at in the aggregate, seem to have shifted somewhat. Formerly, research interests of organizational sociologists often focused on blue-collar workers' perspectives of the relations between labor and capital (or capital's representatives, management). Organization theorists, freed from their link with a traditional academic discipline, seem to have developed a keen market orientation, and lately have been paying acute attention to the concerns of their clientele: corporations, whose resources allow them to offer some professors highly remunerative consulting opportunities; and MBA students training for management roles.

Not surprisingly, these "customers" seem uninterested not only in theory, but in the procedures used by researchers to assess whether the phenomena they observe or manipulate are more than just trivial or random occurrences. That is, as Van de Vall, Bolas, and Kang have found (1976), the more sophisticated the statistical procedures used by organizational social scientists, the *less* favorably their work is regarded by their customers. As has been argued elsewhere (Weiss 1983), appreciation of social scientific, as opposed to less abstract "common sense," explanations of organizational life generally requires some training. But rather than burden students with complicated statistics and abstract theory, scholars of the social science of organizations, most especially those located in business schools, tend to teach on the basis of concrete, qualitative descriptions of organizations (DiTomaso 1985). This "case study method" of post hoc causal interpretation of complex, yet briefly described, business situations provides a dubious basis for generalizing to other organizations or other situations; it is nevertheless seen as appropriate, in part, because it is believed to be less taxing on the paying customers (Kotter, in Jelinek 1980).

THE REDISCOVERY OF THE HARVARD-CHICAGO PERSPECTIVE

This indifference to theory development and contempt for quantification, along with a possible reticence to expose strongly held beliefs to empirical examination, may have contributed to the shift away from the "Weberian" analysis of organizations over the past decade. In its place, many organizational theorists are currently pursuing theoretical agendas that are strikingly similar to the other original theoretical approach to the analysis of organizations. As discussed in Chapter 2, Parsons' misinterpretation of Weber as a structural functionalist, leading ultimately to what Blau and others thought were empirical tests of Weber, was only one of the products of the Pareto Circle's influence at Harvard. The effects of that group's approach extended also to the University of Chicago, transported there by two of its erstwhile members: W. Lloyd Warner, who had worked in close collaboration with Mayo on the Hawthorne studies, and William Foote Whyte, whose participant observation study of a poor neighborhood in Boston, conducted while a Junior Fellow at Harvard, was accepted as a doctoral dissertation at Chicago (and published in 1943 as *Street Corner Society*, now regarded as a classic of sociological analysis).

At Chicago, the melding of the Harvard group's perspective with the viewpoint of Chicago sociology (discussed in Chapter 3) produced many of the classic quasi-anthropological descriptions of organizations and occupations. The compatibility of these two perspectives has a number of sources. For example, the basic dilemmas in modern society were seen by both groups as rooted in the dissolution of traditional societies in which individuals had a strong sense of their place in the community and their role in life. In Henderson's version of Pareto, this societal transformation was seen as disruptive to social order because individuals were nonlogical and incapable of functioning effectively in the absence of a social structure in which the means to fulfill one's physical and emotional needs are strictly preordained. The Pareto group's solution to the social problems of industrial society was that the "captains of industry," once supplied with some guidance on how to satisfy their employees' psychic needs, were the appropriate persons to supply the leadership and direction that people wanted and required. The Chicago sociologists saw the rise of urban, industrialized, "mass society" as decreasing the effectiveness of the social controls that they viewed as having a salutary effect on society and on its individual members. Their research was directed toward gaining an understanding of the developing patterns of deviance from societal norms.

As discussed in Chapter 3, the basic concerns shared by the Chicago School and the Pareto Circle were also those of the mainstream of European sociology. However, the responses by these scholars in the United States to the basic sociological question of how the social order is maintained were not the same as those of the Europeans. At Harvard and Chicago the central question seems to have been how to bring individuals' behavior into line with a norm; the appropriateness of the particular norm was not generally questioned. In contrast, the classic tradition of European sociological theory—the tradition of Max Weber—examined the modernization of society and how its concomitantly higher differentiation affected both the distribution of the increasing material surpluses that it yielded and the distribution of power to establish the norms with which others could be made to comply.

These basic theoretical concerns are related to the choices of variables in the research inspired by these approaches. Fundamentally, the Harvard-Chicago approach emphasized ideal, subjective factors as explanatory mechanisms. For example, Mayo and his colleagues interpreted the Hawthorne studies as demonstrating that productivity was determined by workers' feelings that they were being supervised by individuals who cared about their personal happiness, and that workers' desires to adhere to groups' social norms more successfully predicted their level of productivity than did opportunities for economic gain. The decades of empirical behavioral science investigations that have searched, with very limited success, for the effects of job satisfaction on job performance are, in no small part, a result of that famous legend (Baritz 1960). A concern with the influence of subjective factors was always integral to Weber's sociology as well, as exemplified in his discussion of the ideologies that legitimate authority; however, objective, material factors were also considered. For example, although the work carried out by Blau and his students on the "Weberian" sociology of organizations may have been based on a misunderstanding of Weber's view of the roles of the various material, structural characteristics of organizations, the research variables that were extrapolated from Weber's model do reflect his concerns with objective aspects of social structure.

The Harvard-Chicago approach to the sociology of organizations has reappeared in contemporary organizational research, perhaps most prominently in the recent attention to the concept of "organizational culture." The current literature on this topic is notably similar to a body of qualitative research on the cultural and social character of worklife conducted four decades ago at Chicago by a group of sociologists and social anthropologists. Moore (1946) and Cottrell (1940) discussed the use of special jargons or argots, which they viewed as facilitating group cohesiveness and identification among members of particular occupations. Myers (1948) argued that all work groups have elaborate and enduring myths about themselves and about others, which serve functions such as the dramatic symbolization of the group's values and the maintenance of morale. Miller and Form (1951) discussed the roles of ceremonies and rituals, which "are important because they may reveal the basic ideas and beliefs of the group." For example, they argued that rites of passage are very important because they function to "maintain, reinforce, and express feelings of solidarity.... They also symbolize the common values" (p. 293). However, by the end of the 1950s, having used their descriptive data to draw thought-provoking analogies between aspects of some modern work roles and those of primitive societies, scholars pursuing this line of research seemed to lose direction. In "A Field in Search of a Focus" (1965) Whyte indicated that his students eventually "began to look for methods of data gathering and analysis that would enable them to make comparative studies of a number of cases (p. 307)."

Warner's influences on these studies are readily identifiable, and appear to have gone substantially beyond the mere insertion of anthropological terms such as "symbolization of values" and "myth." Rather, this work also seems to have incorporated the functionalist orientation of Warner and his mentor Malinowski, who had argued that intensive observation of a culture would reveal that the structures that existed in a society did so because they served some function in increasing the survivability of that culture and its members (1960). These studies illustrate, in a number of ways, the bases of Merton's (1949) critique of functionalism as assuming that structures functioned equally for all of society. That is, although jargon, myths, and rituals may function to facilitate cohesiveness, maintain morale, or symbolize common values, they might also be used by certain individuals to impose their own values and goals on others.

Regrettably, the current round of writings on "culture" seems not to have addressed this long-standing concern. Not only the objections to the Chicago studies of the 1940s, but the studies themselves, seem to have been forgotten. Van Maanen and Barley (1984), in an article entitled

"Occupational Communities: Culture and Control in Organizations," stated their purpose as demonstrating "the utility of viewing behavior in organizations through an occupational rather than organizational lens" (p. 288). Such an essay was necessary, they contended, because although "considerable lip service has been paid to such a perspective by organizational theorists . . . focused and conceptually-driven research based on such a perspective has been notably absent" (p. 288). To help fill this supposed lacuna, Van Maanen and Barley drew on Van Maanen's ethnographic studies of police work to demonstrate that "jargon and argot," such as referring to certain styles of automobiles as "pimpmobiles" and certain types of citizens as "dirtbags," function to encourage "positive identification with an occupation." Although Merton and countless other sociologists over the past few decades have warned of the problems of functionalist explanations, no alternative interpretations of these field data were offered. For example, the use of language that seems to encourage racist stereotyping and in general degrade civilians might be functional for veteran police officers to instill in rookies a cynical view of their work, but it might be less functional for the citizenry whom the police are charged to protect. Nonetheless, Van Maanen and Barley cannot be accused of being the only ones unaware of the Chicago School's work on occupational cultures, the functionalist orientation of those studies, and the critiques of that position; their paper received the 1985 "New Concept Award" from the Organizational Behavior Division of the Academy of Management.

Many of the current generation of organizational culture papers also have in common with the Chicago School the subjectivist theoretical perspective known as Symbolic Interactionism, although the connection to that old and substantially unsuccessful (Coser 1975; Huber 1973; Mullins 1973) paradigm is recognized explicitly in the organizational culture literature only rarely (e.g., Evered 1983; Gray, Bougon, and Donnellon 1985; Wexler 1983). In light of the norm in academic writing of acknowledging the roots of one's theoretical position, and the absence of acknowledgement of symbolic interactionists' work in most organizational culture studies, it seems that many contemporary culture writers are unaware of this link. That this connection exists even for those whose work does not specifically mention the earlier perspective, however, is apparent in comparing the following definition of culture from the introductory essay to a special issue on organizational culture in the *Administrative Science Quarterly* to Coser's explanation of the basic standpoint of Symbolic Interactionism:

> Culture—another word for social reality—is both product and process, the shaper of human interaction and the outcome of it, continually created and recreated by people's ongoing interactions (Jelinek, Smircich and Hirsch 1983, p. 331).

Meanings are constructed and reconstructed in the process of social action.... Social reality, far from being stable, is the result of ongoing negotiations between mutually involved sets of actors (Coser 1976, p.176).

The similarity between the organizational culture literature and a theory that argues that the social world is built up purely from interpersonal interactions would not seem consistent with the contention that the culture literature is isomorphic to the work of the Pareto Circle or the Chicago School theorists. Those groups have been portrayed here as having focused on the question, central to European social theory, of the nature of social control. However, the symbolic interactionist perspective was initially formulated as an attempt to construct a theory that would fill in the social psychological details of the macrosocial processes described by theorists concerned with social control, including Durkheim, Freud, and Marx. Symbolic Interactionism, named Blumer (1937) but founded by George Herbert Mead, proposed that the necessary precondition for social order was the ability of individuals to assume the role of a "generalized other." This was done, Mead (1934) argued, through the vocal gesture, which is to say, language. Contending that social integration rests, most basically, on the use of these shared vocal symbols, he alluded to the issues addressed by Durkheim and Marx in stating: "The process of communication is one which is more universal that that of the universal religion or universal economic process in that it is one that serves them both" (1934, p. 259). Nevertheless, Mead was entirely aware that the exchange of vocal symbols ultimately had to be *about* something, such as normative or economic processes, and that this symbolic interaction not only influenced but was influenced by these structural phenomena.

The view of the Symbolic Interactionist approach that influenced the Chicago School organization theorists, however, was that of Blumer, who served as a member of Chicago's Committee on Human Relations in Industry, the academic unit that had sponsored these studies. Neglecting the dialectical understanding offered by Mead, Blumer advocated a purely idealist perspective that decried conceiving of "human society in terms of structure or organization" or of considering "social action as an expression of such structure or organization" (1937, p. 189). Criticizing Blumer's approach, Zeitlin has asked: "If some men control property and other resources while other men do not, and the latter are able to earn their livelihood only by working for the former, would Blumer deny that this relationship is a determinant of action?" (1973, p. 217).

Those influenced by Blumer who conducted research in capitalist work organizations did not specifically deny the significance of the social relations of production; it simply was not of particular theoretical concern. From Blumer's perspective the social world did not have an objective reality: phenomena existed only insofar as their meaning had been constructed, generally employing language as the medium, through interactions with others. This influence is evident in studies, such as those of Moore and Cottrell, in which the focus was on the development of linguistic forms—jargon and argot—rather than on the substance of what those media were communicating *about*. Coser (1976) has noted that Symbolic Interactionism has been rejected by most sociologists as "a kind of scientific Luddism," arguing that:

> it rejects conceptual generalization and abstraction and allows concepts to perform at best a sensitizing function. Since the world is constructed from interpretative processes arising in transactions between individuals it is only amenable to careful descriptions aided by sensitizing, as opposed to theoretically grounded, concepts (p. 156).

Nevertheless, organization culture scholars, many of whom were trained in business schools rather than sociology departments, are currently pursuing topics that are highly similar to those that occupied the attention of the group at Chicago. The table of contents of a collection of readings entitled *Organizational Symbolism* (Pondy, Frost, Morgan, and Dandridge 1983) shows the focus on language rather than content that the Symbolic Interactionists pursued many years ago. Among the topics offered in the collection were "The Language of Organizations," "Organizational Stories as Symbols Which Control the Organization," "The Value of a Good War Story," "The Language of Corporate Takeovers," and "Humor in a Machine Shop."

Yet another parallel between the Harvard-Chicago viewpoint and that of the contemporary organizational culture writers is the propensity to analogize between primitive cultures and the "cultures" inside modern corporations. For example, the writing of William Ouchi (author of a best-selling book on management, and recipient of a doctorate in sociology from Chicago) not only indicates a sharing of Mayo's interest in Durkheim's analysis of the bases of social solidarity, but offers a strikingly similar interpretation of that sociologist's work. Noting Durkheim's view that the occupational group is the most viable replacement for the social integrative mechanisms lost in the transition from primitive to modern society, Ouchi and Johnson (1978) argued, much as Mayo (1933) did, that in modern societies "the work organization may be the one social institution which can provide primary relations" (1978, p. 287). However, when Durkheim wrote of occupational groups, often using the term corporation for that purpose, he was referring to guildlike associations of individuals engaged in the same craft, not to individuals who happened to work for the same employer (1933).

Ouchi (1980), in describing what he called the clan form of organization—that is, one based on members' congruity of values, beliefs, and traditions—again cited Durkheim, this time as support for his view that "any occupational group which has organic solidarity may be considered a clan. Thus, a profession, a labor union, or a corporation may be considered a clan" (1980, p. 136). However, two paragraphs after the one cited by Ouchi, Durkheim reiterated his view that capitalist enterprises (which would appear to be *Ouchi's* use of the term corporation) could never attain organic solidarity. The similarity of Ouchi's misconceptions of Durkheim to those of Mayo is also suggested by Ouchi and Johnson's observation, in summarizing their description of what they called the "Type Z" organization, that "Mayo foresaw a work organization with very much the same kind of wholistic and broad community relations as we described" (p. 311).

An illustration, from the contemporary organizational culture literature, of the direct analogizing from primitive to modern society is provided by Martin, who employed terms and concepts remarkably similar to those of the original culture researchers. Rather than misconstruing Durkheim, she appears to have been unaware of his argument. The following quote illustrates as well her use of the functionalist orientation of Parsons, Warner, and the Chicago researchers:

> When anthropologists discuss the functions that such myths serve in tribal societies, the organizational relevance of this research becomes clear. Myths serve to maintain and express solidarity among members of a community, legitimate the power structure of the community's institutions, and validate the rituals of the tribe (Martin 1981, p. 263).

However, the organizational relevance of such research may be less clear than Martin suggests, especially in light of her apparently interchangeable use of the terms tribe and community. In Durkheim's analysis, myths and rituals may serve to maintain and express solidarity among members of a tribe or other premodern collectivity. Solidarity in a modern community, however, in which there is a division of labor, is based on exchanges rooted in the interdependencies of individuals who each carry out relatively unique roles. That is, the less primitive the society, the more irrelevant for social solidarity are phenomena such as myths and symbols. Additionally, her functionalist approach seems open to the same challenge of that perspective that Merton posed more than three decades ago: Do myths, for example, "express solidarity among members," or might they just as well enhance subordination of the majority by a dominant clique?

That the rediscovery of organizational culture has restored the influence of the Harvard group is also suggested by Schein's recent conversion to advocacy of the culture perspective. He has noted that "this shift takes me back full circle" (1985 p. xi) to graduate work at Harvard almost four decades ago. The influences of Mayo's version of Durkheim, which views an absence of shared values as causing anomie, and Henderson's version of Pareto, which argues that powerful leaders bring a feeling of security to the masses, do seem apparent in his statement that:

> At the core of every culture will be assumptions about the proper way for individuals to relate to each other in order to make the group safe and comfortable. When such assumptions [regarding "power, influence, and hierarchy" and "intimacy, love, and peer relationships"] are not widely shared, we speak of "anarchy" and "anomie" (Schein 1985, p.104).

Although Schein may define a situation in which there is a lack of consensus on issues such as power as one of anarchy and anomie, others might describe those conditions as "pluralism" and "tolerance of others." Schein, however, took the position of the Harvard group, claiming that shared assumptions are a universal of healthy societies. By then placing shared assumptions at the center of his definition of organizational culture, Schein could argue that the creation of an organizational culture serves the benign function of reducing anarchy and anomie. His conclusion that *"the unique and essential function of leadership is the manipulation of culture"* (p. 317) compares closely to the view expressed by Henderson and Mayo's epigone, Chester Barnard, that "the inculcation of belief in the real existence of a common purpose is an essential executive function" (1938, p. 233).

The influence of the Pareto Circle on the organizational culture literature is not restricted to purely theoretical discussions. In his essay on "How to Decipher and Change Organizational Culture" (1984, 1985), Sathe, a current member of the Harvard Business School faculty, wrote purely prescriptively when he stated that:

> One must get people to see the inherent worth of what it is they are being asked to do . . . [and] one way to do this is to persuade people to unlearn or question their current pattern of beliefs and values by helping them to see that their assumptions are not confirmed by reality testing, or are actually disconfirmed (1984, pp. 20-21; 1985, p. 20-21).

Consistent with Henderson's version of Pareto, Sathe took the role of the leader to be that of straightening out subordinates' nonlogical sentiments. Consistent with Barnard, who asserted that organizations, as cooperative systems, could only have outputs that were moral and worthwhile, he assumed that there *is* an inherent worth to what employees are asked to do.

Much of the prescriptive literature on organizational culture is essentially hortatory, and much of the rest uses qualitative data to make its case. In more theoretically-oriented writings, and when the description is of some length and detail, the research is often referred to as "ethnographic" (see Van Maanen, Dabbs, and Faulkner 1982). Reviewing a number of these studies, however, a noted anthropologist (Harris 1984) considered their self-description as ethnographies to be merely presumptuous. Some recent culture studies have attempted to buttress their recommendations by providing quantitative analyses to demonstrate the importance of the culture concept for understanding organizations. For example, Pozner, Kouzes, and Schmidt (1985), in an article entitled "Shared Values Make a Difference: An Empirical Test of Corporate Culture," reported a survey in which almost 1,500 managers provided information on their salary, level in the organization, gender, and educational attainment. Additionally, the respondents completed a number of Likert scales addressing such issues as their perceived career success, their willingness to work long hours, and the extent to which their personal values were compatible with those of their organization, their coworkers, their superiors, and their subordinates.

In Pozner, Kouzes, and Schmidt's study, the theoretical orientation underlying the data collection and analysis seems, again, to be remarkably reminiscent of the Harvard perspective of the 1920s and 1930s. They stated that "In our free society, we permit a wide variety of groups to form and disband on the assumption that those . . . which do not serve a useful purpose will in time fail to attract sufficient individuals who share their values" (1985, p. 304). In doing so, Pozner and his associates seem to have combined Parsonian functionalism with Barnard's view that organizations, because they are composed of individuals who have freely joined together to engage in an enterprise that expresses their shared value orientation, all have moral outcomes. To illustrate their point, the authors—who otherwise discussed only large, private sector corporations in the article—offered only a list of voluntary associations, such as The Moral Majority and the ACLU. The reader is left to wonder how the authors would explain the ability of companies in the tobacco industry to hire and retain clerks, truck drivers, and direct laborers.

More significant than the choice of illustrative examples is the apparent influence of this theoretical perspective on their choice of analyses to conduct with their quantitative data. Only the Likert-scaled opinion items were analyzed; the dependent variable was a "Shared Values Index" composed of responses to two items, which asked whether the respondents' personal values were congruent with those of their organization, and whether working for their employer caused them to compromise their moral principles. Not too surprisingly, this measure was found to predict opinions concerning, for example, whether the respondents' personal values were congruent with those of their coworkers, subordinates, and superiors, and whether their broader moral values were congruent with those others. Respondents who felt that they shared values with their organization also perceived their careers as more successful, and expressed greater willingness to work long hours. The authors concluded that these findings demonstrated that creating a "corporate culture," an environment in which values are held in common, causes these salutary outcomes.

However, their subjectivist orientation seems to have led them to not consider alternative interpretations of their findings. For example, perceived success and sharing of values might not be causally, but only spuriously, related, as both might be associated with respondents' organizational levels. As Aiken and Bacharach (1976) have shown, subjective reactions to an organization seem to result from one's objective location in its hierarchy; thus those near the top are likely to share the values of others in that stratum. Moreover, individuals in higher level positions would be likely to perceive themselves as successful.

Ouchi and Wilkins, vigorous proponents of the organizational culture perspective, have recently reviewed the literature on this topic (1985), contending that the source of its current popularity is rooted in organizational researchers' disenchantment with the objectivist, "Weberian" study of bureaucracy. For example, they described Lincoln, Olson, and Hanada's (1978) frustration over the inability of what Ouchi and Wilkins referred to as the "size-complexity-administrative ratio model" to help them understand the differences between the workings of organizations in Japan and in the United States. According to Ouchi and Wilkins, this failure (and others) of "the paradigm of formal organizational structure" was a major impetus to the focus on culture rather than structure as the prime determinant of organizational behavior.

Their assessment of the reason for the current interest in organizational culture is one with which the analysis offered in the present study certainly concurs. Nonetheless, having featured the work of Lincoln and his associates, they might have mentioned that these particular researchers, rather than slipping into the "despair" that Ouchi and Wilkins characterized as the emotional state of many organizational scholars at the end of the 1970s, continued their investigation into differences between Japanese and U.S. firms. In a later publication (Lincoln, Hanada, and Olson 1981) they were able to explain a substantial proportion of the differences they sensed to exist between companies in those two cultural contexts. To achieve this, however, they did not revert to impressionistic observations, nor to surveys focusing on subjective assessments and disregarding objective structural criteria. Rather, they retained their data on formal organizational structure, and added demographic characteristics of individual employees, as well as those employees' subjective reactions to the workplace. This attention to both objective and subjective factors, at both the individual and organizational levels, is, this book has argued, precisely the research strategy that Max Weber advocated.

THE ANALYSIS OF IDEOLOGY IN CONTEMPORARY ORGANIZATION THEORY

The concept of ideology has been of central interest for both the study that has been reported in the present book and the current round of studies of organizational culture. Not only has ideology been included as one of the defining elements of organizational culture (Pettigrew 1979; Strand 1983), but William Starbuck, a former editor of the *Administrative Science Quarterly*, has announced that ideology is the answer to the question of what determines the structure of organizations:

> Organization theorists have carried out numerous studies of so-called objective phenomena, and their aggregate finding is that almost nothing correlates strongly and consistently with anything else. This null finding fits the hypothesis that organizational structures and technologies are primarily arbitrary, temporary, and superficial characteristics. These characteristics are determined by complex interactions among ideologies (Starbuck, 1982, p. 1).

Unfortunately, Starbuck did not identify the source of the evidence that led him to this conclusion. Although data have not yet been published to confirm Starbuck's assertion, in recent years a number of organization theorists based in business schools have offered analyses of ideology. These studies and theoretical essays, although largely agreeing among themselves as to what ideology means, work from an understanding of the term that is highly discrepant from that which has been employed in the present study and in most discussions of this concept in twentieth-century social science. In these recent writings ideology has been subjected to a remarkable transformation, in which it has been stripped of its political content.

In essence, these papers have defined the term ideology with no reference to the particular interests that an ideology serves to advance. In an influential essay, Beyer defined ideologies as "relatively coherent sets of beliefs that bind some people together and that explain their worlds in terms of cause-and-effect relations" (1981, p. 166). Somewhat similarly, Abravanel defined organizational ideology as "a set of fundamental ideas and operative consequences linked together into a dominant belief system often producing contradictions but serving to define and maintain the organization" (1983, p. 274). Ideology was defined by Dunbar, Dutton, and Torbert as "shared beliefs which reflect the social experiences in a particular context at a given time" (1982, p. 91), and by Starbuck as "a logically integrated cluster of beliefs, values, rituals, and symbols" (1982, p. 1). Brunsson stated "an ideology is a set of ideas" (1982, p. 38).

From where might these authors have gotten definitions of this term that, in passing over the interest-based nature of ideology, are so much at variance with the concept's standard usage in the social sciences? Only two of the five writings mentioned above provided sources for their definition. Beyer cited Apter (1964) as having defined ideology as a "generic term applied to general ideas potent in specific situations of conduct ... it is the link between action and fundamental belief (Beyer 1981, p. 166). However, filling in the parts of Apter's definition for which Beyer substituted ellipses provides a very different sense than the version she presented, in which ideologies appear as simply general linking mechanisms between affect and behavior. Apter described as ideological "not *any* ideals, only political ones; not *any* values, only those specifying a given set of preferences; not *any* beliefs, only those governing a particular mode of thought" (1964, p. 17). In his previous paragraph Apter was far more direct, indicating that ideology may be viewed as lending "a more honorable and dignified complexion to social conduct" or as "a cloak for shabby motives and appearances" (1964, p. 16).

Whereas Beyer's omission of Apter's explanation of the political nature of ideology conceivably could be explained by editorial exigencies, Abravanel's depoliticized definition more clearly is based on a distortion of his source. He claimed to be directly quoting Berger and Luckmann as describing ideology as "a particular definition of reality that comes to be attached to an organizaton or group" (Abravanel 1983, p. 274). In fact, the precise quote is "When a particular definition of reality comes to be attached to a concrete power interest, it may be called an ideology" (1967, p. 123). Among sociologists, Berger and Luckmann's "social construction of reality" perspective is criticized because it directs too *little* attention to issues of political power, seeing processes such as domination as socially constructed, rather than as inherent in social facts such as the relations of production (Abercrombie 1980; Light 1969). Yet, by removing Berger and Luckmann's reference to "concrete power interest," Abravanel altered their definition of ideology to direct even less attention to issues of power, instead leaving the impression that ideology had been defined simply as what groups of people happen to be thinking.

Abravanel continued his analysis of ideology, stating that "Ideology, though not directly observable, is a construct that requires empirical validation if it is to be taken seriously" (p. 277). As empirical validation for his view that "In order to survive, [organizations] must have a solid ideological basis" (p. 285) (in which the contradictions between the fundamental and operative ideologies are mediated by myths) he presented four "brief case studies" averaging two-thirds of a page in length. For example, one of the studies that served as empirical validation for his viewpoint consisted of the assertion that the fundamental ideology of IBM was the "freedom and independence of employees," that the operative ideology involved conformity in such areas as attire, and that the mediating myth was that "freedom comes with restraint."

Meyer made use of Beyer's conception of ideology in his investigation of ideology's effects on organizational structure and performance. Defining "harmony" as an ideology, and noting that it was correlated negatively with formalization and complexity in a small sample of hospitals, he concluded that harmony obviates formalization and complexity. In concluding that ideology causally influenced organizational structure, Meyer failed to address obvious alternative causal interpretations of his data—for example, that complexity may have been a cause of disharmonies (as was found by Lawrence and Lorsch 1967). Not only did he argue that ideology influenced organizational structure, but that it shaped responses to the environment as well. That is, analyzing three hospitals' responses to a strike, he noted that each of them responded differently; having characterized the hospitals as exhibiting different ideologies, he concluded that it must have been the ideologies that caused these different responses. The possibility that the ideology and the response to the environment might both be explained by some underlying reality was not considered.

Beyer and Trice also reported (1981) a quantitative investigation of ideology in organizations. They studied the use of managerial discipline, based on an evaluation they had conducted of a large corporation's alcoholism program. They reasoned that "personal and work histories help to create and alter managerial ideologies, which then, moderated by situational variables and expectations, lead managers to take certain actions to deal with deviant behaviors among subordinates" (1981, p. 260). On the basis of additive scales of two to five Likert-type questionnaire items, five ideologies (i.e., "coherent sets of beliefs") were constructed, with an average scale reliability of .54. Examining the first of their hypotheses, regression analyses of whether "personal and work histories help to create and alter" these ideologies yielded adjusted r^2s "that ranged from .00 to .02" (Beyer and Trice 1981, p. 261). Addressing their final hypothesis, concerning the effects of these views on managers' behavior, their most substantial finding was that supervisors who agreed with statements such as "I feel an obligation to help out others who are in trouble" and "Everyone has problems at one time or another and needs help from others" were more likely to state that they talk with their subordinates about personal problems.

In contrast to Meyer's study, Beyer and Trice's design permitted independent assessments of both the presumed causes and effects of managerial ideologies. However, they failed to demonstrate that the clusters of questionnaire items that they called ideologies were distorted, oversimplifying ideas that legitimate self-serving action. Rather, they were able to find only that a very few highly specific opinions were linked to some very closely related behaviors.

Although these studies have attempted to provide somewhat more justification for their claims of ideology's importance than did Starbuck in his simple declaration that ideology determines organizational structure, it is not clear what these uses of the term ideology have to do with the concept discussed in Chapter 3. Neither "harmony" nor agreement with the statement "everyone has problems at one time or another" constitute "selected or distorted ideas about a social system [that] purport to be factual, and also carry a more or less explicit evaluation of the 'facts'" (Johnson 1968, p. 77). Nor do they "define a particular program of social action as legitimate and worthy of support" (Johnson 1968, p. 81) or provide "a relatively simple definition of a complex situation" (Johnson 1968, p. 83). These key elements of Johnson's description of ideology—written from what is considered to be the most conservative of theoretical perspectives in sociology—are entirely missing from all of the contemporary conservative organization theory that makes use of the term ideology. For the vast majority of social scientists, of both radical and conservative persuasions, over a period of many decades, a "set of beliefs" has been merely a set of beliefs, and not an ideology. The opinion that "everyone has problems at one time or another" is merely an opinion and not an ideology—unless perhaps, it can be shown that agreement with this viewpoint serves "to activate [people] according to a common definition of the situation and a common plan" (Johnson 1968, p. 83). The findings Beyer and Trice presented, however, indicated that individuals' espousal of these opinions generally did not activate behaviors.

Discussions of ideology in organizations have not been restricted to the work of professors of business administration; some are found among the writings of Marxian scholars as well. They appear to use the term primarily to signify a type of analysis, typically a discursive critique that attempts to reveal the class-interest bases of ideas that have been presented as factual and neutral. That is, this usage of the term ideology often denotes analyses intended to show how those whose views are different from the authors' are promoting purposeful, deceptive bunkum. Salaman and Thompson's (1980) edited volume of readings written from a Marxian perspective on organizations was entitled *Control and Ideology in Organizations*. However, only two of the 13 chapters even mentioned ideology, and in both cases the analysis was theoretical rather than empirical. Fischer and Sirianni's (1984) edited volume of *Critical Studies in Organization and Bureaucracy* included an essay by the first coeditor on "Ideology and Organization Theory." It consisted of a summary of Bendix's *Work and Authority in Industry*.

A quantitative analysis of organizations' use of ideology was reported by Seider (1974), who analyzed "American Big Business Ideology." Writing from a Marx-Mannheim sociology of knowledge perspective, he echoed the doubts expressed by Marxian scholars that such questions are amenable to investigation with standard sociologists' techniques, arguing that "Questionnaire responses may be useful for specific issues but are probably too narrow in scope to encompass a world view or ideology"

(1974, p. 805). His resolution of this conundrum was to content-analyze executives' speeches; he then related the speeches' contents to the industry in which the speaker was employed. Seider found, for example, that aerospace executives were more likely to use nationalistic themes and to advocate military spending than were retail executives. Although these findings would seem to support the basic notion of the sociology of knowledge perspective, namely, that consciousness is shaped by material existence, Seider offered no evidence that these speeches contained distorted oversimplifications of their subject matter. Moreover, the general public is quite aware that speeches are often made to advance the speaker's interests. As a result these particular findings seem painfully unenlightening.

The present study's claim to have identified causes and effects of a managerial ideology, in contrast to both the Marxian and the conservative analyses reviewed here, would appear to satisfy the criteria set forth in Johnson's (1968) essay on the characteristics of an ideology. The medical disease model of alcoholism is indeed based on "selected or distorted ideas" that "purport to be factual"; for example, the number of individuals found by systematic research to have had some problem with alcohol is cited as the number of victims of the disease of alcoholism. The medical model provides "a relatively simple definition of a complex situation," as in company policy statements that explain that the disease exists when an individual's job performance is substandard. It attempts to "define a particular program of social action as legitimate and worthy of support," for instance, by explaining that because of "denial," forcing an employee into the program "is the kindest thing [the supervisor] can do." Finally, the quantitative analyses have suggested that the disease model can "activate [people] according to a common definition of the situation"; companies that started an EAP to improve productivity, and that hired an administrator who advocated the disease model, were more likely than others to provide training to supervisory personnel, who were more inclined to refer subordinates to the program, which was rated by the personnel executive as having been more effective in improving productivity.

SOCIAL THEORY AND THE ANALYSIS OF ALCOHOLISM AND EMPLOYEE ASSISTANCE PROGRAMS

Most writing and research on occupational alcoholism and employee assistance programs has not been directed toward the testing and development of sociological theory. The present study, however, has attempted to illustrate the usefulness of the application of Weberian theory to the interpretation of this contemporary organizational phenomenon. The argument has been made here, as well, that Weber's theoretical perspective on organizations, understood as Weber had intended, is a more useful scientific theory than the currently fashionable versions of the half-century-old Harvard-Chicago perspectives.

Fortunately, the opportunity exists to compare the ability of these two theoretical traditions to provide an understanding of occupational programs. Trice and his associates, whose work has figured so prominently in the occupational alcoholism field, have worked from an avowedly sociological perspective. Although most of their work on these programs has had an applied orientation, their theoretical leanings have been made clear in a number of papers.

Trice and Sonnenstuhl (1985b, p. 6) noted that "the findings of sociological research on social control" comprised one of three sources (along with studies of affiliation with A.A. and the concept, in industrial relations, of "progressive discipline") for Trice's development of the constructive confrontation strategy. Addressing this connection between sociological research and coercive managerial strategies in a more detailed analysis of this technique and its social control implications, Trice and Beyer (1982) identified social control as a pivotal concept in the social sciences, associating it with the work of E. A. Ross, W. I. Thomas, and Charles H. Cooley, early members of the Chicago School; Everett C. Hughes, a later member of that group; Emile Durkheim and George Simmel, from the mainstream of European social theory; and Talcott Parsons, George Homans, and William F. Whyte, members of the Harvard Pareto Circle. Trice and Beyer noted that a common concern among these theorists was the means by which society maintains conformity to the normative order. However, reviewing the history of debates over the value of the Chicago School social control perspective, they asserted their disagreement with the criticism that it was biased toward the assumption of normative conformity, stating that "the concept does not necessarily embrace the status quo" (p. 24) and that "all forms of social and class conflict . . . can be analyzed with the concept of social control" (1982, p. 23).

Nevertheless, their analysis of the use of the constructive confrontation strategy in occupational alcoholism and employee assistance programs, presented as an application of this honored sociological tradition, was not a convincing demonstration of either the value freedom or sensitivity to conflict of the social control approach. They noted that the constructive confrontation strategy "assumes that the social controls used in work settings are expressions of the beliefs and values of American society" (Trice and Beyer 1982, p. 28), although they neither cited nor supplied evidence that this assumption is justified. Nevertheless, they emphasized the theme that the activities of corporate management are reflective of the values of the general public, arguing that "work settings have a legitimate basis for intervention that is largely absent in other groups and institutions—namely, the right to expect performance in exchange for wages and salary" (p. 26).

Not only were the goals and activities of management said to be consistent with the values of the general public, but individual employees were said to accept managements' perspectives so completely that they make them their own: "Most members of a society internalize values that are compatible with role expectations. Consequently, external controls—such as formal expectations to perform efficiently on a job—are often consistent with individual values derived from the larger culture" (Trice and Beyer 1982, p. 24). Trice and Sonnenstuhl (1985a) applied this theme directly to the use of constructive confrontation, asserting not only that managements' performance norms are held by individual members of society, but that deviants will find that their co-workers have internalized and are committed to those norms. The discussion by these authors of the process of dealing with deviant employees noted that "the confrontational part of such discussions ... reiterates internalized values upheld by the group (in this case, expectations of work performance)" (Trice and Sonnenstuhl 1985b, p. 9).

Although these assertions were made in the absence of any supporting evidence, the opinion that remunerative rewards to employees legitimate an employer's expectation for efficient performance is not particularly counterintuitive. However, it is frequently recognized that the level of legitimacy accorded managements' work norms hinges on the specific definition of efficient performance. The Harvard and Chicago studies in industrial sociology documented that workers felt that they owed their employers "a fair day's work" for "a fair day's pay" (Whyte 1955); nevertheless, the specifics of what constituted such a level of work effort (or of pay, for that matter) were, and obviously still are, a matter of dissensus between labor and management. In neglecting this ubiquitous phenomenon, Trice and Beyer's denial that the social control perspective is insensitive to the analysis of class conflict seems contradicted by their own analysis.

The inappropriateness of applying the Chicago School's broad conceptualization of social control to the analysis of work organizations, as Trice and Beyer have done, was discussed in Chapter 3, in which it was argued that for those employed in capitalist work organizations conformity to norms generally means conformity to the will of management. The insensitivity of the Chicago School social control approach to differences between compliance with broadly legitimated regulations, and compliance based on the calculative, instrumental involvement (Etzioni 1968) characteristic of wage labor, is in distinct contrast to the tradition in European social thought that this book has attempted to follow. As discussed in previous chapters, a central interest for Rousseau, Hegel, Marx, and others in this tradition was the dialectical relationship between individuals' roles as members of the state (the domain of universalistic concerns) and of civil society (in which particularistic interests predominate). Once the division of labor had created a civil society of individuals and groups pursuing differing, often competing, economic activities, the role of normative consensus in the maintenance of social solidarity became more limited than when actions benefitting one member of the community were likely to benefit all.

The theoretical outgrowths of the Harvard-Chicago perspective of the 1920s and 1930s, such as the social control approach, and, more recently, organizational culture, generally have ignored the effects of this great societal transformation. Rather, they appear to view norms as simply emerging, perhaps on the basis of some functional need of the group, but certainly not as representative of the particular interests of one individual or subgroup. Compliance and even internalization are then assumed to follow, nonproblematically. The prescriptively oriented organizational culture literature, as management theory rather than social science theory, leaves no doubt as to what the source of those norms should be, unabashedly advising management to manipulate organizational norms so that they are isomorphic with their own goals. In light of the emphasis in these theoretical perspectives on value consensus, and the present study's concern with deviance, their explanations for the existence of noncompliant behavior are of particular interest. In the organizational culture literature poor fits between the corporate culture and individual behavior are often explained in terms of imperfect socialization; letting new employees in on the company's myths, legends, stories, sagas, and so on, is recommended as the way to get them "on the team." The explanation of why some employees might not conform to the group's (that is, the company's) performance norms provided by the social control perspective of Trice and his associates' apparently is that noncompliant employees are sick. Suffering from alcoholism or perhaps depression, these employees are purported to be in need of treatment through constructive confrontation, consisting of "crisis precipitation" through the use of the "job threat."

Max Weber and Reinhard Bendix analyzed the nature of control in society without assuming that healthy, properly socialized individuals simply comply with whatever commands are put forward as norms. They assumed, instead, that individuals first attempt to assess whether others have the right to impose their norms on them. From Weber's and Bendix's perspective, following in the tradition of European social thought, the central problem of social domination becomes the means by which those who wish to control others justify their position. One such means is through the advocacy of an ideology that, once legitimated, is a key to a system of domination that is enforced through a bureaucratic administrative structure. Examining specific hypotheses derived from these theorists, this study has been able to find a number of statistically significant, nonobvious, associations among variables of organizational structure and process and individuals' beliefs. Objective measures of organizational structure were found to be related to executives' subjective impressions of managerial control problems. These subjective impressions were associated with the beliefs held by other individuals about the causes of alcohol problems, which in turn were associated with the presence of particular EAP features, and with objective and subjective (as rated by the personnel executive) outcomes.

The present study also endeavored to make use of certain aspects of the social control perspective that has developed in the United States. In particular, it examined two that Parsons' student Pitts (1968), writing from the more narrowly defined perspective in which social control refers to the institutional mechanisms for managing deviance, noted as having potential for facilitating the analysis of conflict. The data that have been presented here have provided empirical support for his statement that the redefinition of deviance as a medical problem can facilitate social control by establishing tenable criteria for negative sanctioning. That is, this study has shown that in many organizations employees' frequent absenteeism and lateness can result in their being diagnosed as alcoholic, and that the consequence of that diagnosis often is exposure to very credible threats of job loss. The means by which this medicalization of deviance is accomplished illustrates the other of Pitts' contentions noted in Chapter 3, that ideology serves an important role in social control by clarifying the substantive content of norms. This study has indicated that the medical disease model of alcoholism tends to be adopted by companies concerned about increasing their employees' productivity, and that a number of its corollaries, such as the identification of alcoholics and other "troubled" employees on the basis of poor job performance, aid in clarifying the company's performance norms by defining employees in need of "assistance" as those whose behavior is outside of the boundaries of those norms.

SUMMARY

This study has attempted to investigate what have been argued here to be the central questions in Weber's essays on bureaucracy, questions that, prior to this study, had only been addressed by Bendix's *Work and Authority in Industry*. Specifically, in his analysis of the sociology of domination, Weber theorized that bureaucratic modes of control and ideologies of management are the mechanisms brought into play when those in possession of the means of administration experience problems of social control. Both qualitative and quantitative data have been offered here as evidence that the medical disease ideology of alcoholism constitutes a managerial ideology, a set of ideas that are "espoused by or for those who exercise authority in economic enterprises, and which seek to explain and justify that authority" (Bendix 1956, p. 2). Data also have addressed Weber's hypothesis that the various social structural elements of his ideal-type model of bureaucracy serve to facilitate domination; higher levels of both formalization and centralization were found in organizations that expressed problems with employee work performance.

Reviewing three books of theoretical essays on Weber, Seidman (1985) noted "a virtual explosion of discourse on the classics." He stated that "for the sociologist who does empirical research or theory construction, such a massive expenditure of collective intelligence may be puzzling, even dismaying," and questioned whether "this turn back to the classics [signifies] a romantic disillusionment with the scientific demands of contemporary sociology" (p. 673). Perhaps the sociologist who would be most puzzled and dismayed by the concentration on theoretical discourse and the implied incompatibility among various sociological endeavors would be Max Weber, who devoted much of his career to survey research. In 1909 he refused to join the Heidelberg Academy of Sciences until it agreed to fund a survey that he considered to be of particular importance. The following year he was a founder of the German Sociological Society, chartered with the primary purpose of advancing "social science knowledge through the undertaking of scientific investigations and surveys" (Oberschall 1965, p. 142). It is in Weber's spirit (if not with his breadth and brilliance of insight) that this study has attempted to examine issues in classical theory not only through discourse, but through empirical research. In having done so, it hopes to have demonstrated that theoretical and empirical analyses may be combined to illuminate problematic contemporary social phenomena.

More specifically, this book has sought to test Weber's hypotheses regarding processes of social domination, and simultaneously to examine their value for the investigation of the nature of alcoholism and employee assistance programs. By testing those hypotheses, it has been able to go considerably beyond testimonials to the humanitarian spirit behind corporations' adoption of these programs, to show that the programs vary systematically according to organizations' material interests and objective structures. It has also gone beyond the general assertions of others that alcoholism and employee assistance programs seem to have something to do with controlling employees. It has shown specific conditions under which such control attempts tend to be made, how they are carried out, and the particular explanation of alcohol problems that is most useful for such purposes.

Contrary to the skepticism of some scholars, this study has been able to assess the intentions underlying the actions of business executives. Rather than being subjected to what has been called the "tyranny of data," this study has made use of various sources of information to address a central question in the historical debate over the nature of dominancy relations. Theory has been used to guide this research to an analysis of the implementation of a new, sophisticated, and insidious means of social control in organizations. In the guise of a health care benefit, and often using individuals who have suffered from alcohol problems and who wish only to help others, corporate alcoholism and employee "assistance" programs function in many cases to intimidate workers into higher productivity. It is an illustration of what Sherrill (1979) has called "America's unique talent for combining ruthlessness and innocence."

References

Abercrombie, Nicholas. 1980. *Class, Structure and Knowledge*. New York: New York University Press.

Abravanel, Harry. 1983. "Mediatory Myths in the Service of Organizational Ideology." In *Organizational Symbolism*, edited by Louis R. Pondy et al., pp. 273–94. Greenwich, Conn.: JAI Press.

Agarwal, Naresh C. 1979. "On the Interchangeability of Size Measures." *Academy of Management Journal* 22: 404–9.

Aiken, Michael, and Samuel Bacharach. 1976. "Structural and Process Constraints of Influence in Organizations: A Level Specific Analysis." *Administrative Science Quarterly* 21: 623–42.

Albrow, Martin. 1970. *Bureaucracy*. New York: Praeger.

Alcoholics Anonymous. 1939. *Alcoholics Anonymous*. New York: Works.

Aldrich, Howard E. 1972. "Technology and Organizational Structure: A Reexamination of the Findings of the Aston Group." *Administrative Science Quarterly* 17: 26–43.

————. 1979. *Organizations and Environments*. Englewood Cliffs, N. J.: Prentice-Hall.

Allen, Robert F. 1980. "The Corporate Health-Buying Spree: Boon or Boondoggle?" *Advanced Management Journal* 45: 4–22.

Altman, Steven, Enzo Valenzi, and Richard M. Hodgetts. 1985. *Organizational Behavior*. Orlando, Fla.: Academic Press.

American Medical Association. 1967. *Manual on Alcoholism*. Washington, D.C.: American Medical Association.

Anderson, Carl R. 1984. *Management*. Dubuque, Iowa: William C. Brown.

Antonio, Robert J. 1979. "The Contradiction of Domination and Production in Bureaucracy: The Contribution of Organizational Efficiency to the Decline of the Roman Empire." *American Sociological Review* 44: 894–912.

Apter, David E. 1964. "Introduction: Ideology and Discontent." In *Ideology and Discontent*, edited by David E. Apter. New York: Free Press.

Argyris, Chris. 1957. *Personality and Organization*. New York: Harper.

Armor, David J., J. Michael Polich, and Harriet B. Stambul. 1978. *Alcoholism and Treatment*. New York: John Wiley.

Azumi, Koya, and Charles McMillan. 1974. "Subjective and Objective Measures of Structure." Paper read at the Annual Meetings of the American Sociological Association, New York.

Back, Kurt W. 1972. *Beyond Words*. New York: Russell Sage Foundation.

Bales, Robert F. 1944. "The 'Fixation Factor' in Alcohol Addiction." Ph.D. dissertation, Department of Sociology, Harvard University.

Baritz, Loren. 1960. *The Servants of Power*. Middletown, Conn.: Wesleyan University Press.

Barnard, Chester I. 1938. *The Functions of the Executive*. Cambridge, Mass.: Harvard University Press.

Barnes, Gordon. 1979. "The Alcoholic Personality." *Journal of Studies on Alcohol* 40: 571–634.

Bartell, Ted. 1976. "The Human Relations Ideology: An Analysis of the Social Origins of a Belief System." *Human Relations* 29: 737–49.

Baxter, James. 1979. Personal communication.

Beauchamp, Dan E. 1980. *Beyond Alcoholism*. Philadelphia: Temple University Press.

Bedeian, Arthur G. 1984. *Organizations: Theory and Analysis*. Chicago: Dryden Press.

Bendix, Reinhard. 1956. *Work and Authority in Industry*. New York: John Wiley.
_____. 1960. *Max Weber: An Intellectual Portrait*. Berkeley: University of California Press.

Bennis, Warren G. 1970. *American Bureaucracy*. Chicago: Aldine.

Benson, J. Kenneth. 1977. "Organizational Analysis: Critique and Innovation." Special issue, *Sociological Quarterly* 18 (3).

Berger, Peter L., and Thomas Luckmann. 1967. *The Social Construction of Reality*. New York: Doubleday.

Berkly, George. 1978. *The Craft of Public Administration*. Boston: Allyn and Bacon.

Berry, Ralph E., and James P. Boland. 1977. *The Economic Cost of Alcohol Abuse*. New York: Free Press.

Bertrand, S., and J. Masling. 1969. "Oral Imagery and Alcoholism." *Journal of Abnormal Psychology* 74: 50–53.

Beyer, Janice M. 1981. "Ideologies, Values, and Decision-Making in Organizations." In *Handbook of Organizational Design*, vol. 2, edited by Paul C. Nystrom and William H. Starbuck, pp. 166–203. New York: Oxford University Press.

Beyer, Janice M., and Harrison M. Trice. 1978. *Implementing Change: Alcoholism Policies in Work Organizations*. New York: Free Press.
_____. 1979. "A Reexamination of the Relations between Size and Various Components of Organizational Complexity." *Administrative Science Quarterly* 24: 48–64.
_____. 1981. "Managerial Ideologies and the Use of Discipline." In *Academy of Management Proceedings*, edited by Kae H. Chung, pp. 259–63. Wichita, Kans.: Academy of Management.

Biggort, Nicole Woolsey, and Gary G. Hamilton. 1984. "The Power of Obedience." *Administrative Science Quarterly* 29: 540–49.

Blau, Peter M. 1955. *Dynamics of Bureaucracy*. Chicago: University of Chicago Press.
_____. 1956. *Bureaucracy in Modern Society*. New York: Random House.
_____. 1957. "Formal Organization: Dimensions of Analysis." *American Journal of Sociology* 63: 58–69.

———. 1965. "The Comparative Study of Organizations." *Industrial and Labor Relations Review* 18: 323–38.

———. 1970. "A Formal Theory of Differentiation in Organizations." *American Sociological Review* 35: 201–18.

Blau, Peter M., et al. 1976. "Technology and Organization in Manufacturing." *Administrative Science Quarterly* 21: 20–40.

Blau, Peter M., and Richard A. Schoenherr. 1971. *The Structure of Organizations.* New York: Basic Books.

Blauner, Robert. 1964. *Alienation and Freedom: The Factory Worker and His Industry.* Chicago: University of Chicago Press.

Blumer, Herbert. 1937. "Social Psychology." In *Man and Society,* edited by Emerson P. Schmidt, pp. 144–198. New York: Prentice-Hall.

Bobbitt, H. Randolph, et al. 1978. *Organizational Behavior.* 2nd ed. Englewood Cliffs, N. J.: Prentice-Hall.

Boroson, Warren. 1978. "The Myth of the Unhealthy Executive." *Across the Board* 15: 10–16.

Borthwick, R. 1977. "Summary of Cost-Benefit Study Results for Navy Alcoholism Rehabilitation Programs." Arlington, Va.: Presearch.

Bramel, Dana, and Ronald Friend. 1981. "Hawthorne, the Myth of the Docile Worker, and Class Bias in Psychology." *American Psychologist* 36: 867–78.

Brandes, Stuart D. 1976. *American Welfare Capitalism.* Chicago: University of Chicago Press.

Braverman, Harry. 1974. *Labor and Monopoly Capital.* New York: Monthly Review Press.

Brunsson, Nils. 1982. "The Irrationality of Action and Action Rationality: Decisions, Ideologies and Organizational Action." *Journal of Management Studies* 19: 29–44.

Burack, Elmer H. 1975. *Organization Analysis.* Hinsdale, Ill.: Dryden.

Burawoy, Michael. 1978. "Braverman and Beyond." *Politics and Society* 8: 247–312.

———. 1979. *Manufacturing Consent: Changes in the Labor Process under Monopoly Capitalism.* Chicago: University of Chicago Press.

Bureau of National Affairs. 1973. *Employee Conduct and Discipline.* Washington, D.C.: Bureau of National Affairs.

Burrell, Gibson, and Gareth Morgan. 1979. *Sociological Paradigms and Organizational Analysis.* London: Heinemann.

Cahalan, Don. 1970. *Problem Drinkers: A National Survey.* San Francisco: Jossey-Bass.

———. 1979. "Why Does the Alcoholism Field Act Like a Ship of Fools?" *British Journal of Addiction* 74: 235–38.

Cahalan, Don, and Ira Cisin. 1976. "Drinking Behavior and Drinking Problems in the United States." In *The Biology of Alcoholism,* vol. 4, edited by Benjamin Kissin and Henry Begleiter, pp. 77–115. New York: Plenum Press.

Cahalan, Don, Ira Cisin, and H.M. Crossley. 1969. *American Drinking Practices: A National Survey of Behaviors and Attitudes.* New Brunswick, N. J.: Rutgers Center of Alcohol Studies.

Cahalan, Don, and Robin Room. 1974. *Problem Drinkers among American Men.* New Brunswick, N. J.: Rutgers Center of Alcohol Studies.

Campbell, Donald T., and Julian C. Stanley. 1966. *Experimental and Quasi-*

Experimental Designs for Research. Chicago: Rand McNally.

Campbell, John P., et al. 1974. *The Management of Organizational Effectiveness: A Review of the Relevant Research and Opinion*. Report TR-71-1. San Diego: Navy Personnel Research and Development Center.

Carey, Alex. 1967. "The Hawthorne Studies: A Radical Criticism." *American Sociological Review* 32: 403–16.

Carman, Roderick S. 1971. "Expectations and Socialization Experiences Related to Drinking among U.S. Servicemen." *Quarterly Journal of Studies on Alcohol* 32: 1040–47.

Champion, Dean J. 1975. *The Sociology of Organizations*. New York: McGraw-Hill.

Cherrington, Ernest H. 1920. *The Evolution of Prohibition in the United States of America*. Montclair, N. J.: Patterson Smith.

Child, John. 1972a. "Organization and Strategies of Control: A Replication of the Aston Study." *Administrative Science Quarterly* 17: 163–77.

———. 1972b. "Organizational Structure, Environment and Performance—The Role of Strategic Choice." *Sociology* 6: 1–22.

———. 1973. "Predicting and Understanding Organization Structure." *Administrative Science Quarterly* 18: 168–85.

Chopra, K. S., D. A. Preston, and L. W. Gerson. 1979. "The Effect of Constructive Coercion on the Rehabilitative Process." *Journal of Occupational Medicine* 21: 749–52.

Clark, Walter, and Don Cahalan. 1976. "Changes in Problem Drinking over a Four-Year Span." *Addictive Behaviors* 1: 251–59.

Clinard, Marshall B. 1963. *Sociology of Deviant Behavior*. New York: Holt, Rinehart, and Winston.

Clyne, R. M. 1965. "Detection and Rehabilitation of the Problem Drinker in Industry." *Journal of Occupational Medicine* 9:265–68.

Cohen, Jacob, and Patricia Cohen. 1983. *Applied Multiple Regression/ Correlation Analysis for the Behavioral Sciences*. 2nd ed. Hillsdale, N. J.: Erlbaum Associates.

Cohen, Jere, Lawrence Hazelrigg, and Whitney Pope. 1975. "De-Parsonizing Weber: A Critique of Parsons' Interpretation of Weber's Sociology." *American Sociological Review* 40: 229–41.

Coppolino, Carl A., and Carmela M. Coppolino. 1965. *The Billion Dollar Hangover*. New York: A. S. Barnes.

Corneil, Wayne. 1980. Personal communication.

Coser, Lewis A. 1975. "Presidential Address: Two Methods in Search of a Substance." *American Sociological Review* 40: 691–700.

———. 1976. "Sociological Theory from Chicago Dominance to 1965." *Annual Review of Sociology* 2: 145–60.

Coser, Lewis A., and Bernard Rosenberg. 1969. *Sociological Theory*. New York: MacMillan.

Cosper, Rod. 1979. "Drinking as Conformity: A Critique of Sociological Literature on Occupational Differences in Drinking." *Journal of Studies on Alcohol* 40: 868–91.

Cottrell, W. F. 1940. *The Railroader*. Stanford: Stanford University Press.

Dalton, Dan R., et al. 1980. "Organization Structure and Performance: A Critical Review." *Academy of Management Review* 5: 49–64.

Davidson, A. R., and J. J. Jaccard. 1979. "Variables That Moderate the Attitude-Behavior Relation: Results of a Longitudinal Study." *Journal of Personality and Social Psychology* 37: 1364–76.

Davies, David L. 1974. "Is Alcoholism Really a Disease?" *Contemporary Drug Problems* 3: 197–212.

_____. 1976. "Definitional Issues in Alcoholism." In *Alcoholism*, edited by Ralph E. Tarter and A. Arthur Sugarman, pp. 53–74. Reading, Mass.: Addison-Wesley.

Davis, Keith. 1967. *Human Relations at Work*. New York: McGraw-Hill.

Davis, Mary F. 1984. "Worksite Health Promotion." *Personnel Administrator* 29: 45–50.

Dennis, N., F. Henriques, and C. Slaughter. 1956. *Coal Is Our Life: An Analysis of a Yorkshire Mining Community*. London: Eyre and Spottiswoode.

Dentler, Robert A., and Kai T. Erikson. 1959. "The Functions of Deviance in Groups." *Social Problems* 7: 98–107.

Denzin, Norman K. 1978. *The Research Act*. 2nd ed. Chicago: Aldine.

Dessler, Gary. 1980. *Organization Theory: Integrating Structure and Behavior*. Englewood Cliffs, N. J.: Prentice-Hall.

_____ 1982. *Organization and Management*. Reston, Virginia: Reston.

Dewar, Robert, and Jerald Hage. 1978. "Size, Technology, Complexity, and Structural Differentiation: Toward a Theoretical Synthesis." *Administrative Science Quarterly* 23: 111–36.

DiTomaso, Nancy. 1985. "Sociologists Teaching in Business Schools: Occupational and Intellectual Prospects and Opportunities." Paper read at the Annual Meetings of the American Sociological Association, Washington, D.C.

Dorfman, Rhonda A. 1982. "The History, Design, and Results of the National Occupational Alcoholism Assistance Program Standards Survey." *The ALMACAN* 12: 14–15.

DuBrin, Andrew J. 1985. *Contemporary Applied Management*. 2nd ed. Plano, Tex.: Business Publications.

Dunbar, Roger L.M., John M. Dutton, and William R. Torbert. 1982. "Crossing Mother: Ideological Constraints on Organizational Improvement." *Journal of Management Studies* 19: 91–108.

Duncan, W. Jack. 1978. *Organizational Behavior*. Boston: Houghton Mifflin.

Durkheim, Emile. 1933. *The Division of Labor in Society*. New York: Macmillan.

Dwyer, Paul S. 1984. "National Crisis Grows." *EAP Digest* 7: 46–50.

Edwards, Daniel W. 1975. "The Evaluation of Troubled Employee and Occupational Alcoholism Programs." In *Occupational Alcoholism Programs*, edited by R. Williams and G. Moffatt, pp. 40–135. Springfield, Ill.: Charles C. Thomas.

Edwards, Griffith, et al. 1977. "Alcoholism: A Controlled Trial of 'Treatment' and 'Advice.'" *Journal of Studies on Alcohol* 38: 1004–31.

Ends, E. J., and C. W. Page. 1959. "Group Psychotherapy and Concomitant Psychological Change." *Psychological Monographs* 73: 1–31.

Engle, Kenneth B., and Thomas K. Williams. 1972. "Effect of an Ounce of Vodka on Alcoholics' Desire for Alcohol." *Quarterly Journal of Studies on Alcohol* 33: 1099–1105.

Erfurt, John C., and Andrea Foote. 1977. *Occupational Employee Assistance Programs for Substance Abuse and Mental Health Problems*. Ann Arbor: Institute of Labor and Industrial Relations, University of Michigan–Wayne State University.

Etzioni, Amitai. 1968. "Social Control: Organizational Aspects." In *International Encyclopedia of the Social Sciences*, edited by David L. Sills, pp. 396–402. New York: Macmillan and Free Press.

Feinberg, Samuel. 1983. "From Where I Sit." *Women's Wear Daily*, March 30, p. 44.

Fenichel, Otto. 1945. *The Psychoanalytic Theory of Neuroses*. New York: Norton.

Fennell, Mary B., Mirian B. Rodin, and Glenda K. Kantor. 1981. "Problems in the Work Setting, Drinking, and Reasons for Drinking." *Social Forces* 60: 114–32.

Festinger, Leon. 1957. *A Theory of Cognitive Dissonance*. Evanston, Ill.: Row, Peterson.

Festinger, Leon, Henry W. Riecken, and Stanley Schachter. 1956. *When Prophecy Fails*. Minneapolis: University of Minnesota Press.

Feuer, Lewis S. 1959. *Marx and Engels: Basic Writings on Politics and Philosophy*. Garden City, N. Y.: Doubleday.

Feuerbach, Ludwig. 1957. *The Essence of Christianity*. Translated by George Eliot. New York: Harper.

Fischer, Frank. 1984. "Ideology and Organization Theory." In *Critical Studies in Organization and Bureaucracy*, edited by Frank Fischer and Carmen Sirianni, pp. 172–90. Philadelphia: Temple University Press.

Fischer, Frank, and Carmen Sirianni, eds. 1984. *Critical Studies in Organization and Bureaucracy*. Philadelphia. Temple University Press.

Follmann, Joseph F. 1976. *Alcoholics and Business*. New York: Amacom.

Foote, Andrea, et al. 1978. *Cost-Effectiveness of Occupational Employee Assistance Programs: Test of an Evaluation Method*. Ann Arbor: Institute of Labor and Industrial Relations, University of Michigan–Wayne State University.

Ford, Robert C., and Frank S. McLaughlin. 1981. "Employee Assistance Programs: A Descriptive Survey of ASPA Members." *Personnel Administrator* 26: 29–35.

Franke, Richard H., and James D. Kaul. 1978. "The Hawthorne Experiments: First Statistical Interpretation." *American Sociological Review* 43: 623–43.

Freedberg, E. J., and W. E. Johnston. 1980. "Outcome with Alcoholics Seeking Treatment Voluntarily or after Confrontation by Their Employer." *Journal of Occupational Medicine* 22: 83–86.

Freedberg, E. J., and S. E. Scherer. 1977. "Ontario Problem Assessment Battery for Alcoholics." *Psychological Reports* 40: 743–46.

Freud, Sigmund, 1930. *Civilization and Its Discontents*. London: Hogarth.

Friedson, Eliot. 1970. *Professional Dominance*. New York: Atherton.

Gaeta, E., R. Lynn, and L. Grey. 1982. "AT&T Looks at Program Evaluation." *EAP Digest* 3: 28, 30.

Gibson, James L., John M. Ivancevich, and James H. Donnelly, Jr. 1985. *Organization: Behavior, Structure, Processes*. Plano, Tex.: Business Publications.

Giddens, Anthony. 1971. *Capitalism and Modern Social Theory*. Cambridge, England: Cambridge University Press.

Glassner, Barry, and Bruce Berg. 1980. "How Jews Avoid Alcohol Problems." *American Sociological Review* 45: 84–93.

Glatt, Max M. 1958. "Group Therapy in Alcoholism." *British Journal of Addiction* 54: 84–93.

Goldman, Paul. 1983. "The Labor Process and the Sociology of Organizations." In *Research in the Sociology of Organizations*, vol. 2, edited by Samuel B. Bacharach, pp. 49–81. Greenwich, Conn.: JAI Press.

Goldman, Paul, and Donald Van Houten. 1977. "Managerial Strategies and the Worker: A Marxist Analysis of Bureaucracy." *Sociological Quarterly* 18: 108–125.

Goodwin, Donald, et al. 1974. "Drinking Problems in Adopted and Non-Adopted Sons of Alcoholics." *Archives of General Psychiatry* 31: 164–69.

Googins, Bradley. 1985. "Can Change Be Documented?: Measuring the Impact of EAPs." In *The Human Resource Management Handbook*, edited by Samuel H. Klarreich, James L. Francek, and C. Eugene Moore, pp. 222–31. New York: Praeger.

Gordon, Gerald, and Edward V. Morse. 1975. "Evaluation Research." *Annual Review of Sociology* 1: 339–62.

Gouldner, Alvin. 1954. *Patterns of Industrial Bureaucracy*. New York: Free Press.

_____. 1970. *The Coming Crisis of Western Sociology*. New York: Basic Books.

Gove, Philip, ed. 1976. *Webster's Third New International Dictionary of the English Language*. Springfield Ill.: G. and C. Merriam.

Gray, Robert H., et al. 1983. "Convergent Results of Two Methods of Estimating the Prevalence of Problem Drinking." *Journal of Occupational Medicine* 25: 531–33.

Greden, John F., Sinai I. Frenkel, and Donald W. Morgan. 1975. "Alcohol Use in the Army: Patterns and Associated Behavior." *American Journal of Psychiatry* 132: 11–16.

Guerin, Philip J. 1976. "Family Therapy: The First Twenty-Five Years." In *Family Therapy: Theory and Practice*, edited by Philip J. Guerin, pp. 2–22. New York: Gardner Press.

Gupta, Nina. 1980. "Some Alternative Definitions of Size." *Academy of Management Journal* 23: 759–66.

Gusfield, Joseph R. 1963. *Symbolic Crusade: Status Politics and the American Temperance Movement*. Urbana: University of Illinois Press.

Habbe, Stephen. 1969. *Company Controls for Drinking Problems*. New York: Conference Board.

_____. 1973. "Controlling the Alcohol Problem: Not by Management Alone." *Conference Board Record* 10: 31–33.

Hacker, Andrew. 1955. "The Use and Abuse of Pareto in Industrial Sociology." *American Journal of Economics and Sociology* 14: 321–33.

Hage, Jerald. 1965. "An Axiomatic Theory of Organizations." *Administrative Science Quarterly* 10: 289–320.

Hage, Jerald, and Michael Aiken. 1967. "Program Change and Organizational Properties: A Comparative Analysis." *American Journal of Sociology* 72: 503–19.

_____. 1970. *Social Change in Complex Organizations*. New York: Random House.

Hall, Richard H. 1963. "The Concept of Bureaucracy: An Empirical Assessment." *American Journal of Sociology* 72: 503–19.

———. 1982. *Organizations: Structure and Process*. 3rd ed. Englewood Cliffs, N. J.: Prentice-Hall.

Hannan, Michael T., and John Freeman. 1977. "The Population Ecology of Organizations." *American Journal of Sociology* 82: 929–64.

Harris, Marvin. 1984. "Review of J. Van Maanen, J. Dabbs, and R. Faulkner, *Varieties of Qualitative Research.*" *Academy of Management Review* 9: 166–69.

Harrison, E. F. 1978. *Management and Organizations*. Boston: Houghton Mifflin.

Haug, Marie. 1973. "Deprofessionalization: An Alternate Hypothesis for the Future." In *Professionalization and Social Change*, edited by Paul Halmos, Sociological Review Monograph no. 20, pp. 195–211.

Hawkins, Richard, and Gary Tiedeman. 1975. *The Creation of Deviance*. Columbus, Ohio: Charles E. Merrill.

Hayward, Becky J., William E. Schlenger, and Jerome B. Hallan. 1975. "Characteristics of Selected Occupational Programs." Technical Report FR18-76. Raleigh, N. C.: Human Ecology Institute.

Hegel, G. W. F. 1952. *Philosophy of Right*. Translated by T. M. Knox. Oxford: Oxford University Press.

Helvetius, Claude Adrien. 1758. *De L'esprit*. Paris: Durand.

Heydebrand, Wolf. 1977. "Organizational Contradictions in Public Bureaucracies: Toward a Marxian Theory of Organizations." *Sociological Quarterly* 18: 83–107.

Heyman, Margaret M. 1976. "Referral to Alcoholism Programs in Industry: Coercion, Confrontation and Choice." *Journal of Studies on Alcohol* 37: 900–7.

Hickson, David J., Derek S. Pugh, and Diana C. Pheysey. 1969. "Operations Technology and Organizational Structure: An Empirical Reappraisal." *Administrative Science Quarterly* 14: 378–97.

Hingson, Ralph W., Ruth I. Lederman, and Diana W. Chapman. 1985. "Employee Drinking Patterns and Accidental Injury: A Study of Four New England States." *Journal of Studies on Alcohol* 46: 298–303.

Hinings, C. R., and G. L. Lee. 1971. "Dimensions of Organization Structure and Their Context: A Replication." *Sociology* 5: 83–93.

Hirschi, Travis. 1969. *Causes of Delinquency*. Berkeley: University of California Press.

Hitchcock, Lyman, and Mark Sanders. 1976. *A Survey of Alcohol and Drug Abuse Programs in the Railroad Industry*. Washington, D.C.: U.S. Department of Transportation, Federal Railroad Administration.

Hitz, Danielle. 1973. "Drunken Sailors and Others: Drinking Problems in Specific Occupations." *Quarterly Journal of Studies on Alcohol* 34: 496–505.

Hodgson, Ray. 1979. "Much Ado about Nothing Much: Alcoholism Treatment and the Rand Report." *British Journal of Addiction* 74: 227–34.

Hoffman, Helmut. 1970. "Personality Characteristics of Alcoholics in Relation to Age." *Psychological Reports* 27: 167–71.

Hoffman, Helmut, Rodney G. Loper, and Mary L. Kammeier. 1974. "Identifying Future Alcoholics with MMPI Alcoholism Scales." *Quarterly Journal of Studies on Alcohol* 35: 490–98.

Howland, Richard, and Joe Howland. 1978. "200 Years of Drinking in the United States: Evolution of the Disease Concept." In *Drinking*, edited by John Ewing and Beatrice Rouse, pp. 39–60. Chicago: Nelson-Hall.

Huber, Joan. 1973. "Symbolic Interactionism as a Pragmatic Perspective: The Bias of Emergent Theory." *American Sociological Review* 38: 274–83.

Huse, Edgar. 1979. *The Modern Manager*. St. Paul, Minn.: West.

Inkson, J. H. K., D. J. Hickson, and D. S. Pugh. 1970. "Organization Context and Structure: An Abbreviated Replication." *Administrative Science Quarterly* 15: 318–29.

Iutcovich, Joyce M. 1982. "The Employee Assistance Program as a Mechanism of Control over Problem-Drinking Employees." Ph.D. dissertation, Department of Sociology, Kent State University.

Jackson, John H., and Cyril P. Morgan. 1982. *Organization Theory*. 2nd ed. Englewood Cliffs, N. J.: Prentice-Hall.

Janowitz, Morris. 1975. "Sociological Theory and Social Control." *American Journal of Sociology* 81: 82–108.

Jelinek, Marian. 1980. "Comments on the Panel Discussion at the 1980 OBTC." *Exchange: The Organizational Behavior Teaching Journal* 5: 19–21.

Jelinek, Marian, Linda Smircich, and Paul Hirsch. 1983. "Introduction: A Code of Many Colors." *Administrative Science Quarterly* 28: 331–38.

Jellinek, E.M. 1952. "Phases of Alcohol Addiction." *Quarterly Journal of Studies on Alcohol* 18: 240–62.

———. 1960. *The Disease Concept of Alcoholism*. Highland Park, N. J.: Hillhouse.

Johnson, Harry M. 1968. "Ideology and the Social System." In *International Encyclopedia of the Social Sciences*, vol. 7, edited by David Sills, pp. 76–85. New York: Macmillan.

Jonsson, E., and T. Nilsson. 1968. "Alcohol Consumption in Monozygotic and Dizygotic Pairs of Twins." *Nordisk Hygienish Tidskrift* 49: 21–25.

Kaij, L. 1960. *Alcoholism in Twins: Studies on the Etiology and Sequels of Abuse of Alcohol*. Stockholm: Almquist and Wiksell.

Kalberg, Stephen. 1980. "Max Weber's Types of Rationality: Cornerstones for the Analysis of Rationalization Processes in History." *American Journal of Sociology* 85: 1145–79.

Kammeier, Mary L., Helmut Hoffman, and Rodney G. Loper. 1973. "Personality Characteristics of Alcoholics as College Freshmen and at the Time of Treatment." *Quarterly Journal of Studies on Alcohol* 34: 390–99.

Kanuk, Leslie, and Conrad Berenson. 1975. "Mail Surveys and Response Rates: A Literature Review." *Journal of Marketing Research* 12: 440–53.

Kearns, Robert. 1980. "Alcoholism Programs Have Own Abuses." *Chicago Tribune*, October 8, 1980, p. 10.

Keller, Mark, and Mairi McCormick. 1968. *A Dictionary of Words about Alcohol*. New Brunswick, N. J.: Rutgers Center of Alcohol Studies.

Keller, Robert T. 1984. "The Harvard 'Pareto Circle' and the Development of Organization Theory." *Journal of Management* 10: 193–203.

Kimberly, John R. 1976. "Organizational Size and the Structuralist Perspective: A Review, Critique and Proposal. *Administrative Science Quarterly* 21: 571–97.

Klein, Stuart M., and R. Richard Ritti. 1984. *Understanding Organizational Behavior*. 2nd ed. Boston: Kent.

Kochan, Thomas. 1980. *Collective Bargaining and Industrial Relations*. Homewood, Ill.: Irwin.

Kristianson, P. A. 1970. "A Comparison Study of Two Alcoholic Groups and a Control Group." *British Journal of Medical Psychology* 43: 161–75.

Krygier, Martin. 1979. "State and Bureaucracy in Europe: The Growth of a Concept." In *Bureaucracy*, edited by Eugene Kamenka and Martin Krygier, pp. 1–33. London: Edward Arnold.

Kuhn, Thomas S. 1962. *The Structure of Scientific Revolutions*. Chicago: University of Chicago Press.

Kurtz, Norman R., Bradley Googins, and William C. Howard. 1984. "Measuring the Success of Occupational Alcoholism Programs." *Journal of Studies on Alcohol* 45: 33–45.

Langner, Thomas S., and Stanley T. Michael. 1963. *Life Stress and Mental Health*. Glencoe, Ill.: Free Press.

Langton, John. 1984. "The Ecological Theory of Bureaucracy." *Administrative Science Quarterly* 29: 330–54.

LaVan, Helen, Nicholas Mathys, and David Drehmer. 1983. "A Look at the Counseling Practices of Major U.S. Corporations." *Personnel Administrator* 28: 76–146.

Lawrence, Paul R., and Jay W. Lorsch. 1967. *Organization and Environment: Managing Differentiation and Integration*. Boston: Graduate School of Business Administration, Harvard University.

Lemere, F. 1956. "What Causes Alcoholism." *Journal of Clinical Experimental Psychopathology* 17: 202–6.

Lemert, Edwin. 1967. *Human Deviance, Social Problems, and Social Control*. Englewood Cliffs, N. J.: Prentice-Hall.

Lester, D. 1966. "Self-Selection of Alcohol by Animals, Human Variation and the Etiology of Alcoholism." *Quarterly Journal of Studies on Alcohol* 27: 395–439.

Levine, Hermine Z. 1985. "Consensus on . . . Employee Assistance Programs." *Personnel* 62: 14–19.

Lewis, Karen A. 1981. "Employee Assistance Programs: The State of the Art of Mental Health Services in Government and Industry." Ph.D. dissertation, Department of Counseling Psychology, Northwestern University.

Light, I. 1969. "The Social Construction of Uncertainty." *Berkeley Journal of Sociology* 14: 189–99.

Lincoln, James R., Mitsuyo Hanada, and Jon Olson. 1981. "Cultural Orientations and Individual Reactions to Organizations: A Study of Employees of Japanese-owned Firms." *Administrative Science Quarterly* 26: 93–115.

Lincoln, James R., Jon Olson, and Mitsuyo Hanada. 1978. "Cultural Effects on Organizational Structure: The Case of Japanese Firms in the United States." *American Sociological Review* 43: 829–47.

Linsky, Arnold S. 1970. "The Changing Public Views of Alcoholism." *Quarterly Journal of Studies on Alcohol* 31: 692–704.

_____. 1975. "Stimulating Responses to Mailed Questionnaires: A Review." *Public Opinion Quarterly* 29: 82–101.

Linsky, Arnold S., Murray A. Straus, and John P. Colby. 1985. "Stressful Events, Stressful Conditions and Alcohol Problems in the United States: A Partial Test of Bales's Theory." *Journal of Studies on Alcohol* 46: 72–79.

Loper, Rodney G., Mary L. Kammeier, and Helmut Hoffman. 1973. "MMPI

Characteristics of College Freshmen Males Who Later Became Alcoholics." *Journal of Abnormal Psychology* 82: 159–62.

Ludwig, Arnold. 1972. "On and off the Wagon: Reasons for Drinking and Abstaining by Alcoholics." *Quarterly Journal of Studies on Alcohol* 23: 91–97.

––––––. 1985. "Cognitive Processes Associated with 'Spontaneous' Recovery from Alcoholism." *Journal of Studies on Alcohol* 46: 53–58.

Ludwig, Arnold, Abraham Wikler, and Louis Stark. 1974. "The First Drink: Psychological Aspects of Craving." *Archives of General Psychiatry* 30: 539–47.

Luft, H. S. 1975. "The Impact of Poor Health on Earnings." *The Review of Economics and Statistics* 57: 43–57.

Makela, Klaus, et al. 1981. *Alcohol, Society, and the State*. Toronto: Addiction Research Foundation.

Malinowski, Bronislaw. 1960. *A Scientific Theory of Culture*. New York: Oxford University Press.

Mann, Marty. 1958. *Marty Mann's New Primer on Alcoholism*. New York: Holt, Rinehart, and Winston.

Mannello, Timothy A. 1979. *Problem Drinking among Railroad Workers: Extent, Impact, and Solutions*. Washington, D.C.: University Research Corporation.

Mannheim, Karl. 1936. *Ideology and Utopia*. Translated by Louis Wirth. New York: Harcourt Brace.

March, James, and Herbert Simon. 1958. *Organizations*. New York: Wiley.

Marlatt, G. Alan. 1973. "A Comparison of Aversive Conditioning Procedures in the Treatment of Alcoholism." Paper read at the Annual Meetings of the Western Psychological Association, Anaheim, California.

Marlatt, G. Alan, Barbara Demming, and John B. Reid. 1973. "Loss of Control Drinking in Alcoholics; An Experimental Analogue." *Journal of Abnormal Psychology* 81: 233–42.

Martin, Joanne. 1981. "Stories and Scripts in Organizational Settings." In *Cognitive Social Psychology*, edited by Albert H. Hastorf and Alice M. Isen, pp. 255–305. New York: Elsevier.

Marx, Karl. 1970. *Critique of Hegel's 'Philosophy of Right.'* Translated by Joseph O'Malley. Cambridge, England: Cambridge University Press.

––––––. 1977. "Theses on Feuerbach." In *Karl Marx: Selected Writings*, edited by David McLellan, pp. 156–58. Oxford: Oxford University Press.

Marx, Karl, and Friedrich Engels. 1947. *The German Ideology*. New York: International.

Masi, Dale A. 1984. *Employee Counseling Services*. New York: American Management Association.

Maslow, Abraham H. 1954. *Motivation and Personality*. New York: Harper.

Matthews, Clara M. 1976. *Effects of Treatment on Job Performance*. Raleigh, N. C.: Human Ecology Institute.

Maxwell, Milton A. 1960. "Early Identification of Problem Drinkers in Industry." *Quarterly Journal of Studies on Alcohol* 21: 655–78.

Mayhew, Leon. 1971. *Society: Institutions and Activity*. Glenview, . Ill.: Scott, Foresman.

Mayo, Elton. 1933. *The Human Problems of an Industrial Civilization*. New York: Macmillan.

McKelvey, Bill. 1982. *Organizational Systematics*. Berkeley: University of California Press.

Mead, George H. 1934. *Mind, Self and Society*. Chicago: University of Chicago Press.

Medeiros, James A., and David E. Schmitt. 1977. *Public Bureaucracy: Values and Perspectives*. North Scituate, Mass.: Duxbury.

Mello, Nancy K. 1972. "Behavioral Studies of Alcoholism." In *Biology of Alcoholism*, vol. 2, edited by Benjamin Kissin and Henri Begleiter, pp. 219–91. New York: Plenum Press.

Mellon, Lawrence J. 1969. "How Boeing Handles Alcoholism." *Industrial Medicine* 38: 37–43.

Melossi, Dario. 1983. "A Politics without a State: The Concepts of 'State' and 'Social Control' from European to American Social Science." *Research in Law, Deviance and Social Control* 5: 205–22.

Merton, Robert K. 1936. "The Unanticipated Consequences of Purposive Social Action." *American Sociological Review* 1: 894–904.

———. 1940. "Bureaucratic Structure and Personality." *Social Forces* 23: 405–15.

———. 1949. *Social Theory and Social Structure*. Glencoe, Ill.: Free Press.

Meyer, Alan D. 1982. "How Ideologies Supplant Formal Structures and Shape Responses to Environments." *Journal of Management Studies* 19: 45–61.

Meyer, Marshall W. 1972. "Size and the Structure of Organizations: A Causal Analysis." *American Sociological Review* 37: 434–41.

Mid-America ALMACA Chapter. 1980. "Conference Board Report on EAPs." *Mid-America ALMACA Chapter News* (December), pp. 1–2.

———. 1981. "Conference Board Report on EAPs: Part II." *Mid-America ALMACA Chapter News* (January), pp. 1–2.

Miles, Robert H. 1980. *Macro Organizational Behavior*. Santa Monica: Goodyear.

Miller, Delbert C., and William H. Form. 1951. *Industrial Sociology*. New York: Harper.

Miller, W. R., and R. K. Hester. 1981. "Treating the Problem Drinker: Modern Approaches." In *The Addictive Behaviors: Treatment of Alcoholism, Drug Abuse, Smoking and Obesity*, edited by W.R. Miller, pp. 11–141. Oxford: Pergamon.

Mills, C. Wright. 1960. "Introduction: The Classic Tradition." In *Images of Man: The Classic Tradition in Sociological Thinking*, edited by C. Wright Mills, pp. 1–17. New York: Braziller.

Miner, John B. 1985. *The Practice of Management*. Columbus, Ohio: Charles E. Merrill.

Miner, John B., and Mary G. Miner. 1977. *Personnel and Industrial Relations*. 3rd ed. New York: Macmillan.

Mitchell, Terence R. 1985. "An Evaluation of the Validity of Correlational Research Conducted in Organizations." *Academy of Management Review* 10: 192–205.

Moore, Wilbert E. 1946. *Industrial Relations and the Social Order*. New York: Macmillan.

Morley, Eileen D. 1971. "Human Services in Complex Work Organizations." Ph.D. dissertation, Graduate School of Education, Harvard University.

Muchinsky, Paul. 1977. "Employee Absenteeism: A Review of the Literature." *Journal of Vocational Behavior* 10: 316–40.

Mulford, Harold A., and Donald E. Miller. 1964. "Measuring Public Acceptance of the Alcoholic as a Sick Person." *Quarterly Journal of Studies on Alcohol* 25: 314–22.

Mullins, Nicholas C. 1973. *Theories and Theory Groups in Contemporary American Sociology.* New York: Harper and Row.

Munch, Richard. 1981. "Talcott Parsons and the Theory of Action. 1. The Structure of the Kantian Core." *American Journal of Sociology* 86: 709–39.

Myers, Donald W. 1984. *Establishing and Building Employee Assistance Programs.* Westport, Conn.: Quorum.

Myers, M. M. 1948. "Myth and Status Systems in Industry." *Social Forces* 31: 331–37.

Myers, Phyllis S., and Donald W. Myers. 1985. "Are Employers Conforming to Standards?" *EAP Digest* 6: 55–62.

National Council on Alcoholism. 1976a. *Facts on Alcoholism.* New York: National Council on Alcoholism.

———. 1976b. *A Joint Union-Management Approach to Alcoholism Recovery Programs.* New York: National Council on Alcoholism.

National Industrial Conference Board. 1958. *The Alcoholic Worker.* New York: National Industrial Conference Board.

National Institute on Alcohol Abuse and Alcoholism. 1972. *Alcohol and Alcoholism: Problems, Programs, and Progress.* Washington, D.C.: Government Printing Office.

Nicholson, Nigel. 1977. "Absence Behavior and Attendance Motivation: A Conceptual Synthesis." *Journal of Management Studies* 14: 231–52.

Niven, Robert G. 1985. "Introduction." In *Preventing Alcohol Problems through a Student Assistance Program.* National Institute on Alcohol Abuse and Alcoholism, pp. vii–viii. Washington, D. C.: Government Printing Office.

Nystrom, Paul C., and William H. Starbuck. 1984. "Organizational Facades." In *Academy of Management Proceedings,* edited by John A. Pearce and Richard B. Robinson, pp. 182–85. Boston: Academy of Management.

Oberschall, Anthony. 1965. *Empirical Social Research in Germany 1848–1914.* New York: Basic Books.

Opinion Research Corporation. 1972. *Executive's Knowledge, Attitudes and Behavior Regarding Alcoholism and Alcohol Abuse.* Princeton, N. J.: Opinion Research Corporation.

———. 1974. *Executive's Knowledge, Attitudes and Behavior Regarding Alcoholism and Alcohol Abuse,* Study II. Princeton, N. J.: Opinion Research Corporation.

———. 1976. *Executive's Knowledge, Attitudes and Behavior Regarding Alcoholism and Alcohol Abuse,* Study III. Princeton, N.J.: Opinion Research Corporation.

———. 1979. *Executive's Knowledge, Attitudes and Behavior Regarding Alcoholism and Alcohol Abuse,* Study IV. Princeton, N. J.: Opinion Research Corporation.

Orcutt, James D. 1976. "Ideological Variations in the Structure of Deviant Types." *Social Forces* 55: 419–37.

Orcutt, James D., R. E. Cairl, and E. T. Miller. 1980. "Professional and Public Conceptions of Alcoholism." *Journal of Studies on Alcohol* 41: 652–61.

Orford, Jim, and Ann Hawker. 1974. "Investigation of an Alcoholism Rehabilitation Halfway House, 2. Complex Question of Client Motivation." *British Journal of Addiction* 69: 315–23.

Osborn, Richard N., Jerald G. Hunt, and Lawrence R. Jauch. 1980. *Organization Theory: An Integrated Approach.* New York: Wiley.

Ortega, Suzanne T., and William A. Rushing. 1983. "Interpretation of the Relationship between Socioeconomic Status and Mental Disorder: A Question of the Measure of Mental Disorder and a Question of the Measure of SES." In *Research in Community and Mental Health*, vol. 3, edited by James R. Greenley and Roberta G. Simmons, pp. 141-61. Greenwich Conn.: JAI Press.

Ouchi, William. 1980. "Markets, Bureaucracies, and Clans." *Administrative Science Quarterly* 25: 129-40.

Ouchi, William, and Jerry B. Johnson. 1978. "Types of Organizational Control and Their Relationship to Emotional Well-being." *Administrative Science Quarterly* 25: 293-317.

Ouchi, William G., and Alan L. Wilkins. 1985. "Organizational Culture." *Annual Review of Sociology*. 11: 457-83.

Pace, Nicolas A. 1981. "A Prescription for Help." *EAP Digest* 2 (November/December): 24-26.

Park, Peter. 1962. "Drinking Experiences of 805 Finnish Alcoholics in Comparison with Similar Experiences of 192 English Alcoholics." *Acta Psychiatrica Scandinavica* 38: 227-46.

_____. 1973. "Developmental Ordering of Experiences in Alcoholism." *Quarterly Journal of Studies on Alcohol* 34: 473-89.

Parker, Douglas A., and Jacob A. Brody. 1982. "Risk Factors for Alcoholism and Alcohol Problems among Employed Women and Men." In *Occupational Alcoholism: A Review of Research Issues,* pp. 99-128. Washington, D.C.: Government Printing Office.

Parsons, Talcott. 1937. *The Structure of Social Action.* New York: McGraw-Hill.

_____. 1947. "Introduction." In Max Weber, *The Theory of Social and Economic Organization*, translated by A. M. Henderson and Talcott Parsons, pp. 3-86. New York: Oxford University Press.

_____. 1951. *The Social System.* New York: Free Press.

_____. 1956a. "Suggestions for a Sociological Approach to the Theory of Organizations-I." *Administrative Science Quarterly* 1: 63-85.

_____. 1956b. "Suggestions for a Sociological Approach to the Theory of Organizations-II." *Administrative Science Quarterly* 1: 225-39.

_____. 1960. "Review of R. Bendix, *Max Weber: An Intellectual Portrait*." *American Sociological Review* 25: 750-52.

_____. 1970. "On Building Social System Theory: A Personal History." *Daedalus* 99: 826-81.

_____. 1975. "Comment on Cohen, Hazelrigg and Pope." *American Sociological Review* 40: 666-70.

Partanen, J., K. Bruun, and T. Markkanen. 1966. *A Study on Intelligence, Personality, and Use of Alcohol in Adult Twins*. Helsinki: Finnish Foundation for Alcohol Studies.

Pattison, E. Mansell. 1976. "Nonabstinent Drinking Goals in the Treatment of Alcoholics." In *Research Advances in Alcohol and Drug Problems*, vol. 3, edited by Robert J. Gibbons et al., pp. 401-55. New York: Wiley.

Pattison, E. Mansell, Mark Sobell, and Linda Sobell. 1977. *Emerging Concepts of Alcohol Dependence*. New York: Springer.

Pell, Sidney, and C. Anthony D'Alonzo. 1970. "Sickness Absenteeism of Alcoholics." *Journal of Occupational Medicine* 12: 198-210.

Pennings, Johannes M. 1973. "Measures of Organization Structure: A Methodological Note." *American Journal of Sociology* 79: 686–704.

Pettigrew, Andrew. 1979. "On Studying Organizational Cultures." *Administrative Science Quarterly* 24: 87–104.

Pfeffer, Jeffrey. 1976. "Beyond Management and the Worker." *Academy of Management Review* 1: 36–46.

Pitts, Jesse. 1968. "Social Control: The Concept." In *International Encyclopedia of the Social Sciences*, vol. 14. edited by David L. Sills, pp. 381–96. New York: Macmillan and Free Press.

Plamenantz, John P. 1970. *Ideology*. New York: Praeger.

Polich, J. Michael, and Charles T. Kaelber. 1985. "Sample Surveys and the Epidemiology of Alcoholism." In *Alcohol Patterns and Problems*, edited by Marc A. Schuckit, pp. 43–77. New Brunswick, N.J.: Rutgers University Press.

Pozner, Barry Z., James H. Kouzes, and Warren H. Schmidt. 1985. "Shared Values Make a Difference." *Human Resource Management* 24: 293–309.

Pugh, Derek S., et al. 1963. "A Conceptual Scheme for Organizational Analysis." *Administrative Science Quarterly* 8: 289–315.

Pugh, Derek S., et al. 1968. "Dimensions of Organization Structure." *Administrative Science Quarterly* 13: 65–105.

Pugh, Derek S., et al. 1969. "The Context of Organization Structures." *Administrative Science Quarterly* 14: 91–114.

Pugh, Derek S., David J. Hickson, and Charles R. Hinings. 1969. "An Empirical Taxonomy of Structures of Work Organizations." *Administrative Science Quarterly* 14: 115–26.

Randolph, Theron. 1956. "The Descriptive Features of Food Addiction: Addictive Eating and Drinking." *Quarterly Journal of Studies on Alcohol* 17: 198–224.

Ravin, Iver S. 1975. "Formulation of an Alcoholism Rehabilitation Program at Boston Edison Company." In *Occupational Alcoholism Programs*, edited by Richard L. Williams and Gene H. Moffat, pp. 194–223. Springfield, Ill.: Charles C. Thomas.

Reichman, Walter. 1981a. "The Need for Quality Research." *Labor-Management Alcoholism Journal* 11: 76–78.

———. 1981b. "Conference Board Report: Must Be Dismissed as Invalid and Meaningless." *The ALMACAN* 11: 5.

Reichman, Walter, et al. 1981. "Women's Occupational Alcoholism Demonstration Project." *Labor-Management Alcoholism Journal* 10: 209–18.

Rice, Berkeley. 1982. "The Hawthorne Defect: Persistence of a Flawed Theory." *Psychology Today* 16: 70–74.

Ritzer, George, and James Belasco. 1969. "Cooperating on Alcoholism: A Union Dilemma." In *Company Controls for Drinking Problems*, by Stephen Habbe, pp. 34–36. New York: National Industrial Conference Board.

Robbins, Stephen P. 1983. *Organization Theory*. Englewood Cliffs, N. J.: Prentice-Hall.

Roebuck, J. B., and R. G. Kessler. 1972. *The Etiology of Alcoholism: Constitutional, Psychological and Sociological Approaches*. Springfield, Ill.: Charles C. Thomas.

Rohan, William P. 1972. "MMPI Changes in Hospitalized Alcoholics: A Second Study." *Quarterly Journal of Studies on Alcohol* 33: 65–76.

Rohan, W. P., R. L. Tatro, and S. R. Rotman. 1969. "MMPI Changes in Alcoholics during Hospitalization." *Quarterly Journal of Studies on Alcohol* 30: 389–400.

Roizen, R., et al. 1978. "Spontaneous Remission among Untreated Problem Drinkers." In *Longitudinal Research in Drug Use: Empirical Findings and Methodological Issues*, edited by D. B. Kandel, pp. 197–221. New York: Wiley.

Roman, Paul M. 1980. "Medicalization and Social Control in the Workplace: Prospects for the 1980's." *Journal of Applied Behavioral Science* 16: 407–22.

_____. 1981. "Corporate Pacesetters Making EAP Progress." *Alcoholism: The National Magazine* 1: 37–41.

_____. 1982. "Employee Assistance Programs in Major Corporations in 1979: Scope, Change, and Receptivity." In *Alcohol and Health Monograph* 3, *Prevention, Intervention and Treatment: Concerns and Models*, pp. 177–202. Washington, D. C.: Government Printing Office.

_____. n.d. "Existing Programs and Executive Receptivity: The 1974 Executive Caravan." Mimeographed.

Roman, Paul M., and Lisa A. Thomas. 1978. "Structure and Outcome in Employee Assistance Programs: Exploratory Observations. *Labor-Management Alcoholism Journal* 8: 34–43.

Roman, Paul M., and Harrison M. Trice. 1970. "The Development of Deviant Drinking Behavior: Occupational Risk Factors." *Archives of Environmental Health* 20: 424–35.

_____. 1976. "Alcohol Abuse and Work Organizations." In *Social Aspects of Alcoholism*, edited by Benjamin Kissin and Henri Beglieter, pp. 445–519. New York: Plenum Press.

Rorabaugh, W. J. 1979. *The Alcoholic Republic: An American Tradition*. New York: Oxford University Press.

Rose, H. K., and M. M. Glatt. 1961. "A Study of Alcoholism as an Occupational Hazard of Merchant Seamen." *Journal of Mental Sciences* 107: 18–30.

Ross, Edward A. 1901. *Social Control: A Survey of the Foundations of Order*. New York: Macmillan.

Rouse, Kenneth A. n.d. *What to Do about the Employee with a Drinking Problem*. Long Grove, Ill.: Kemper Insurance Companies.

Rousseau, Jean Jacques. 1951. *The Social Contract*. New York: Oxford University Press.

Ruben, H. L. 1974. "A Review of the First Year's Experience in the U.S. Army Alcohol and Drug Abuse Program." *American Journal of Public Health* 64: 999–1001.

Salaman, Graeme. 1978. "Towards a Sociology of Organisational Structure." *Sociological Review* 26: 519–54.

Salaman, Graeme, and Kenneth Thompson. 1980. *Control and Ideology in Organizations*. Cambridge, Mass.: MIT Press.

Salazar, Lee, and Robert Doyle. 1978. "The Alcoholism Program at the Bethlehem Steel Company: The Importance of Supervisory Training." *Maryland State Medical Journal* (July): 80–81.

Sathe, Vijay. 1984. "How to Decipher and Change Organizational Culture." Paper read at the Conference on Managing Corporate Cultures, Pittsburgh.

_____. 1985. "How to Decipher and Change Organizational Culture." Paper read at the Annual Meeting of the Academy of Management, San Diego.

Saunders, W. M., and P. W. Kershaw. 1979. "Spontaneous Remission from Achoholism—A Community Study." *British Journal of Addiction* 74: 251–65.

Schacht, Richard. 1970. *Alienation*. New York: Doubleday.

Schein, Edgar H. 1985. *Organizational Culture and Leadership*. San Francisco: Jossey Bass.

Schlenger, William E., Jerome B. Hallan, and Becky J. Hayward. 1976. *Characteristics of Selected Occupational Programs*. Raleigh, N.C.: Human Ecology Institute.

Schlenger, William E., and Becky J. Hayward. 1975. *Assessing the Impact of Occupational Programs*. Raleigh, N. C.: Human Ecology Institute.

Schlenger, William E., Becky J. Hayward, and Jerome B. Hallan. 1976. *Simulation Study of the Impact of Occupational Programs*. Raleigh, N. C.: Human Ecology Institute.

Schollaert, Paul T. 1977. "Job-Based Risks and Labor Turnover among Alcoholic Workers." In *Alcoholism and Its Treatment in Industry*, edited by Carl J. Schramm, pp. 177–85. Baltimore: Johns Hopkins University Press.

Schuckit, M., D. Goodwin, and G. Winokur. 1972. "A Study of Alcoholism in Half Siblings." *American Journal of Psychiatry* 128: 1132–36.

Schwartz, David. 1984. *Introduction to Management*. New York: Harcourt Brace Jovanovich.

Scott, W. Richard. 1981. *Organizations*. Englewood Cliffs, N.J.: Prentice-Hall.

Seider, Maynard S. 1974. "American Big Business Ideology: A Content Analysis of Executive Speeches." *American Sociological Review* 39: 802–15.

Seidman, Steven. 1985. "Max Weber: A Classic Analyzed." *Contemporary Sociology* 14: 673–77.

Selznick, Philip. 1949. *TVA and the Grass Roots*. Berkeley: University of California Press.

Shaffer, J. W., et al. 1962. "Nialamide in the Treatment of Alcoholism." *Journal of Nervous and Mental Diseases* 135: 222–32.

Shain, Martin, and Judith Groeneveld. 1980. *Employee-Assistance Programs*. Lexington, Mass.: Lexington Books.

Sherrill, Robert. 1979. "Review of Marshall Frady, *Billy Graham*." *New York*, July 30, pp. 65–66.

Shils, Edward. 1970. "Tradition, Ecology, and Institution in the History of Sociology." *Daedalus* 99: 760–825.

Shirley, Charles E. 1985. "The Alcoholic Executive." New York: Alcoholism Council of Greater New York, Inc. Mimeographed.

Shostak, Arthur B. 1980. *Blue-Collar Stress*. Reading, Mass.: Addison-Wesley.

Sills, David. 1958. *The Volunteers*. Glencoe, Ill.: Free Press.

Smart, Reginald G. 1974. "Employed Alcoholics Treated Voluntarily and under Constructive Coercion: A Follow-Up Study." *Quarterly Journal of Studies on Alcohol* 35: 196–209.

———. 1976. "Spontaneous Recovery in Alcoholics: A Review and Analysis of the Available Literature." *Drug and Alcohol Dependence* 1: 227–85.

Smircich, Linda. 1983a. "Organizations as Shared Meanings." In *Organizational Symbolism*, edited by Louis R. Pondy et al., pp. 55–65. Greenwich, Conn.: JAI Press.

———. 1983b. "Studying Organizations as Cultures." In *Beyond Methodology*, edited by Gareth Morgan, pp. 160–72. Beverly Hills: Sage.

Smith, Franklin. 1980. "Companies Give It Straight to Alcoholics: Stop Drinking or Face Losing Your Job. *American Banker*, November 3, 1980, p. 12.

Snyder, Charles. 1978. *Alcohol and the Jews*. Carbondale: Southern Illinois University Press.

Sonnenstuhl, William J. 1980. "A Comment on Medicalization in the Workplace." *Journal of Applied Behavioral Science* 18: 123–25.

Speigel, D., P. A. Hadley, and R. G. Hadley. 1970. "Personality Test Patterns of Rehabilitation Center Alcoholics, Psychiatric Inpatients and Normals." *Journal of Clinical Psychology* 26: 366–71.

Stanford, Dick. 1981. "Labor Speaks." *EAP Digest* 2: 39.

Starbuck, William H. 1982. "Congealing Oil: Inventing Ideologies to Justify Acting Ideologies Out." *Journal of Management Studies* 19: 1–27.

Starr, Ann, and Ginger Byram. 1985. "Cost–Benefit Analysis for Employee Assistance Programs." *Personnel Administrator* 30: 55–62.

Sternhagen, C. J. 1972. "Absenteeism and Tardiness." In *Handbook of Modern Personnel Administration*, edited by J. J. Famularo, pp. 61-3–61-14. New York: McGraw-Hill.

Stinchcombe, Arthur L. 1982. "Should Sociologists Forget Their Mothers and Fathers?" *American Sociologist* 17: 2–10.

Stivers, Richard. 1976. "Culture and Alcoholism." In *Alcoholism*, edited by Ralph Tarter and Arthur Sugarman, pp. 573–602. Reading, Mass.: Addison-Wesley.

Strand, Rich. 1983. "A Systems Paradigm of Organizational Adaptations to the Social Environment." *Academy of Management Review* 8: 90–96.

Straus, Robert. 1979. "Discussion." In *Research Priorities on Alcohol*, edited by Mark Keller, *Journal of Studies on Alcohol*, Supplement Number 8, p. 302.

Stuart-Kotze, Robin. 1980. *Introduction to Organizational Behavior*. Reston, Va.: Reston Publishing.

Sutherland, Edwin H., and Donald R. Cressey. 1960. *Principles of Criminology*. 6th ed. Chicago: Lippincott.

Swidler, Ann. 1973. "The Concept of Rationality in the Work of Max Weber." *Sociological Inquiry* 43: 35–42.

Szilagyi, Andrew D. 1984. *Management and Performance*. Glenview, Ill.: Scott, Foresman.

Szilagyi, Andrew D., and Marc J. Wallace. 1980. *Organizational Behavior and Performance*. Santa Monica: Goodyear.

Tarter, Ralph, and Dorothea Schneider. 1976. "Models and Theories of Alcoholism." In *Alcoholism*, edited by Ralph Tarter and Arthur Sugarman, pp. 75–106. Reading, Mass.: Addison-Wesley.

Thomas, K. 1980. Personal communication.

Thorpe, J. J., and J. T. Perrett. 1959. "Problem Drinking: A Follow-Up Study." *Archives of Industrial Health* 19: 24–32.

Threatt, Robin M. 1976. *The Influence of Alcohol on Work Performance*. Raleigh, N. C.: Human Ecology Institute.

Tintera, J., and H. Lovell. 1949. "Endocrine Treatment of Alcoholism." *Geriatrics* 4: 274–80.

Toby, Jackson. 1964. "Is Punishment Necessary?" *Journal of Criminal Law, Criminology, and Police Sciences* 55: 332–37.

Tolor, Alexander, and John Tamerin. 1975. "The Attitudes toward Alcoholism

Instrument: A Measure of Attitudes toward Alcoholics and the Nature of Causes of Alcoholism." *British Journal of Addiction* 70: 223–31.

Tournier, Robert E. 1985. "The Medicalization of Alcoholism: Discontinuities in Ideologies of Deviance." *Journal of Drug Issues* 15: 39–49.

Trahair, Richard C. S. 1984. *The Humanist Temper*. New Brunswick, N. J.: Transaction.

Trice, Harrison M. 1957. "Identifying the Problem Drinker on the Job." *Personnel* 34: 527–33.

_____. 1962. "The Job Behavior of Problem Drinkers." In *Society, Culture, and Drinking Patterns*, edited by David J. Pittman and Charles R. Snyder, pp. 493–510. New York: Wiley.

_____. 1964. "New Light on Identifying the Alcoholic Employee." *Personnel* 41: 1–8.

_____. 1966. *Alcoholism in America*. New York: McGraw-Hill.

_____. 1969. *Alcoholism and Industry: Modern Procedures*. 3rd ed. New York: Christopher P. Smithers Foundation.

_____. 1972. *Alcoholism and Industry: Modern Procedures*. 5th ed. New York: Christopher P. Smithers Foundation.

_____. 1984. "Data Based Research, Research Issues and Non-Research: A Critical Appraisal." In *EAP Research: An Annual of Research and Research Issues*, vol. 1, edited by C. Howard Grimes, pp. 136–51. Troy, Mich: Performance Resource Press.

Trice, Harrison M., and James Belasco. 1966. *Emotional Health and Employer Responsibility*. Bulletin No. 57, New York State School of Industrial and Labor Relations, Cornell University.

Trice, Harrison M., and Janice M. Beyer. 1982. "Social Control in Worksettings: Using the Constructive Confrontation Strategy with Problem-Drinking Employees." *Journal of Drug Issues* 12: 21–43.

_____. 1984. "Employee Assistance Programs: Blending Performance-Oriented and Humanitarian Ideologies to Assist Emotionally Disturbed Employees." In *Research in Community and Mental Health*, vol. 4, edited by James R. Greenley, pp. 245–97. Greenwich, Conn.: JAI Press.

Trice, Harrison M., Richard Hunt, and Janice M. Beyer. 1977. "Alcoholism Programs in Unionized Work Settings: Problems and Prospects in Union-Management Cooperation." *Journal of Drug Issues* 6: 103–15.

Trice, Harrison M., and Paul M. Roman. 1972. *Spirits and Demons at Work: Alcohol and Other Drugs on the Job*. Ithaca: New York State School of Industrial and Labor Relations.

_____. 1978. *Spirits and Demons at Work: Alcohol and Other Drugs on the Job*. 2nd ed. Ithaca: New York State School of Industrial and Labor Relations.

Trice, Harrison M., and William J. Sonnenstuhl. 1985a. "Constructive Confrontation and Counseling." *EAP Digest* 6: 31-36.

_____. 1985b. "Contributions of AA to Employee Assistance Programs." *Employee Assistance Quarterly* 1: 7–31.

Udy, Stanley M. 1959. " 'Bureaucracy' and 'Rationality' in Weber's Organization Theory." *American Sociological Review* 24: 794–795.

U. S. Bureau of the Census. 1983. *Statistical Abstract of the United States: 1984*. Washington, D. C.: Government Printing Office.

U. S. Department of Health, Education and Welfare. 1974. *Second Special Report to the U.S. Congress on Alcohol and Health.* Washington, D.C.: Government Printing Office.

U. S. Department of Health and Human Services. 1981. *Fourth Special Report to the U.S. Congress on Alcohol and Health.* Washington, D.C.: Government Printing Office.

_____. 1983. *Fifth Special Report to the U.S. Congress on Alcohol and Health.* Washington, D.C.: Government Printing Office.

U. S. Office of Vital Statistics. 1961. *Mortality in 1950 by Occupation and Industry.* Washington, D. C.: Government Printing Office.

U. S. Senate, Committee on Labor and Public Welfare. 1970. *Hearings before the Special Subcommittee on Alcoholism and Narcotics.* Washington, D.C.: Government Printing Office.

Vaillant, George E. 1983. *The Natural History of Alcoholism.* Cambridge, Mass.: Harvard University Press.

Van de Vall, Mark, Cheryl Bolas, and Tai S. Kang. 1976. "Applied Social Research in Industrial Organizations: An Evaluation of Functions, Theory, and Methods." *Journal of Applied Behavioral Science* 12: 158-77.

Van Maanen, John. 1979. "Qualitative Methods." Special issue, *Administrative Science Quarterly* 24 (4).

Van Maanen, John, and Stephen R. Barley. 1984. "Occupational Communities: Culture and Control in Organizations." *Research in Organizational Behavior* 6: 287-365.

Van Maanen, John, J. M. Dabbs, and Robert R. Faulkner. 1982. *Varieties of Qualitative Research.* Beverly Hills: Sage.

Von Wiegand, Ross A. 1974. "Advances in Secondary Prevention of Alcoholism through the Cooperative Efforts of Labor and Management in Employer Organizations." *Preventive Medicine* 3: 80-85.

Wagner, William G. 1982. "Assisting Employees with Personal Problems." *Personnel Administrator* 27: 59-64.

Walker, Keith, and Martin Shain. 1983. "Employee Assistance Programming: In Search of Effective Interventions for the Problem-Drinking Employee." *British Journal of Addiction* 78: 291-303.

Wallace, Walter L. 1969. *Sociological Theory.* Chicago: Aldine.

Walsh, Diana C. 1982. "Employee Assistance Programs." *Milbank Memorial Fund Quarterly: Health and Society* 60: 492-517.

Ward, David A. 1985. "Concepts of the Nature and Treatment of Alcoholism." *Journal of Drug Issues* 15: 3-16.

Weber, Marianne. 1950. *Max Weber.* Heidelberg: Lambert Schneider.

Weber, Max. 1922. *Wirtschaft und Gesellschaft.* Tubingen: J. C. B. Mohr (Paul Siebeck).

_____. 1924. "Zur Psychophysik der Industriellen Arbeit." in *Gesammelte Aufsatze zur Sociologie und Sozialpolitik*, pp. 61-225. Tubingen: J. C. B. Mohr (Paul Siebeck).

_____. 1927. *General Economic History.* Translated by Frank H. Knight. Glencoe, Ill.: Free Press.

_____. 1930. *The Protestant Ethic and the Spirit of Capitalism.* Translated by Talcott Parsons. London: G. Allen and Unwin.

_____. 1946. *From Max Weber.* Translated by Hans Gerth and C. Wright Mills. New York: Oxford University Press.

_____. 1947. *The Theory of Social and Economic Organization.* Translated by A. M. Henderson and Talcott Parsons. New York: Oxford University Press.

_____. 1949. *The Methodology of the Social Sciences.* Translated by Edward Shils and Henry Finch. New York: Free Press.

_____. 1968. *Economy and Society.* Edited by Guenther Roth and Claus Wittich. New York: Bedminster.

Weiner, Carolyn. 1981. *The Politics of Alcoholism: Building an Arena around a Social Problem.* Berkeley: University of California Press.

Weiss, Richard M. 1980. *Dealing with Alcoholism in the Workplace.* New York: Conference Board.

_____. 1982a. "Evaluations of Industrial Alcoholism and Employee Assistance Programs: A Sobering Review." Paper read at the Annual Meeting of the Evaluation Research Society, Baltimore.

_____. 1982b. "Consulting on Employee Assistance Programs." In *Academy of Management Proceedings*, edited by Kae H. Chung, pp. 129–33. Wichita, Kans.: Academy of Management. ,

_____. 1983. "Getting Applicable Research to Managers: Some Implications of Recent Trends in Theorizing about Organizations." In *Academy of Management Proceedings*, edited by Kae H. Chung, pp. 95–99. Wichita, Kans.: Academy of Management.

_____. 1984. "The Conference Board Report: How and Why." In *EAP Research: An Annual of Research and Research Issues*, vol. 1, edited by C. Howard Grimes, pp. 136–51. Troy, Mich.: Performance Resource Press.

_____. 1985. "Deviance, Discipline, and Social Distance in Organizations: The Role of the Community." Paper read at the Annual Meeting of the Society for Applied Sociology, Erie, Pa.

White, Robert W. 1952. *Lives in Progress.* New York: Holt, Rinehart and Winston.

Whyte, William F. 1943. *Street Corner Society.* Chicago: University of Chicago Press.

_____. 1955. *Money and Motivation.* New York: Harper and Brothers.

_____. 1965. "A Field in Search of a Focus." *Industrial and Labor Relations Review* 18: 305–22.

Wilder, William E. 1976. *Occupational Alcoholism Program Information System.* Reston, Va.: Association of Labor-Management Administrators and Consultants on Alcoholism.

Wilensky, Harold. 1964. "The Professionalization of Everyone?" *American Journal of Sociology* 70: 137–58.

Wilkinson, A. E., et al. 1971. "Psychological Test Characteristics and Length of Stay in Alcoholism Treatment." *Quarterly Journal of Studies on Alcohol* 26: 586–94.

Williams, J. Clifton, Andrew J. DuBrin, and Henry L. Sisk. 1985. *Organization and Management.* Cincinnati: Southwestern.

Wilson, Edward O. 1975. *Sociobiology.* Cambridge, Mass.: Harvard University Press.

Winslow, W. W., et al. 1966. "Some Economic Estimates of Job Disruption from an Industrial Mental Health Project." *Archives of Environmental Health* 13: 213–19.

Wiseman, Jacqueline. 1970. *Stations of the Lost.* Englewood Cliffs, N. J. : Prentice-Hall.

World Health Organization, Expert Committee on Mental Health. 1951. *Technical Report Series, number 42*. Geneva: World Health Organization.

World Health Organization, Expert Committee on Mental Health, Alcoholism Subcommittee. 1952. *Technical Report Series, number 48*. Geneva: World Health Organization.

Worthy, James C. 1950. "Organizational Structure and Employee Morale." *American Sociological Review* 15: 169–79.

Wren, Daniel. 1979. *The Evolution of Management Thought*. 2nd ed. New York: Wiley.

Zeitlin, Irving M. 1968. *Ideology and the Development of Sociological Theory*. Englewood Cliffs, N. J.: Prentice-Hall.

———. 1973. *Rethinking Sociology: A Critique of Contemporary Theory*. Englewood Cliffs, N. J.: Prentice-Hall.

Zey-Ferrell, Mary. 1979. *Dimensions of Organizations*. Santa Monica: Goodyear.

Zwerman, William L. 1970. *New Perspectives on Organization Theory*. Westport, Conn.: Greenwood Press.

Index

About the Author

RICHARD M. WEISS is an Assistant Professor of Business Administration at the University of Delaware. He received a Ph.D. from the School of Industrial and Labor Relations at Cornell University. He is the author of *Dealing with Alcoholism in the Workplace* (New York: Conference Board, 1980), and his writing has appeared in the *Academy of Management Review, Human Relations*, the *American Psychologist, Contemporary Sociology, Administrative Science Quarterly*, the *Employee Assistance Programming Research Annual*, the *Proceedings of the Academy of Management*, and the *Proceedings of the Southern Management Association*.